with love
the
Marcics

the GREAT South African COOK BOOK

EDITORIAL STEERING COMMITTEE

Cass Abrahams, Hilary Biller, Phillippa Cheifitz, David Higgs,
Reuben Riffel, Dorah Sitole, Errieda du Toit, Anna Trapido

PHOTOGRAPHY Toby Murphy **COVER ART** Conrad Botes

EDITORS Libby Doyle, Ruth Hobday, Jules Mercer, Ingeborg Pelser

QUIVERTREE
PUBLICATIONS

In association with PQ Blackwell

Among Madiba's personal papers in the Nelson Mandela Foundation's archive is a wonderful letter about food in which Madiba writes to his two daughters about their developing culinary skills. Reading that letter reiterates to me how much he appreciated good food and recognised that preparing and sharing food was one of the simplest ways to show love for others.

Unfortunately, what should be a simple, achievable act for anyone – providing food for loved ones – is a struggle for far too many. Today, one in four South Africans suffers from hunger, and in some parts of the country one in six children suffer from severe malnutrition. Food insecurity is fed by chronic levels of inequality and coupled with drought and high levels of unemployment. Many South Africans are in need of our help.

In order to reverse these alarming statistics, food security is now a major focus of Mandela Day, a global movement to change the world for the better, led by the Nelson Mandela Foundation. I am therefore delighted that the publication of *The Great South African Cookbook* will directly support the Foundation's food-security work. Not only is it a joyous culinary celebration of our nation's vibrant food culture, but proceeds from sales of the book will be used to develop and support community food and agricultural projects that will improve the lives of those who are in need of food and who need to be freed from poverty.

Creating a book of this magnitude wouldn't have been possible without the expertise and guidance of our eminent editorial steering committee. When we asked for their support, all of them agreed without hesitation, and their participation enriches this project for all of us. Thank you also to Conrad Botes, whose magnificent artwork, including his image of Madiba, provides a unique artistic dimension to the book. Equally, I would like to thank our principal sponsor partner, Tiger Brands. As part of their involvement in this project, Tiger Brands launched a nationwide competition, across all nine provinces, with the Department of Higher Education and Training to find 10 talented trainee chefs. The 10 finalists' recipes, which appear on pages 342–355, show that South Africa's extraordinary culinary culture remains in good hands.

Finally, I would like to thank each and every one of the contributors. By inviting us to your homes, restaurants, farms, community vegetable gardens and even your boats and sharing the food you cook for the people you love, you have taken us on a spectacular journey that shows off the true beauty and spirit of South Africa.

On the occasion of his ninetieth birthday, Madiba said, 'The world remains beset by so much suffering, poverty and deprivation. It is in your hands to make of our world a better one for all, especially the poor, vulnerable and marginalised.' For me, this book is about hope for what can be achieved both now and in the future, and, ultimately, about sharing and changing lives with food.

Sello Hatang
Chief Executive
Nelson Mandela Foundation

gatsby howe ish! HAKALAKA morogo SAMOSAS ma TSO! TINOOit!

CONTENTS

REUBEN RIFFEL
WITH MARYKE, MAX & LATIKA
*MASTERCHEF SOUTH AFRICA
JUDGE, REUBEN'S*

**PRESSURE-COOKED
LAMB KNUCKLES**
CREAMY RISOTTO
PORK & BEANS

*Franschhoek,
Western Cape*

My past has a big impact on how I cook today. I love it when I get to see my kids' smiling faces as they tuck into bowls of hearty goodness, pretty much the same food that I used to enjoy as a child. What more can a parent ask for?

Reuben

PRESSURE-COOKED LAMB KNUCKLES

SERVINGS: 6 | PREP TIME: 5 MINS | COOK TIME: 30 MINS | SKILL LEVEL: 1 (EASY)

INGREDIENTS

8 small onions, peeled
2 cloves garlic, crushed
olive oil
sprig of fresh thyme
10 Rosa tomatoes,
  cut in half
20 small lamb knuckles
2 cups chicken stock

METHOD

Braise the onion and garlic in some olive oil for 2 minutes in a pressure cooker pot. Add the thyme and tomatoes. Cook for another 4 minutes. Add the lamb knuckles, season with salt and pepper and add chicken stock. Place the pressure cooker lid on top and pressure-cook on medium heat for 15–20 minutes. Once the lamb is soft, serve with creamy risotto (see recipe below), gem squash, peas, and carrots mashed with butter and honey.

CREAMY RISOTTO

SERVINGS: 6 | COOK TIME: ABOUT 20 MINS | SKILL LEVEL: 1 (EASY)

INGREDIENTS

1½ cups Arborio rice
olive oil
juice of 1 lemon
4 cups chicken stock,
  warmed
3 tbsp unsalted butter
2 tbsp grated Parmesan

METHOD

Rinse the rice under cold running water for about 1 minute. Add olive oil to a pan and heat slightly. Add the rice, heat through, then squeeze the lemon juice into the pan, followed by two ladlefuls of the warm stock. Keep stirring and as the stock gets absorbed into the rice, add more stock. Do not allow the stock to boil away and also make sure the temperature is not too low. When the last ladle of stock has been added, cook away half of the stock in the pan and remove from the heat. Add the butter and Parmesan and stir slowly to form an emulsion. Season to taste.

PORK & BEANS

SERVINGS: 6 | PREP TIME: 10 MINS | COOK TIME: 2 HOURS PLUS RESTING | SKILL LEVEL: 1 (EASY)

INGREDIENTS

1 tbsp black peppercorns
2 bay leaves, dried
2 sprigs thyme
3 tbsp coarse salt
canola oil
2½ kg boneless pork belly

Beans
olive oil
3 medium red onions,
   coarsely chopped
3 cloves garlic, peeled
   and crushed
3 cups tomato passata
2 cups concentrated
   chicken stock
2 x 410g cans borlotti
   beans
2 x 410g cans red kidney
   beans
1 x 410g can white beans
dried origanum to taste
smoked paprika to taste
200 g Cheddar or
   mozzarella, cubed

METHOD

Pre-heat the oven to 250°C. Crush together the black peppercorns, bay leaves and thyme with the coarse salt and a drizzle of canola oil. Using a sharp knife, score the skin of the pork belly. Rub the aromatics mixture all over the pork. Place in a roasting tray, fat side up, and roast for 15 minutes. Turn the oven temperature down to 170°C and roast for another 1 hour and 20 minutes.

Remove the meat from the oven and place another tray on top with enough weight to press down on the belly very lightly. Allow to cool like this for 2–3 hours. (This process is optional, but I like to have the fat side fairly flat and you also get rid of the excess fat.) Chop the cooled meat into cubes.

To cook the beans, add some olive oil to a wide pan and slowly sweat the onions and garlic in it without allowing them to brown. After about 4 minutes, add the passata and chicken stock, bring quickly to simmering point and then simmer slowly for 4 minutes. Add the beans, heat through, then add the cubed pork. Cook for 8 minutes. Add the origanum and smoked paprika, season to taste and just before you serve the dish, add the cubes of cheese and stir through. By the time you serve the cheese will be nicely melted.

"I remember we used to slaughter pigs once a year, and with the excess of pork my parents had to be creative in their cooking. Pork belly and beans might seem fashionable to people today, but to me it was a staple of the slaughter month in my youth."

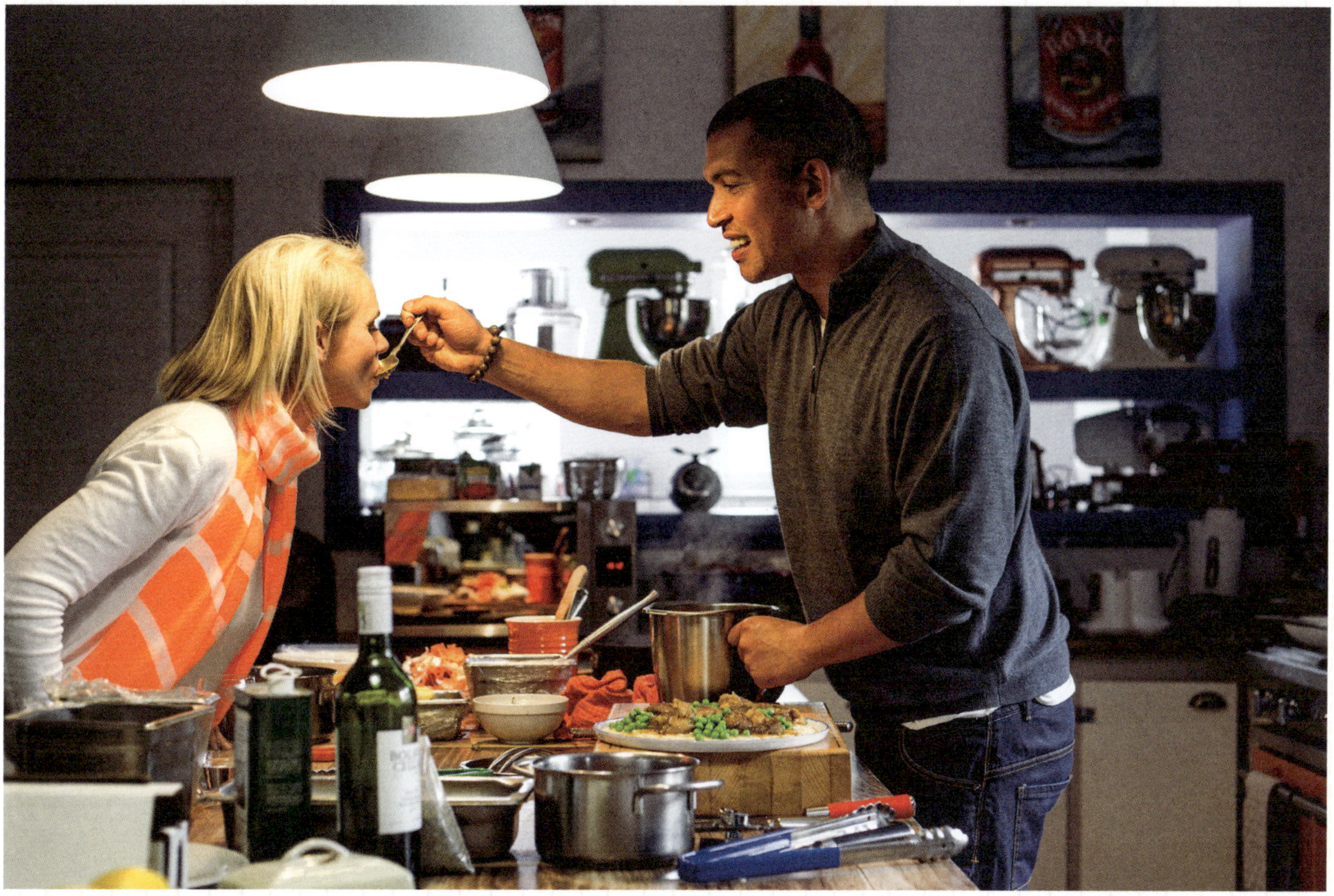

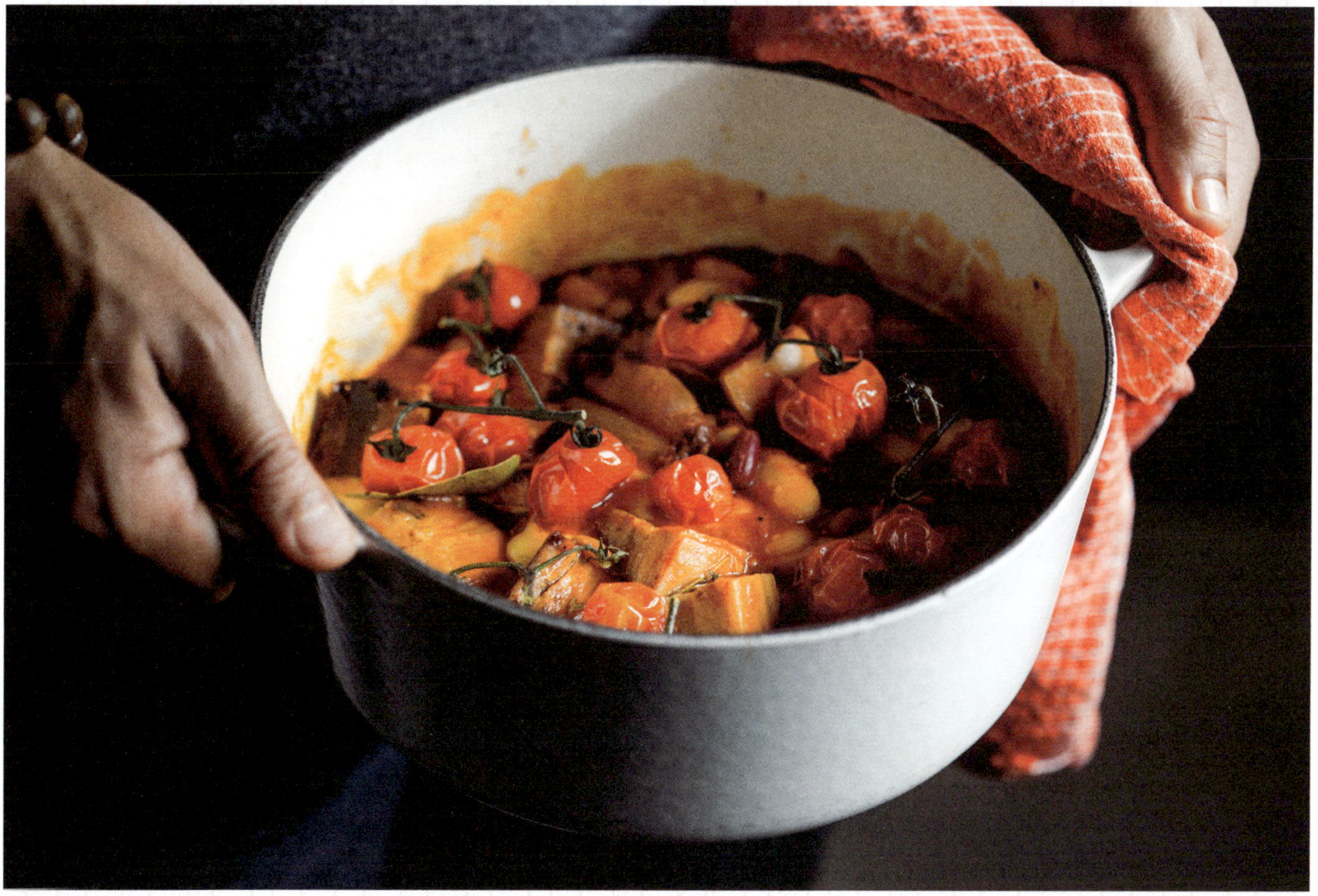

A lifetime is not enough to discover the diversity, the flavours and the history of food in this country. I try to take food from the past and bring it into modern times without losing those aspects that make the dish so well-loved and unique. *Erriede*

Welgemoed,
Western Cape

ERRIEDA DU TOIT

WITH IAN

HUISKOK

MACARONI CHEESE WITH ROASTED TOMATOES
DUTCH BABY WITH GRILLED PEACHES & ALMOND PASTE

MACARONI CHEESE WITH ROASTED TOMATOES

SERVINGS: 6 | PREP TIME: 5 MINS | COOK TIME: 40 MINS | SKILL LEVEL: 1 (EASY)

INGREDIENTS

500 g macaroni

40 ml butter

40 ml flour

2–3 cloves garlic, crushed (optional)

750 ml warm milk

5 ml mustard

250 ml grated Cheddar

freshly grated nutmeg

12 'Rosa' or cherry tomatoes, cut into thick slices or halved

75 g cubed mozzarella for topping

about 50 g cubed leftover bread for topping

METHOD

Pre-heat the oven to 180°C. Bring a large pot of water to the boil, add the macaroni and cook until almost done, then drain.

In a medium saucepan, melt the butter, stir in the flour and add the garlic. Simmer gently till the garlic is soft and somewhat caramelised, not browned. Add half the milk, whisk until smooth, then add the rest and simmer till thickened and very smooth. Remove from the heat and stir in the mustard and half the Cheddar. Season with freshly grated nutmeg and plenty of salt and pepper.

Pour the cheese sauce over the pasta, stir well and put in a baking dish. Top with the rest of the grated Cheddar. Arrange the tomatoes, mozzarella cubes and bread cubes on top. Bake in the oven until bubbly and golden brown (about 20 minutes). The tomatoes must start to 'catch' and have slightly burnt edges.

DUTCH BABY WITH GRILLED PEACHES & ALMOND PASTE

SERVINGS: 2–4 | PREP TIME: 10 MINS | COOK TIME: 25 MINS | SKILL LEVEL: 2 (MODERATE)

INGREDIENTS

125 ml cake flour

125 ml milk

3 large eggs, lightly whisked

pinch of salt

pinch of nutmeg

60 ml butter

lemon juice

icing sugar for dusting

crème fraîche or double-cream yoghurt, to serve

Filling

peaches (you can use any stone fruit available)

Almond paste

1 cup almond flour (ground almonds)

125 ml caster sugar

1 egg white

zest of 1 lemon, finely grated

METHOD

Pre-heat the oven to 220°C with the oven rack placed low. Place a large ovenproof heavy-bottomed pan (preferably cast iron) in the oven till very hot, around 8 minutes.

Whisk cake flour, milk, eggs, salt and nutmeg together in a medium-sized bowl until foamy, or use a blender or food processor. Do not overmix.

Careful now! Add the butter to the hot pan, tilt the bottom to coat, then add the batter. Bake until the puffed sides are well browned and the centre is golden brown, around 20 minutes. Do not even think of opening the oven door while it bakes.

To make the filling, stone peaches and slice. Dip the fruit slices in brown sugar and caramelise on a hot griddle pan. To make the almond paste, place all ingredients in a blender and blend until it binds together. Form into a sausage and roll in plastic wrap or greaseproof paper till ready to use.

Take the pudding out of the oven, squeeze over some lemon juice, add the fruit filling and blobs of almond paste and dust with icing sugar. Serve in the pan and cut into wedges at the table.

TIPS

Vary the fillings according to what's in the cupboard: a simple filling of cinnamon sugar, lemon juice and honey is delicious, or try caramelised bananas and cream with chopped peanut brittle.

CASS ABRAHAMS
AUTHOR & CAPE MALAY CHEF

THREE DHAL CURRY
WATERBLOMMETJIE
BREDIE

*Diep River,
Western Cape*

I realised early on in my career that when you see a plate of food in front of you, you can tell a lot about the history, the geography and the economics of its originating country. Food builds bridges over culture and class systems. We were so separated under apartheid in South Africa, and food broke down those walls that divided us.

THREE DHAL CURRY

SERVINGS: 6 | PREP TIME: 20 MINS PLUS 30 MINS SOAKING | COOK TIME: 30–45 MINS
SKILL LEVEL: 1 (EASY)

INGREDIENTS

125 ml oil dhal
(also known as toor
dhal or yellow lentils)
125 ml moong dhal
125 ml channa dhal
1 large onion, thinly sliced
60 ml oil
2 sticks cassia
(I use Robertson's)
2 cardamom pods
1 sprig curry leaves
2 medium tomatoes,
skinned and chopped
½ tsp chilli flakes
(I use Robertson's)
10 ml crushed garlic
5 ml crushed ginger
2 tsp garam masala
5 ml ground cumin
(I use Robertson's)
5 ml ground coriander
(I use Robertson's)
5 ml ground turmeric
(I use Robertson's)
about 3 cups water
salt to taste
250 ml chopped
coriander leaves

METHOD

Soak all the dhals in a bowl of water for 30 minutes. Place onion, oil, cassia, cardamom and curry leaves in a large saucepan and fry until onions are soft.

Add tomatoes, chilli flakes, garlic, ginger and all the spices and stir well. Drain the dhals and add to the pan together with 3 cups water. Season to taste. Bring to the boil and simmer until dhal is soft and mushy.

Sprinkle with coriander leaves and serve with rice or puri (an unleavened, deep-fried, flaky Indian bread).

"I grew up in a traditional African shanty town. My journey has taken me all over the world, but what still fascinates me is that no matter where you are from – a shanty town or Disney World – it's always a plate that tells a story."

WATERBLOMMETJIE BREDIE

SERVINGS: 6 | PREP TIME: 20 MINS | COOK TIME: ABOUT 1½ HOURS | SKILL LEVEL: 1 (EASY)

INGREDIENTS

2 large onions, chopped

4 whole cloves

2 ml peppercorns

125 ml water

30 ml vegetable oil

1 kg lamb, cut into pieces

10 ml crushed garlic

2 kg fresh
  waterblommetjies
  (see notes)

4 large potatoes, cubed

30 ml lemon juice or
  a bunch suurentjies,
  chopped (see notes)

2 ml ground nutmeg

METHOD

Place the onions, cloves and peppercorns in a large saucepan. Add water, bring to the boil and simmer until the onions are transparent and all the water has evaporated. Add the oil and sauté until the onions are brown. Add the meat and garlic and continue cooking and stirring over low heat until the meat has a beautiful brown colour.

In the meantime, boil half the waterblommetjies in water until just tender. Drain and wash under cold water. Set aside. Add the rest of the waterblommetjies to the meat and cook until the meat is almost tender. Add the potatoes and cook until the potatoes are almost done. Add the parboiled waterblommetjies, lemon juice or suurentjies and salt and pepper to taste, and stir through. Sprinkle nutmeg over and serve with rice.

NOTES

Waterblommetjies are the buds of Cape pondweed, an indigenous vegetable native to the Western Cape.

Suurentjies are also known as suurings, wood sorrel or Cape sorrel: the leaves of this plant, *Oxalis pes-caprae*, contain oxalic acid and thus have a very similar sour taste to lemon juice. They have long been used in Cape cookery when lemons aren't available.

PHILLIPPA CHEIFITZ
WITH ROBERT
AUTHOR & FOOD EDITOR

ROAST DUCK BREAST WITH GRAPES & HANEPOOT SAUCE
ICED BORSCHT WITH HOT POTATOES & SOUR CREAM

I was brought up in a traditional Jewish household, the granddaughter of eastern European immigrants. Friday night was always our big meal of the week, the Sabbath meal. The extended family — my parents, sister, two aunts, three uncles and all the cousins — would gather at the white damask-covered table, the Sabbath candles flickering.

Phillippa

*Camps Bay,
Western Cape*

ROAST DUCK BREAST
WITH GRAPES & HANEPOOT SAUCE

SERVINGS: 4 | PREP TIME: 15 MINS | COOK TIME: 25 MINS | SKILL LEVEL: 1 (EASY)

INGREDIENTS

4 duck breast fillets, about 200 g each

watercress or wild rocket, to garnish (optional)

crispy pan-fried or roasted potato chunks, to serve

Sauce

2 tbsp runny honey

3 tbsp white wine vinegar

½ cup chicken stock

1 tsp cornflour

2 tbsp brandy

½ cup unsweetened pure hanepoot grape juice

½ cup sweet hanepoot wine

lemon juice (if needed)

1 cup small (or halved if larger) hanepoot or seedless grapes

METHOD

First make the sauce. Stir honey and vinegar together in a small heavy saucepan. Boil until syrupy and a good caramel colour. Remove from heat and add stock, stirring constantly. Mix cornflour and brandy to a smooth paste and stir into the sauce. Still stirring, simmer until it comes to the boil and thickens slightly. Stir in the grape juice and wine and bring to the boil. Keep simmering for about 5 minutes until slightly reduced. Season to taste. Check that the sauce is pleasantly sweet and sour, adding lemon juice if necessary.

Pre-heat the oven to 200°C. Prick the skin of the duck breasts. Pour boiling water over, then drain. Slowly brown the skin in a pan on the hob, then flip and briefly brown the other side. Remove and keep the fat for another use. Season. Place duck breasts in a roasting pan. Spoon over the sauce and grapes. Roast for about 15 minutes until glazed and bronzed, and medium rare.

TIP

The much-loved, tawny-speckled hanepoot grape, with its distinctive honey-sweet flavour, is only available in late summer, so I use a seedless variety the rest of the season.

ICED BORSCHT WITH
HOT POTATOES & SOUR CREAM

SERVINGS: 6–8 | PREP TIME: 15 MINS | COOK TIME: 1 HOUR | SKILL LEVEL: 1 (EASY)

INGREDIENTS

8 medium beetroot

1 tbsp salt

8 cups water

sugar

strained fresh lemon juice

fresh cream, to serve

hot boiled potatoes, to serve

METHOD

Wash the beetroot very well but don't peel them. Wear kitchen gloves to avoid staining. Trim the stalks, leaving about 5 cm, and leave on the tails so that the beetroot won't bleed. Place in a saucepan with the salt and water. Bring to the boil, reduce the heat and cook, covered, for about 1 hour or until tender. Remove the beetroot and strain the liquid. Stir in ¼ cup sugar and ⅓ cup lemon juice. Taste for sweet-sour balance, adding more sugar or more lemon juice if necessary. If serving in glasses, add a shot of cream but use the beetroot for a salad. If serving in bowls, stir in some peeled, grated beetroot. Either way, serve well chilled. Pass around the cream and potatoes at table.

DORAH SITOLE
WITH SIFISO, SIBUSISO, AYANDA & NHLANNHLA
AUTHOR & INDIGENOUS FOOD CHAMPION

OXTAIL ON UJEQE
UJEQE MADE FOUR WAYS
MOROGO WITH LEEKS & POTATOES
SEAFOOD SAMP

Since starting my career in food, I've been writing about our local food heroes and encouraging people to enjoy indigenous food in their daily cooking. The whole family is a part of my cooking philosophy. In the kitchen, everyone should take part. This is the new generation, and they are taking it on – good for them!

Dorah

Bryanston, Gauteng

OXTAIL ON UJEQE

SERVINGS: 6 | PREP TIME: 15 MINS | COOK TIME: 3 HOURS | SKILL LEVEL: 1 (EASY)

INGREDIENTS

60 ml (4 tbsp) oil
1½ kg oxtail
2 red onions, sliced
2 sweet red peppers, thickly sliced
2 sweet yellow peppers, thickly sliced
4 cloves garlic, crushed
45 ml (3 tbsp) tomato paste
500 ml (2 cups) beef stock
250 ml (1 cup) dry red wine
1 x 410 g can chopped tomatoes
leaves from 1 long sprig of rosemary
2 bay leaves
30 ml (2 tbsp) chopped fresh basil
ujeqe, to serve (see recipe below)

METHOD

Pre-heat the oven to 180°C. Heat the oil in a large ovenproof casserole over high heat and brown oxtail in batches to seal on all sides. Remove and set aside.

Reduce heat to medium and add onions, peppers and garlic to the casserole. Cook, stirring, for about 5 minutes, until vegetables start to soften. Add tomato paste, stock and red wine, and return oxtail to pan. Add chopped tomatoes, rosemary and bay leaves and season with salt and pepper. Bring to the boil, cover, and cook in the oven for 2 hours. Remove lid and cook for a further 1 hour. Stir in basil, reserving a little to garnish.

To serve, arrange ujeqe slices on individual plates and spoon oxtail over. Serve with morogo (see recipe following page) and garnish with chopped basil.

UJEQE MADE FOUR WAYS
STEAMED BREAD MADE FOUR WAYS

SERVINGS: 4–6 | PREP TIME: 20 MINS PLUS RISING TIME | COOK TIME: 1 HOUR | SKILL LEVEL: 1 (EASY)

INGREDIENTS

720 g (6 cups) cake flour
5 ml (1 teaspoon) salt
15 ml (1 tablespoon) sugar
10 g instant dry yeast
about 375 ml (1½ cups) lukewarm water
1 egg, beaten
65 ml (¼ cup) oil

Variations

250 ml (1 cup) frozen mixed vegetables, thawed
150 g button mushrooms, finely chopped
60 ml (4 tbsp) chopped fresh herbs such as parsley and coriander

METHOD

Sift together cake flour and salt, then add sugar and instant yeast. Make a well in the middle and pour in lukewarm water, beaten egg and oil. Mix together and knead for at least 10 minutes to form a soft, pliable dough. Cover dough with plastic wrap and allow to rise until doubled in size (about 1 hour and 30 minutes).

Remove dough from bowl, form it into a round and place it in a greased bowl. If making variations, divide the dough into 4 equal portions and leave 1 portion plain. Add mixed vegetables to the second portion, mushrooms to the third and herbs to the last portion, kneading each one well. Add the dough rounds next to each other in the same bowl as the first portion of dough.

Immerse the bowl in a pot with boiling water in it; the water must come two thirds of the way up the sides of the bowl. Cover tightly and steam for 1 hour over medium heat (replenish the water if it goes dry). Test by inserting a skewer into the bread – if it comes out clean, the bread is cooked.

MOROGO WITH LEEKS & POTATOES

SERVINGS: 4-6 | PREP TIME: 10 MINS | COOK TIME: 20 MINS | SKILL LEVEL: 1 (EASY)

INGREDIENTS

1 bunch morogo or spinach, chopped

3 medium potatoes,
  peeled and diced

1 bunch spring onions, chopped

5 ml (1 tsp) crushed garlic

2 leeks, cleaned and sliced

50 g butter

METHOD

Wash morogo thoroughly. Place in a saucepan with potatoes, spring onions, garlic and leeks. Cover and cook over medium heat until potatoes are soft. Add butter to vegetables and mix through. Season to taste with salt and pepper.

SEAFOOD SAMP

SERVINGS: 4 | PREP TIME: 15 MINS | COOK TIME: 2½ HOURS | SKILL LEVEL: 1 (EASY)

INGREDIENTS

400 g (2 cups) samp

2 litres (8 cups) water

45 ml (3 tbsp) butter

1 onion, chopped

2 cloves garlic, crushed

5 ml (1 tsp) ground cumin

5 ml (1 tsp) ground coriander

5 ml (1 tsp) paprika

4 large brown mushrooms, sliced

1 green pepper, diced

250 ml (1 cup) dry white wine

6 mussels

45 ml (3 tbsp) oil

12 medium prawns, peeled and cleaned

200 g calamari rings

200 g hake steaks (or any firm-fleshed
  fish)

12 cherry tomatoes

METHOD

Cook samp in 2 litres of salted boiling water until cooked through and very soft (about 2 hours). Keep replenishing the water so that it does not burn. In a pan, melt the butter, add onion, garlic and spices, and sauté until onion is transparent. Add mushrooms and green pepper, and cook until soft. Set aside.

In a separate small saucepan, bring the wine to the boil, add the mussels and simmer for 1 minute. Set aside.

In another pan heat the oil, add prawns, calamari and hake, and fry gently until cooked (about 10 minutes). Add the onion mixture to the seafood mixture, toss lightly, add the samp and cherry tomatoes, and mix in carefully. Season to taste with salt and freshly ground black pepper.

Spoon onto a serving platter and top with mussels. Serve warm.

When I was young, my father would wake me up early to take me fishing from the beach before school. We would come home with our fresh catch and my mum would take over. After school we'd find something on the dining-room table that she had whipped up. Delicious and caught by our own fair hands – always one of my fondest childhood memories. Cooking, for me, is a spontaneous act. It carries influences such as what your parents cooked, but it should be about what you feel and what you love.

DAVID HIGGS
MARBLE

KABELJOU 'BIRYANI'

*Rosebank,
Gauteng*

KABELJOU 'BIRYANI'

SERVINGS: 6 | PREP TIME: 45 MINS PLUS PICKLING | COOK TIME: 30 MINS | SKILL LEVEL: 1 (EASY)

INGREDIENTS

1 kg kabeljou fillet, cut into 2 cm squares
vegetable oil for frying

Lentils

1 onion, finely chopped
2 cloves garlic, finely chopped
vegetable oil for frying
1 tsp ground cumin
1 tsp mustard seeds
¼ tsp turmeric
1 tbsp sweet masala curry powder
2 tomatoes, skinned and finely chopped
1 tsp brown sugar
1 carrot, finely grated
500 g cooked (al dente) brown puy lentils
100 g raisins
200 ml tomato juice
250 ml good vegetable stock

Pickled cucumber

200 ml water
50 ml white wine vinegar
black peppercorns
50 g sugar
a few sprigs of dill
2 small cucumbers, peeled, de-seeded and cut into 4 cm x 5 cm batons

Green salad

3 courgette flowers
60 g green or purple runner beans, sliced lengthways
2 spring onions, sliced at an angle
12 yellow baby Bright Lights spinach leaves (swiss chard)
2 g coriander leaves

Dressing

2 tsp fresh lime juice
1 tsp lime cordial
100 ml olive oil

To garnish

herb and cucumber oil (see tip)
6 fennel flowers
6 fresh lime segments

METHOD

Brown kabeljou squares lightly in a pan. Set aside and keep warm.

To make the lentils, sauté onions and garlic in oil, add the curry spices and sauté briefly. Add tomatoes and brown sugar and cook through, then add grated carrot and cook through. Add lentils and raisins. Add tomato juice and vegetable stock and simmer until the sauce is reduced and the lentils are soft. Check seasoning.

Make the pickled cucumber the night before. Put all the ingredients other than cucumber in a pot and bring to simmering point, then cool. Add cucumber and refrigerate overnight to pickle.

To make the salad and dressing, mix all the dressing ingredients together and use to dress all salad ingredients other than the coriander leaves. Finely slice the coriander leaves just before serving and add to the salad.

To serve, arrange lentils and kabeljou on serving plates and top with dressed green salad. Garnish with pickled cucumbers, fennel flowers and lime segments, and drizzle over a little herb and cucumber oil.

TIP

To make herb and cucumber oil, blend the skin and de-seeding offcuts from the cucumber, and some coriander stalks, with a little olive oil.

HILARY BILLER
WITH THULISILE NZIMANDE
FOOD EDITOR

GRANDMOTHER'S PICKLED FISH
WHOLEWHEAT SEED LOAF
BUTTERMILK DESSERTS WITH NAARTJIE & VAN DER HUM SYRUP

My maternal grandmother was an excellent cook of traditional Afrikaans food, and I have wonderful memories of meals at my grandparents' home in Pretoria. Pickled fish was served at Easter and Christmas, and she'd always make a big quantity the week before each celebration, which we'd greedily eat with thickly buttered, freshly made brown bread. My mother continued the tradition, and her take was even better than my grandmother's original version.

Hilary

Emmarentia,
Gauteng

GRANDMOTHER'S PICKLED FISH

SERVINGS: 6–8 | PREP TIME: 25 MINS | COOK TIME: 20 MINS PLUS PICKLING | SKILL LEVEL: 1 (EASY)

INGREDIENTS

60 g flour
salt
white pepper
1½–2 kg fresh hake, cut into portions
oil for frying

Sauce
1 kg onions, sliced into rings
375 ml (1½ cups) water
30–45 ml (2–3 tbsp) curry powder
100 g soft brown sugar
2 cm piece of fresh ginger, peeled
  and grated
3 bay or lemon leaves
7½ ml (1½ tsp) ground coriander
6 black peppercorns
1 fresh chilli, seeded and sliced
  (or more if desired)
375 ml (1½ cups) good quality white
  vinegar
125 ml (½ cup) water
15 ml (1 tbsp) cornflour
30 ml (2 tbsp) water

METHOD

You need to prepare this dish 3–5 days before you wish to serve. Season the flour with salt and white pepper. Dip the fish pieces into the flour, coating on both sides. Heat the oil and fry the fish on both sides until golden brown and cooked through. Place on paper towel to drain.

To make the curried pickling sauce, place the onion rings in a large pan, add the first amount of water and bring to the boil. Simmer for 5 minutes. Add the remaining ingredients, including the vinegar and second amount of water but excluding the cornflour, to the onions. Bring to the boil and simmer for 5 minutes. Mix the cornflour to a paste with 30 ml (2 tbsp) water and add to the onion mixture. Bring to the boil and simmer, stirring, until thickened, about another 5–8 minutes.

Arrange the fish and curry sauce in layers in a large glass or ceramic dish (don't use a plastic container). Cover and refrigerate for 3–5 days before enjoying with thickly sliced wholewheat seed loaf (see recipe below).

WHOLEWHEAT SEED LOAF

MAKES: 1 LARGE LOAF OR 6 MINI LOAVES | PREP TIME: 15 MINS PLUS RISING | COOK TIME: 1 HOUR
SKILL LEVEL: 1 (EASY)

INGREDIENTS

4 x 250 ml wholewheat flour
3 x 250 ml cake or white bread flour
250 ml (1 cup) bran
20 ml salt
1 x 10 g sachet instant yeast
30 ml brown sugar or runny honey
50 ml oil
750 ml warm water
250 ml mixed seeds (sunflower,
  sesame, poppy, pumpkin)

METHOD

In a large bowl, combine the wholewheat and cake or white bread flours. Stir in the bran, salt and yeast. Mix through. Combine the sugar or honey, oil and warm water and, using a wooden spoon, slowly add to the dry mixture. It may need all the liquid or may require a little extra. You want quite a wet dough, almost like a thick batter. Stir through half the seeds. Spoon the mixture between 2 medium loaf pans sprayed with cooking spray. Sprinkle the remaining seeds on the tops of the two loaves. Lightly press down the seeds so they stick to the dough. Cover lightly and leave in a warm place until the dough rises to be level with the tops of the pans. Pre-heat the oven to 200°C. Bake for 50–60 minutes. Cool in the pans for 10 minutes before removing to cool completely on a cooling rack.

BUTTERMILK DESSERTS WITH NAARTJIE & VAN DER HUM SYRUP

SERVINGS: 8 | PREP TIME: 15 MINS | COOK TIME: 10 MINS PLUS SETTING | SKILL LEVEL: 1 (EASY)

INGREDIENTS

15 ml (1 tbsp) gelatine
  powder
80 ml (⅓ cup) water
500 ml (2 cups) fresh
  cream
seeds of 1 vanilla pod
180 ml (⅔ cup) caster
  sugar
500 ml (2 cups) buttermilk

Syrup
100 g (½ cup) sugar
375 ml (1½ cups) water
juice of 2 naartjies
2 naartjies, sliced thinly
  into rounds with skin on
2 cloves
1 stick cinnamon
grating of fresh nutmeg or
  pinch of ground nutmeg
45–60 ml (3–4 tbsp)
  Van der Hum liqueur,
  warmed

METHOD

Start making the buttermilk desserts the day before. Sprinkle the gelatine over the water and set aside to sponge. In a pot, combine the cream, vanilla seeds and sugar. Stir over a low heat until the sugar has dissolved. Don't allow it to boil. Add the gelatine mixture and stir to dissolve. Remove from the heat and cool. Once cool, add the buttermilk and whisk till smooth. Spray 8 individual pudding moulds with cooking spray and divide the mixture between the moulds. Cover and cool in the refrigerator overnight. Remove from the fridge at least 30 minutes before serving and bring back to room temperature.

Just before serving, make the syrup. Place the sugar and water in a small pan and cook over medium heat until sugar has dissolved. Add the naartjie juice, naartjie slices and spices and cook over medium heat till syrup has thickened and naartjie slices have softened but not fallen apart. Pour over the warmed Van der Hum liqueur and ignite with a match. Once flames have subsided, remove from the heat and cool.

Unmould buttermilk desserts onto serving plates and spoon over naartjie syrup. Finish off with a naartjie slice or two.

ANNA TRAPIDO
WITH JOSIAH GOODE
AUTHOR & FOOD EDITOR

BEEF SHORT RIB STEW
BOEREMEISIES WITH MAAS CURD CHEESE & NAARTJIE SAUCE

I like food to have 'terroir'. I want to hear, taste and feel where that food has come from, and its flavours must communicate this. In Hartbeespoort we have thriving local small farmers. I'm a big dairy person (I always have been) and I really love maas and maas curd cheese. I use locally sourced milk for both, which are incredible when made at home in the traditional way, using unpasteurised milk.

Anna

*Hartbeespoort,
North West*

BEEF SHORT RIB STEW

SERVINGS: 4 | PREP TIME: 25 MINS | COOK TIME: 3½ HOURS | SKILL LEVEL: 1 (EASY)

INGREDIENTS

1½ kg beef short ribs
1 tbsp oil
170 g bacon
1 onion, finely chopped
1 carrot, finely chopped
2 cloves garlic, finely chopped
1 tbsp tomato paste
1 stick cinnamon
2 tbsp cake flour
3 cups (750 ml) brown sherry
  (I use Old Brown Sherry)
2 cups (500 ml) beef stock

METHOD

Pre-heat the oven to 160°C. Seal short ribs in oil in a casserole pot. When browned, remove and set aside. In a separate pan, sauté bacon for 5 minutes, then remove, drain off fat and chop into small pieces. Sauté onion and carrot in the meat browning pot until soft, then add bacon pieces. Add garlic and cook through (about 2 minutes). Add tomato paste and cinnamon and cook until it starts to caramelise and sweeten, then add flour and mix. Return the meat to the pot and pour the liquids over. Cook in the oven until meat is very tender and sauce is rich and thick (about 3 hours).

BOEREMEISIES WITH MAAS CURD CHEESE & NAARTJIE SAUCE

SERVINGS: 4 WITH LEFTOVERS | PREP TIME: 50 MINS PLUS PRESERVING AND CURING
COOK TIME: 10 MINS | SKILL LEVEL: 1 (EASY)

INGREDIENTS

Boeremeisies
500 g fresh apricots
140 g sugar
mampoer to cover (I use apricot
  mampoer, but any flavour will do)

Maas curd cheese
1 litre maas

Sauce
2 cups naartjie juice
zested strips of 2 naartjies
1 vanilla pod
¼ cup white sugar
1 tbsp honey

METHOD

To make the boeremeisies, pack the apricots into sterilised jars. In a saucepan, dissolve the sugar in the mampoer over a low heat. Pour over the apricots. Seal and set aside for as long as you can wait – a few months, if possible.

To make the maas curd cheese, pour maas into a clean muslin cloth and tie it at the top to form a bag. Suspend bag with a dish underneath to catch the liquid whey that will run out of the muslin bag. Refrigerate for 2–3 days. Remove from fridge, untie cloth and there will be a thick, delicious curd cheese inside.

To make the naartjie sauce, place all the ingredients in a saucepan. Bring to the boil and simmer until reduced by three-quarters.

Cape Town,
Western Cape

JAN BRAAI
AUTHOR & FOUNDER OF NATIONAL BRAAI DAY

PERFECT BRAAIED STEAK
BRAAI FREEDOM FIGHTER BURGER
PERI-PERI SAUCE

Being able to braai the perfect steak is something you should be able to do with ease. As long as you stick to a few basic guidelines and pay attention to what you are doing, you will master this skill in no time. The steak must be of a certain quality though. However well you braai it, a bad piece of meat is never going to turn out great.

Jan

PERFECT BRAAIED STEAK

SERVINGS: 2 | PREP TIME: 20 MINS PLUS FIRE PREPARATION | COOK TIME: 7 MINS PLUS RESTING
SKILL LEVEL: 1 (EASY)

INGREDIENTS

2 x 200–250 g T-bone
    steaks, about 2½–3 cm
    thick
coarse salt

METHOD

If you are making a real fire with real wood – and this is the best way to braai – make a big fire from the outset. Do not make a medium-sized fire and add more wood later. If you have to use charcoal, light quite a lot of it. For a small braai, consider half a bag. (It's not uncommon for me to use a whole bag of charcoal when braaiing steaks for a dinner party.) If you are wondering whether or not you have enough heat, then the answer is probably no. It is essential that that your coals are extremely hot. The exact height of your grid is not important. Anything between 5 and 15 cm is fine; I aim for 10 cm.

Remove the steaks from the fridge 20 minutes before you want to braai them, and leave them – covered with a cloth to protect them from flies – in the shade or indoors.

Add salt whenever you want to. I honestly don't think it makes any difference to meat tenderness or juiciness whether you add the salt before, during or after the braai.

The meat should be dry when it goes onto the fire; do not baste until both sides of the meat have been over the coals for 2 minutes each. And use braai tongs, not a fork, to turn the meat. A fork will make holes in the meat and you might lose some juice.

Steaks should be done medium rare. Take note of the time the steaks go onto the grid and take them off after about 7 minutes. Steaks cut to a thickness of 2½ cm to 3 cm, braaied on extremely hot coals, and at a grid height of 10 cm, take about 7 minutes in total to become medium rare. Break up the 7 minutes as follows: after 2 minutes turn the steaks for the first time, then turn them again after another 2 minutes; then turn them after 1½ minutes, with a final turn another 1½ minutes later. They are now ready.

Meat needs to 'rest' for a few minutes before you eat it. This allows the juices to settle down and not all run out when you slice the meat. By the time everyone has sat down and been served, the meat has probably rested enough.

BRAAI FREEDOM FIGHTER BURGER

SERVINGS: 4 | PREP TIME: 10 MINS PLUS FIRE PREPARATION | COOK TIME: 8 MINS PLUS RESTING
SKILL LEVEL: 1 (EASY)

INGREDIENTS

2 tbsp olive oil

2 red onions, sliced or chopped

2 sweet red peppers

2 cloves garlic, crushed or chopped

1 tsp chilli powder or cayenne pepper

2 tbsp paprika

2 tomatoes, chopped

2 tbsp tomato paste

½ cup beef stock

1 kg steak mince

1 tsp sea salt

1 tsp black pepper

4 hamburger rolls, buttered

sour cream, to serve

chopped fresh parsley, to serve

METHOD

Heat the oil in a pan or potjie and fry the onions and peppers for about 4 minutes until they start to soften, then throw in the garlic. Add the chilli powder or cayenne pepper and paprika and stir to release their flavours. Add the tomatoes, tomato paste and beef stock, and stir to combine. Bring to the boil, reduce the heat to a simmer, and allow the flavours to develop and the sauce to thicken. Check the pan or potjie every now and then to stir the sauce and make sure it doesn't cook dry or burn.

Meanwhile, wet your hands with water and divide the mince into 4 equal-sized patties. Shape them into rounds, flattening them out quite well, as they will shrink a little during the braaiing process. Sprinkle with salt and pepper on both sides just before or during braaiing. Braai them over very hot coals for 8 minutes, turning only once.

Remove the patties from the braai and rest them for a few minutes. Meanwhile, briefly toast the insides of the buttered rolls on the braai for bonus points. Assemble the burger as follows: roll, patty, sauce, dollop of sour cream, chopped parsley. Serve immediately.

PERI-PERI SAUCE

SERVINGS: 10 (1 MEDIUM JAR) | PREP TIME: 10 MINS | COOK TIME: 30 MINS | SKILL LEVEL: 1 (EASY)

INGREDIENTS

8 cloves garlic, finely chopped

½ cup oil

½ cup grape vinegar (red or white)

½ cup lemon juice

½ cup water

2 tbsp paprika

2 tbsp chilli powder

2 tbsp coarse salt

a few small, hot chillies (see Tip)

METHOD

Put the garlic, oil, vinegar, lemon juice, water, paprika, chilli powder and salt in a glass jar. Close the lid tightly and shake well until the ingredients are mixed and all the salt has dissolved. Taste the sauce and start adding chopped fresh chilli to taste. Remember that your guests might like much less heat than you do – I often make two batches of this sauce, one with fewer chillies than the other. Remember not to touch your eyes or any other sensitive parts of your body while making this sauce, as you will burn yourself. As soon as you are finished preparing it, wash your hands thoroughly (and then still be careful).

TIP

African bird's eye or piri-piri chillies are my first choice for this sauce – they are small and very hot – but you can use any small, potent chillies. The very best option is to grow your own.

This sauce will improve with age and keeps for several weeks in the fridge.

ABIGAIL DONNELLY
FOOD EDITOR

GNOCCHI WITH SAGE BUTTER & CHILLI
GOOEY PAVLOVA WITH POACHED PEACHES

It is super exciting being part of the culinary industry in SA right now. It's booming, and chefs and producers have never been so good. Every day I live, love and dream food. I chose these recipes because they are always unique – every time I make pavlova it turns out differently – but are always a hit too. My friends and family adore them. *Abigail*

Simonstown,
Western Cape

GNOCCHI WITH SAGE BUTTER & CHILLI

SERVINGS: 4 | PREP TIME: 20 MINS | COOK TIME: 55 MINS | SKILL LEVEL: 2 (MODERATE)

INGREDIENTS

800 g potatoes, unpeeled
1 free-range egg
300 g cake flour
1 tsp freshly ground
   nutmeg
flour for rolling out

Sage butter
125 g butter
8 sage leaves
3 cloves garlic, crushed
juice of 1 lemon
1 red chilli, chopped
   (optional)
grated Parmesan, to serve

METHOD

Pre-heat the oven to 180°C. Place the potatoes on a baking tray and roast for about 45 minutes. Cut each potato in half and scoop out the flesh into a bowl. Put the potato flesh through a potato ricer twice (this will ensure a silky-smooth consistency). Add the egg, flour and nutmeg, and season to taste. Mix gently. The mixture should be soft.

Gently flour a surface and your hands, take a handful of potato and gently roll into a log – use just enough flour and not too much. The roll should be about 2 cm thick. Using a sharp knife, cut off pieces about 2 cm long – don't let them touch each other – and continue until you have used up all the dough.

Bring a large pot of salted water to the boil and cook about 10 gnocchi at a time. Remove with a slotted spoon when they rise to the surface.

To make the sage butter, melt the butter with the sage in a frying pan. Add the garlic and cook until the butter turns golden brown. Squeeze in the lemon juice and add the chilli, if using. Season.

To serve the dish, place the gnocchi on a platter and spoon over the sage butter. Scatter with grated Parmesan.

GOOEY PAVLOVA WITH POACHED PEACHES

SERVINGS: 8 | PREP TIME: 15 MINS | COOK TIME: 3 HOURS | SKILL LEVEL: 2 (MODERATE)

INGREDIENTS

12 free-range eggs,
   separated
660 g caster sugar
full-cream yoghurt, to serve

Peaches
12 ripe peaches
400 g caster sugar
3 cups (750 ml) verjuice
1 vanilla pod, cut in half
   lengthwise
4 bay leaves
rose-water (optional)

METHOD

Pre-heat the oven to 120°C. Place the egg whites in a very clean bowl. Beat until frothy, then add the sugar in stages. Beat until the meringue is thick, white and a glorious mass. Dollop onto a large baking tray lined with a silicone baking mat (I use a Silpat) or greased baking paper. Spread out into a circle and make peaks up the sides. Bake for 3 hours.

To make the peaches, cut a cross in the bottom of each peach. Place them, with all the rest of the ingredients except the rose-water, in a deep pan. Cover with a piece of greaseproof paper and tuck it in around the peaches. Simmer for 20 minutes or until they're soft but still whole. Remove the peaches and reduce the liquid by simmering it until reduced. Slip the skins off the peaches and put them back into the liquid. If you like, add a dash of rose-water. Set aside to cool slightly.

Serve the meringue topped with the peaches and dolloped with yoghurt.

TIP

When making the meringue, warm the sugar in the oven for a few minutes: this helps it to dissolve into the egg whites more easily and also makes them whip up into a greater volume of meringue.

COCO REINARHZ
SEL ET POIVRE

THE GREAT
SOUTH AFRICAN
BREAKFAST

For me, food and cooking reflect who I am. I'm a pan-Africanist and love to mix the cooking of places where I've lived, from Belgium to France and Congo to South Africa. I love the idea of cooking a breakfast for all the great South Africans out there. And I think if you are feeding people, then you're a hero.

Coco

Morningside, Gauteng

THE GREAT SOUTH AFRICAN BREAKFAST

SERVINGS: 4 | PREP TIME: 5 MINS | COOK TIME: 70 MINS | SKILL LEVEL: 1 (EASY)

INGREDIENTS

1 tbsp olive oil
1 large onion, chopped
500 g beef mince
1 clove garlic, crushed
200 ml beef stock
2 tsp mixed herbs
1 x 400 g can chopped
   tomatoes
1 tbsp tomato purée
1 tsp sugar
1 x 400 g can baked
   beans
4 vetkoek (see recipe on
   page 150)
fresh herbs, to garnish

METHOD

Heat the olive oil in a heavy pan on medium heat. Add the onion and cook until softened. Add the mince and fry until browned. Add the crushed garlic and cook for a further minute. Add the beef stock, mixed herbs, chopped tomatoes, tomato purée and 500 ml water, and bring to a simmer. Cook, covered, for 40 minutes. Add the baked beans and simmer for another 20 minutes.

Garnish with fresh herbs from the garden and serve with vetkoek.

SKYE FEHLMANN
WITH CREED
NATURALLY ORGANIC

HOME-MADE BASIL PESTO
BRAAIED COURGETTES
WITH TORTILLAS & PESTO

For me, food is soil, and soil is the lifeblood of good food.
Nourishing the soil is a large part of what we do on the farm —
compost is king! I started farming organically when I realised
I was eating food that was damaging nature, the world and, in
effect, us as humans. Our land is constantly under threat as the
city sprawls, so a big part of what we do is educating people
about the importance of the land as a food source.

*Philippi,
Western Cape*

HOME-MADE BASIL PESTO

SERVINGS: 6 | PREP TIME: 5 MINS | SKILL LEVEL: 1 (EASY)

INGREDIENTS

10 handfuls basil
½ handful Italian parsley
6 cloves garlic
3 handfuls Parmesan
1 handful almonds
  (or nuts of preference)
juice of 1 large lemon
1½ cups olive oil
olive oil, for covering

METHOD

Blend all the ingredients except the olive oil for covering in a food processor until the desired consistency is reached. Taste and season well. Store in an airtight jar, covered with extra olive oil, until needed.

TIP

If your budget doesn't stretch to almonds, try using sunflower seeds. The flavour of the pesto is just as good but it has a slightly different nuttiness.

BRAAIED COURGETTES WITH TORTILLAS & PESTO

SERVINGS: 4 | PREP TIME: 10 MINS | COOK TIME: 15 MINS | SKILL LEVEL: 1 (EASY)

INGREDIENTS

6 courgettes,
  sliced in half lengthways
olive oil
12 corn tortillas (I use
  Santa Anna's non-GMO)
3 balls mozzarella, torn
1 cup home-made basil
  pesto (see recipe above)
250g sour cream
  or crème fraîche
green leaves, to serve
edible flowers, to serve

METHOD

In a large bowl, toss the courgette slices with olive oil and season really well with salt and pepper. Once the braai coals are ready, grill the courgettes for a few minutes on each side until just cooked through (a little crunch is good). Remove from heat and set aside. Heat the tortillas on the braai for a few minutes on each side. Serve the warm tortillas stuffed with the braaied courgettes and torn mozzarella, plus dollops of pesto and sour cream, green leaves and edible flowers.

SIPHOKAZI MDLANKOMO
MASTERCHEF SOUTH AFRICA RUNNER-UP

SPINACH & FETA
GNOCCHI ROULADE
BAKED NECTARINES

I fell in love with Italian food as soon as I started to use Italian cookery books. It is so simple and unfussy. With only three ingredients you can have a meal in no time at all, which is great when you are a busy working woman. I met Marco Pierre White and he showed me a version of this nectarine dish using plums. I've changed it to nectarines because in South Africa they are the best fruit.

Siphokazi

Newlands,
Western Cape

SPINACH & FETA GNOCCHI ROULADE

SERVINGS: 6 | PREP TIME: 25 MINS | COOK TIME: 50 MINS | SKILL LEVEL: 2 (MODERATE)

INGREDIENTS

6 potatoes,
  peeled and cubed
½ cup flour
1 egg yolk
⅓ cup grated Parmesan
1 bunch spinach
½ small onion, chopped
1 clove garlic
2 blocks or rounds feta
olive oil for frying
grated Parmesan, to serve

Napolitana sauce
30 ml olive oil
1 clove garlic, sliced
1 x 410 g can tomatoes,
  blended
1 tbsp Italian herbs
1 tsp sugar

METHOD

Place the potatoes in a pot and cover with water, bring to the boil and cook until soft.

While the potatoes are cooking, make the Napolitana sauce. Heat the olive oil in a pan and fry the garlic. Add the tomatoes, herbs and sugar and cook for 10 minutes. Keep warm.

Drain the potatoes and pass through fine sieve. Add flour, egg and Parmesan to the sieved potato, season with salt and pepper and stir to combine. Set aside.

Place the spinach, onion and garlic in a food processor and pulse, then add the feta cheese and pulse to mix.

Lay a large sheet of plastic wrap on top of a clean tea towel. Spoon the potato mixture on top of the plastic wrap and spread out to 1 cm thick, then spread the spinach filling on top of the potato layer. Roll up tightly and secure the ends to make a firm roll, then wrap with the tea towel and secure the ends.

Bring a pot of salted water to the boil and cook the roll for 20 minutes. Remove roll from pot and remove the cloth and plastic wrap. Cut roll into slices and fry the slices on both sides.

Serve with the Napolitana sauce, sprinkled with extra Parmesan.

BAKED NECTARINES

SERVINGS: 6 | PREP TIME: 15 MINS | COOK TIME: 25 MINS | SKILL LEVEL: 1 (EASY)

INGREDIENTS

80 g butter
½ cup caster sugar
1 star anise
1 cinnamon stick
6 nectarines
vanilla ice cream, to serve

METHOD

Pre-heat the oven to 180°C. In a pan, melt the butter and add the caster sugar, followed by the spices and nectarines. Cook on the stove for 2 minutes, then transfer to the oven and cook for 20 minutes or until the nectarines are soft. Serve with the ice cream, drizzled with the pan juices from the nectarines.

Our Karoo cooking has the plaas (farm) touch. But it's also the balance of flavours that interests me. As the old saying goes: 'Food must never taste like rainwater.' I make our boerewors with my right-hand man, Henk van Rooi (see page 77). We've been experimenting with boerewors made from venison and Karoo lamb for years.

Annatjie

ANNATJIE REYNOLDS
KAROO QUEEN OF VENISON

VENISON BOBOTIE
VENISON BOEREWORS
HOME-MADE
TAMATIESMOOR

Richmond,
Northern Cape

VENISON BOBOTIE

SERVINGS: 6 | PREP TIME: 20 MINS | COOK TIME: 25–30 MINS | SKILL LEVEL: 1 (EASY)

INGREDIENTS

20 ml oil

20 ml butter

1 kg minced venison

2 thick slices bread, crusts removed

250 ml (1 cup) full-cream milk

2 onions, finely chopped

50 ml oil

3 large cloves garlic, finely chopped

25 mm piece fresh ginger, peeled and finely chopped, or 8 ml ground ginger

25 ml fresh lemon juice

15 ml smooth apricot jam

45 ml mild (or according to taste) curry powder

1 large egg

100 ml cream

40 ml seedless raisins (optional)

60 ml blanched almonds (optional)

3 fresh lemon or bay leaves

steamed rice, to serve

stewed dried fruit, to serve

Topping

3 eggs, beaten

250 ml cream

2 ml ground turmeric

METHOD

Pre-heat the oven to 180°C. Heat the oil and butter and fry the meat until cooked and brown. Soak the bread in the milk and mash with a fork. Braise the onions in oil until soft and transparent (cover with a lid to prevent the onions from browning). Add the garlic and ginger, and stir-fry briefly. Remove from heat and cool slightly, then stir in the lemon juice and apricot jam. Sprinkle the curry powder over the onion mixture, return to medium heat and stir-fry again. If it sticks to the pan, add small quantities of water. Beat together the egg and cream, season with salt and pepper and combine with the meat, onion mixture and bread. Mix lightly with a large two-pronged fork. Stir in the raisins and almonds, if using. Spoon into a greased ovenproof dish and push a few lemon or bay leaves into the mixture.

To make the topping, beat together the eggs, cream and turmeric and season with salt and pepper. Pour over the meat mixture in the ovenproof dish and bake for approximately 40 minutes, until the topping is brown and firm. Serve with rice and stewed dried fruit.

"We live a simple life on the farm, and are often reminded that we need each other and cannot live a selfish life out here. My friend Lynne Minnaar, who lives 'just around the corner' – 120km away – makes a great venison pie. It's definitely worth driving that distance for!"

VENISON BOEREWORS

MAKES: ABOUT 3½ KG | PREP TIME: 10 MINS PLUS STANDING | SKILL LEVEL: 1 (EASY)

INGREDIENTS

2 kg venison (use cuts from the forequarter such as shoulder and neck)

500 g pork

500 g fatty mutton

50 ml coriander seeds, toasted, ground and sifted

2 ml ground cloves

2 ml freshly grated nutmeg

25 ml salt

5 ml freshly ground black pepper

150 ml brown grape vinegar

500 g bacon

natural sausage casings

METHOD

Cut the venison, pork and mutton into cubes. Combine with the spices and seasoning. Leave to stand in a cool place for a few hours for the flavours to develop and be absorbed. Sprinkle the meat mixture with the vinegar. Add the bacon to the mixture and mince it all coarsely (do not overwork the minced meat). Stuff into sausage casings.

TIP

The total quantity of meat you use should remain consistent as suggested above, but the ratios can be adjusted according to taste. Pork could be omitted, for example, and replaced with more mutton or fatty beef. Sheep's tail fat can be used instead of bacon.

HOME-MADE TAMATIESMOOR
(BRAISED TOMATO SAUCE)

SERVINGS: 8 | PREP TIME: 10 MINS | COOK TIME: 30–50 MINS | SKILL LEVEL: 1 (EASY)

INGREDIENTS

80 ml oil

2 large onions, finely chopped

3 cloves garlic, finely chopped

8 large ripe red tomatoes, skinned and chopped into small cubes

150 ml tomato purée

15 ml brown sugar

METHOD

Heat the oil and, in a covered pan, braise the onions and garlic slowly over low heat until transparent and soft. Add the tomato cubes, tomato purée and sugar. Simmer slowly until most of the liquid has been absorbed and the sauce has thickened. Enjoy at once, or bottle in sterilised glass jars for later use.

TIPS

Tamatiesmoor (braised tomato sauce) is a delicious way to preserve your tomato crop and the sauce is a favourite during the cold, lean Karoo winter months. Bottle the sauce and keep on your pantry shelf – it's delicious in pasta dishes or served with boerewors over mashed potatoes or mieliepap.

Fresh or dried basil and origano are delicious additions to this sauce: simply add during the final stage of the cooking process. Chop the herbs very finely or use the dried variety. Chopped chillies can also be added.

FRANCK DANGEREUX
THE FOOD BARN

GRILLED SUSTAINABLE FISH WITH MINTED BABA GHANOUSH, BURNT ONION SHELL & GREEN OIL
PLUMS IN VERBENA SYRUP WITH ALMOND GRATIN, GRANOLA & HAZELNUT ICE CREAM

Juggling the life of a restaurant chef and father is not easy, but I love the days when I can sit down and enjoy food with my family and friends. Our food is classically simple and inspired by the seasons. The baba ghanoush recipe makes loads because it goes with everything and will keep in the fridge, and the plums, for me, signify the end of summer, when the last of them are picked and the lemon verbena is drying in the shed.

franck

*Noordhoek,
Western Cape*

GRILLED SUSTAINABLE FISH WITH MINTED BABA GHANOUSH, BURNT ONION SHELL & GREEN OIL

SERVINGS: 4 | PREP TIME: 1 HOUR | COOK TIME: 1 HOUR PLUS FILTERING | SKILL LEVEL: 2 (MODERATE)

INGREDIENTS

8 baby heirloom yellow and red tomatoes

1 medium onion, peeled

4 x 120 g fillets red-skinned sustainable gurnard or santer, skin on and bones removed

olive oil

micro coriander leaves, to garnish

12 mint leaves, to garnish

Green oil

70 g each of fresh parsley, coriander, mint, washed

300 ml sunflower oil

1 tsp ground cinnamon

Baba ghanoush

2 large aubergines

olive oil

1 tsp crushed garlic

1 tsp chopped fresh marjoram

4 tbsp chopped fresh mint

2 tbsp chopped fresh coriander

3 tbsp chopped fresh flat-leaf parsley

1 tbsp melted goat's milk butter

2 tbsp tahini paste

juice of 1 lemon

120 ml home-made mayonnaise

METHOD

Make the green oil the day before. Place a large pot of salted water on the heat and bring to the boil. Add all the herbs and blanch for 3 minutes. Strain and refresh the herbs in iced water. When cool, squeeze most of the water out of the cooked herbs. Place in a powerful blender (I use a Nutribullet) with the oil and cinnamon and blitz for 1 minute. Place a paper coffee filter over a jar, pour the green mixture into the filter and allow to drip through overnight.

The following day, prepare the rest of the dish. Slice the larger tomatoes in half and set aside. Place the peeled onion on a small plate, cover in plastic wrap and cook for 1 minute in the microwave. Remove and allow to cool. Place a non-stick pan on high heat, halve the onion and place it, cut-side down, in the hot pan. Cook until blackened, separate the burnt onion 'shells', and set aside.

To make the baba ghanoush, pre-heat the oven to 180°C. Place the whole aubergines on a baking tray and bake for about 1 hour until soft. Take out of the oven and leave to cool slightly. Slice off the aubergine stems, cut the aubergines in half and scoop out the flesh with a spoon, adding it to the bowl of a food processor. Retain half of the cooked skin from one of the aubergines and add to the flesh in the processor. Add all the remaining ingredients except the mayonnaise. Blend until the baba ghanoush is completely blended but still retains some texture. Add the mayonnaise, blend and season to taste with salt and pepper. If the consistency is a little thick, add a splash of water to thin it down.

To cook the fish, heat a large non-stick frying pan, season the fish with salt and pepper, and rub it with olive oil. Place a little olive oil in the pan and cook the fish, skin-side down, until the skin is crispy around the edges. Turn over and fry briefly until just cooked – the cooking time will vary according to the thickness of the fish fillets, and the fish will continue to cook slightly while it rests.

To assemble the dish, spoon some baba ghanoush onto plates, add some tomatoes and the burnt onions, add some coriander micro leaves and the mint leaves, place the rested fish in the middle and drizzle with the green oil. I serve with polenta tubes and grilled aubergine slices.

PLUMS IN VERBENA SYRUP WITH ALMOND GRATIN, GRANOLA & HAZELNUT ICE CREAM

SERVINGS: 4 | PREP TIME: 1 HOUR | COOK TIME: 55 MINS PLUS FREEZING
SKILL LEVEL: 2–3 (MODERATELY CHALLENGING)

INGREDIENTS

4 ripe red plums, washed, cut in half and pips removed

Hazelnut ice cream

250 ml milk

3 egg yolks

75 g sugar

1 tsp cornflour, diluted in 2 tbsp cold water

2 tbsp Nutella

Verbena syrup

150 g sugar

150 ml water

a small handful of lemon verbena leaves

1 tsp cornflour diluted in a little cold water

Granola

50 g whole almonds

50 g whole hazelnuts

50 g rolled oats

50 g sunflower seeds

50 g whole macadamia nuts

60 g honey

Almond cream

2 egg yolks

40 g sugar

30 g ground almonds

110 ml fresh cream, whipped

METHOD

First make the ice cream: scald the milk over medium heat and in the meantime, cream together the egg yolks, sugar and cornflour, whisking the mixture continuously until it turns a pale yellow colour. By now your milk should be simmering. Whisking constantly, pour a little of the milk into the egg mixture to warm and dilute it slightly, gradually adding in up to half the milk. When well mixed, carefully return all the egg mixture to the milk in the pot, whisking constantly. Watch out: this is where it can all go wrong! Return to medium heat and stir continuously with a wooden spoon, ensuring the cream doesn't catch at the bottom of the pot. After just a couple of minutes, the custard will start to thicken: you need to cook it until it coats the back of the spoon. Remove from the heat and decant immediately into a large cold bowl. Allow to cool a little and whisk in the Nutella. If you have an ice-cream machine, churn the ice cream to freeze. If not, place in the freezer, whisking from time to time to prevent ice crystals from forming.

Make the verbena syrup by combining the sugar and water in a pot. Place on the heat and add the lemon verbena leaves. Bring to the boil and cook gently for 10 minutes. Remove the verbena and add the halved plums to the syrup. Cover the pot with a lid and cook gently for 5 minutes (or until the plums are cooked but not falling apart). Remove the plums from the syrup and set aside to cool. Bring the syrup in the pot to the boil and whisk in the diluted cornflour. Bring to the boil again. Decant into a container and refrigerate.

To make the granola, pre-heat the oven to 180°C. Combine all the ingredients in a large bowl and mix together with your hands. Place a sheet of baking paper on a baking tray and place the nut mixture on the paper. Spread it out evenly over the surface of the paper. Bake for 20 minutes. Remove from the oven and allow to cool on the tray. Set aside.

Make the almond cream by creaming the egg yolks and sugar together until slightly pale. Fold in the ground almonds and whipped cream, and refrigerate.

To finish the dish, pre-heat the oven grill. Place the cooked plums, cut-sides up, on a baking tray, and add a tablespoon of almond cream to the top of each plum half. Place under the grill and watch closely as it gratinates, as this happens quite quickly. Remove from the oven when done. Drizzle some of the verbena syrup onto each plate and sprinkle with granola. If using, add a few raspberries to each plate. Place 2 plum halves on each plate and finish by scooping a dollop of ice cream onto each plate. I serve with the ice cream in a tuile to prevent it melting onto the plate, and garnish with fresh raspberries and edible flowers.

YUDHIKA SUJANANI
HOLI COW DELI AND COOKING SCHOOL

PEPPERED CRAYFISH
CHICKEN & SPINACH CURRY
LAYERED LAMB BIRYANI
TURKISH DELIGHT CAKE

I grew up doing my homework at the kitchen table, cherishing the warm aromas and hearing the gentle swish of my gran's sari as she moved about from one kitchen task to the next. The kitchen was the heart of our home, and the heartbeat was the food that came out of it. Love is always the secret ingredient that turns ordinary food into magnificent feasts.

Fourways,
Gauteng

PEPPERED CRAYFISH

SERVINGS: 4 | PREP TIME: 15 MINS | COOK TIME: 15 MINS | SKILL LEVEL: 1 (EASY)

INGREDIENTS

60 ml sunflower oil
5 ml mustard seeds
5 ml cumin seeds
1 onion, finely chopped
7 ml coarse salt
2 sprigs curry leaves
15 ml crushed garlic
15 ml red chilli powder
2 x 400 g cans chopped tomatoes
10 ml ground coriander
5 ml ground cumin
2½ ml turmeric
2 medium crayfish tails, shelled
  and deveined
100 ml fresh cream
5 ml sugar
10 ml dried fenugreek (optional)
15 ml freshly ground black pepper
fresh curry leaves, to garnish
fresh coriander, to garnish

METHOD

Heat sunflower oil in a pot. Add mustard seeds, and when they begin to splutter, sprinkle in cumin seeds. When cumin seeds turn golden brown, add the onion, salt and curry leaves. Sauté until onion is light golden brown. Add crushed garlic and stir until fragrant, taking care not to let it burn. Sprinkle in chilli powder and stir-fry the onions for 3 to 5 seconds. Pour in the tomatoes and stir well. Sprinkle in ground coriander, cumin and turmeric and simmer on a medium heat until the tomatoes soften.

Place crayfish tails in the tomato sauce and simmer until tails change colour and start to coil up. Add a little boiling water if the sauce is too thick. Pour fresh cream over the tails and add a pinch of sugar. Use your fingertips to crush dried fenugreek (if using) over the pan, then simmer until the tails are cooked through. Sprinkle freshly ground black pepper over the cooked tails and stir gently.

Serve garnished with curry leaves and coriander.

TIP

The crayfish tails can be substituted with fresh prawns.

LAYERED LAMB BIRYANI

SERVINGS: 4–6 | PREP TIME: 20 MINS | COOK TIME: 1½ HOUR 30 MINS | SKILL LEVEL: 2 (MODERATE)

INGREDIENTS

4 medium potatoes
sunflower oil for frying
2 onions, finely sliced
60 ml sunflower oil
1 large stick cinnamon
2 bay leaves
4 cardamom pods
5 ml cumin seeds
1 large onion, finely
  chopped
7½ ml coarse salt
15 ml crushed garlic
20 ml crushed ginger

METHOD

Peel potatoes and slice into thick rounds. Heat a little sunflower oil in a pan and fry the potatoes until tender. Remove from the oil and leave to drain. Gently dab the excess oil with paper towel. Fry sliced onion until light golden brown, then remove from the oil and drain. Spread onion slices out on paper towel to drain further.

Heat 60 ml sunflower oil in a large heavy-bottomed pot. Fry cinnamon and bay leaves until fragrant. Add cardamom pods and cumin seeds. When the cumin seeds start to sizzle, add chopped onion and salt. Sauté until onion is light golden brown. Add crushed garlic and ginger. Stir for a few seconds and then add the chilli powder. Stir well and add the lamb knuckles. Mix the knuckles into the chilli paste and continue stirring until the meat begins to stick. Lower the heat and scrape the bottom of the pot with a wooden spoon. Add ground coriander, cumin, garam masala and turmeric. When the spices

30 ml red chilli powder
1¼ kg lamb knuckles
10 ml ground coriander
10 ml ground cumin
7½ ml garam masala
2½ ml turmeric
100 ml fresh cream
2 x 400 g cans brown
  lentils, drained
500 g basmati rice,
  half cooked
60 g butter, chopped
200 ml boiling water
egg-yellow food colouring
fresh coriander, to garnish

on the bottom of the pot start to brown, pour in enough boiling water to cover the knuckles. Simmer the knuckles on a low heat, adding more water if necessary, for about 1 hour or until tender.

When the knuckles are tender and the sauce has reduced, layer the fried potatoes over the lamb. Pour cream over and then layer half the lentils over the potatoes. Layer half-cooked basmati rice over the lentils and scatter the remaining lentils on top. Dot the rice with chopped pieces of butter. Pour 200 ml boiling water into the pot and sprinkle a few drops of egg-yellow food colouring over the rice. Scatter the fried onion slices over the rice and cover the pot with a tight-fitting lid.

Simmer on the lowest heat setting until the rice has steamed through. Then gently toss the biryani, garnish with coriander and serve.

TIP

The rice must be par-cooked and left to cool completely before being added to the pot to ensure that the grains do not become mushy when the biryani is steamed.

CHICKEN & SPINACH CURRY

SERVINGS: 4 | PREP TIME: 20 MINS | COOK TIME: 15 MINS | SKILL LEVEL: 1 (EASY)

INGREDIENTS

2 tomatoes
400 g baby spinach
60 ml sunflower oil
1 stick cinnamon
1 bay leaf
5 ml cumin seeds
1 onion, finely chopped
5 ml coarse salt
5 ml crushed ginger
5 ml crushed garlic
20 ml red chilli powder
750 g chicken thigh fillets, sliced
5 ml ground cumin
5 ml ground coriander
5 ml garam masala
2 ml turmeric
100 ml boiled water
60 ml fresh cream
chopped fresh coriander,
  to garnish

METHOD

Blanch, peel and chop the tomatoes. Set aside. Roughly chop the baby spinach and set aside.

Heat sunflower oil in a pot. Fry cinnamon and bay leaf until they turn a shade or two darker. Add cumin seeds and when they start to sizzle add chopped onion. Add salt and sauté until the onion is light golden brown in colour. Add crushed ginger and garlic to the onion and fry for a few seconds until the moisture evaporates. Then add chilli powder and fry for a few seconds. Add the sliced chicken, stirring it in well so that it is coated in the fried onion. Once the chicken is sealed, add ground cumin, coriander, garam masala and turmeric. Stir-fry the chicken until the spices start to stick to the base of the pot.

Stir in the chopped tomatoes and, using a wooden spoon, loosen the spices stuck to the pan. Continue stirring until the sauce thickens and coats the chicken. Then add 100 ml boiled water and simmer for 2–3 minutes. Pour in cream, add chopped spinach and simmer for 1 minute.

Garnish with chopped coriander and serve with rotis (see recipes on pages 343 and 346), raita (see recipe page 306) and sambals.

TURKISH DELIGHT CAKE

SERVINGS: 8 | PREP TIME: 20 MINS PLUS COOLING | COOK TIME: 20 MINS | SKILL LEVEL: 2 (MODERATE)

INGREDIENTS

8 eggs
370 ml sugar
500 ml cake flour
20 ml baking powder
pinch of salt
120 ml cold water
250 ml sunflower oil
5 ml pure rose essence
5 ml vanilla essence

Icing
125 g butter
750 g icing sugar
2 x 230 g tubs cream
  cheese
2 ml vanilla essence
pink food colouring

Garnish
Turkish delight
a few pistachio nuts
strawberries

METHOD

Pre-heat the oven to 180°C. Grease and line 3 x 20 cm cake tins. Beat eggs until light and fluffy with an electric beater, gradually adding sugar. Continue beating until thick and creamy (the mixture should leave a trail on the surface for 3 seconds). Fold flour, baking powder and salt into the egg mixture. Add water, sunflower oil, rose essence and vanilla essence, then fold the mixture again. Divide mixture into tins and bake for 20 minutes or until a skewer comes out clean when inserted. Turn cakes out onto a wire cooling rack and leave to cool.

To make the icing, cream butter and icing sugar well until light in colour. Add the cream cheese and continue beating until well combined. Add vanilla essence and continue beating until the icing softens, taking care not to overbeat as the icing can split. Tint icing with a few drops of pink food colouring.

Sandwich the cakes together with the icing, reserving enough to be able to smooth it over the top and sides. Garnish with Turkish delight and pistachios and serve with strawberries.

TIP

When making the cake, ensure that the mixing bowl is completely free of oil before whisking the eggs, as oil prevents eggs from incorporating air.

MICK & SALLY HAIGH
CAFÉ BLOOM

GRILLED AUBERGINE ON
WHOLEWHEAT TOAST WITH SWEET
TAHINI & TOMATO-ONION SMOOR

We are crazy about weeds. Our aim at Café Bloom is to present new ideas for eating well. We believe what we put in our mouths alters the way we are, and so at all times we are experimenting and growing. Grow whatever you can in whatever space you have, and don't chuck the weeds – they're free food!

Mick

Nottingham Road, KwaZulu-Natal

GRILLED AUBERGINE ON WHOLEWHEAT TOAST WITH SWEET TAHINI & TOMATO-ONION SMOOR

SERVINGS: 1 | PREP TIME: 10 MINS | COOK TIME: 20 MINS | SKILL LEVEL: 1 (EASY)

INGREDIENTS

1 medium aubergine,
  cut into 5 mm slices

olive oil

1 small onion, finely
  chopped

2 ripe tomatoes, cubed

1 tsp tahini

2 tsp honey

1 slice of your favourite
  wholewheat bread

½ cup mint leaves,
  shredded

½ cup rocket flowers or
  other edible flowers

METHOD

Pre-heat the oven to 180°C. Rub aubergine slices with olive oil and place on a baking tray. Roast in the oven for about 10 minutes or until soft and golden brown. Meanwhile, fry the onion till just beginning to brown before adding the tomato and seasoning to taste. Reduce heat and simmer until consistency is smooth. Set aside.

Pop the bread into the toaster and mix the tahini and honey together.

Once the aubergine is done, you are ready to assemble: place a pinch of shredded mint on your plate, smear toast with the tahini-honey mix and place over the mint. Arrange the aubergine pieces on the toast and dress with the tomato-onion smoor (sauce). Sprinkle with the flowers and the remaining mint, turn off your phone and enjoy.

LISA MARAIS & KEVIN RUCK
WITH LINDELO MADLEVE & JULES MERCER

THE OYSTER LADY

———————————

SMOKED BLACK MUSSELS
WITH AVOCADO
FRESH WEST COAST OYSTERS
WITH GOOSEBERRIES
& ASIAN SESAME SAUCE

We try to present the ocean with minimal intervention. Our oysters and mussels are a great sign of the state of the biosphere down in the water: if there's a healthy ecosystem, there are healthy oysters and mussels. Served fresh and straight from the sea, oysters still contain all of their living chi energy. They are truly nature's bounty.

Lisa

Saldanha Bay,
Western Cape

SMOKED BLACK MUSSELS WITH AVOCADO

SERVINGS: 4 | PREP TIME: 10 MINS | SKILL LEVEL: 1 (EASY)

INGREDIENTS

150 g rocket leaves (optional)

2 avocados, peeled and cut into chunks

a big handful of fresh basil leaves

200 g smoked black mussels (we use The Oyster Lady's Smoked Black Mussels)

crème fraîche, to garnish (optional)

toasted sesame seeds, to garnish (optional)

Dressing

200 ml coconut cream

4 tsp horseradish sauce

1 tsp salt

2 tsp wasabi paste (optional)

METHOD

Mix the dressing ingredients together. Arrange the rocket (if using), avocado and basil leaves on a platter and top with the mussels. Drizzle over the dressing. If using, garnish with dollops of crème fraîche and/or toasted sesame seeds.

FRESH WEST COAST OYSTERS WITH GOOSEBERRIES & ASIAN SESAME SAUCE

SERVINGS: 2 | PREP TIME: 5 MINS | SKILL LEVEL: 1 (EASY)

INGREDIENTS

1 dozen medium West Coast oysters

2 tbsp soy sauce

1 tbsp sesame seeds

a small handful of gooseberries, sliced

tabasco (Original Red or Green Jalapeño)

lime wedges

METHOD

Shuck the oysters and arrange on a platter, loosened on the half shell. Mix together the soy sauce and sesame seeds. Scatter the sliced gooseberries in half of the oyster shells, add a drop or two of Tabasco to each of these shells and squeeze lime juice over them. Add the soy and sesame sauce to the rest of the oysters and serve.

TIP

Oysters have amazing delicate flavours to be savoured, so don't just swallow them, chew them…

MIMI JARDIM
COOKING WITH MIMI

PRAWNS IN BEER
CHOCOLATE SALAMI

I'm a great believer in fresh produce and simple recipes, which I think are both so important in Portuguese cooking. The ingredients list may be short but the flavours are bold and rely heavily on really great quality ingredients. Then of course we must keep cooking and kitchen time quick and easy, so we've got more time for talking and socialising at the family table!

MiMi

Johannesburg,
Gauteng

PRAWNS IN BEER

SERVINGS: 4–6 | PREP TIME: 10 MINS PLUS MARINATING | COOK TIME: 15 MINS | SKILL LEVEL: 1 (EASY)

INGREDIENTS

1 kg medium prawns
25 ml lemon juice
15 ml coarse salt
5 ml pepper
1 bay leaf
small bunch of fresh
  coriander
100 ml butter
75 ml olive oil
5 cloves garlic, crushed
peri-peri sauce
  (see recipes on pages 54
  and 300), to taste
500 ml beer
fresh chillies, to garnish
lemon wedges, to serve

METHOD

Pre-heat the oven to 180°C. Devein the prawns and marinate in the lemon juice, salt, pepper, bay leaf and a sprig of coriander for 10 minutes. Place in a roasting pan.

Melt the butter in a saucepan and add the olive oil, garlic, peri-peri sauce and beer. Pour over the prawns and leave to marinate for 10 minutes. Bake for 10–15 minutes, then place under the grill for 5–6 minutes.

Garnish with fresh chillies and fresh coriander sprigs. Serve immediately with lemon wedges.

CHOCOLATE SALAMI

MAKES: 2 X 20 CM ROLLS | PREP TIME: 10 MINS PLUS SETTING | SKILL LEVEL: 1 (EASY)

INGREDIENTS

20 ml soft butter
200 g sugar
2 eggs
200 g drinking chocolate
  powder
200 g Marie biscuits,
  roughly crushed
sugar for sprinkling

METHOD

Mix together the butter, sugar, eggs and chocolate powder and beat lightly. Fold in the crushed biscuits. If the mixture is too soft, place it in the refrigerator for a while. Turn the mixture onto a sheet of greaseproof paper sprinkled with sugar and shape into 2 rolls of about 20 cm in length. Wrap in the greaseproof paper and refrigerate until set. Cut into slices to serve.

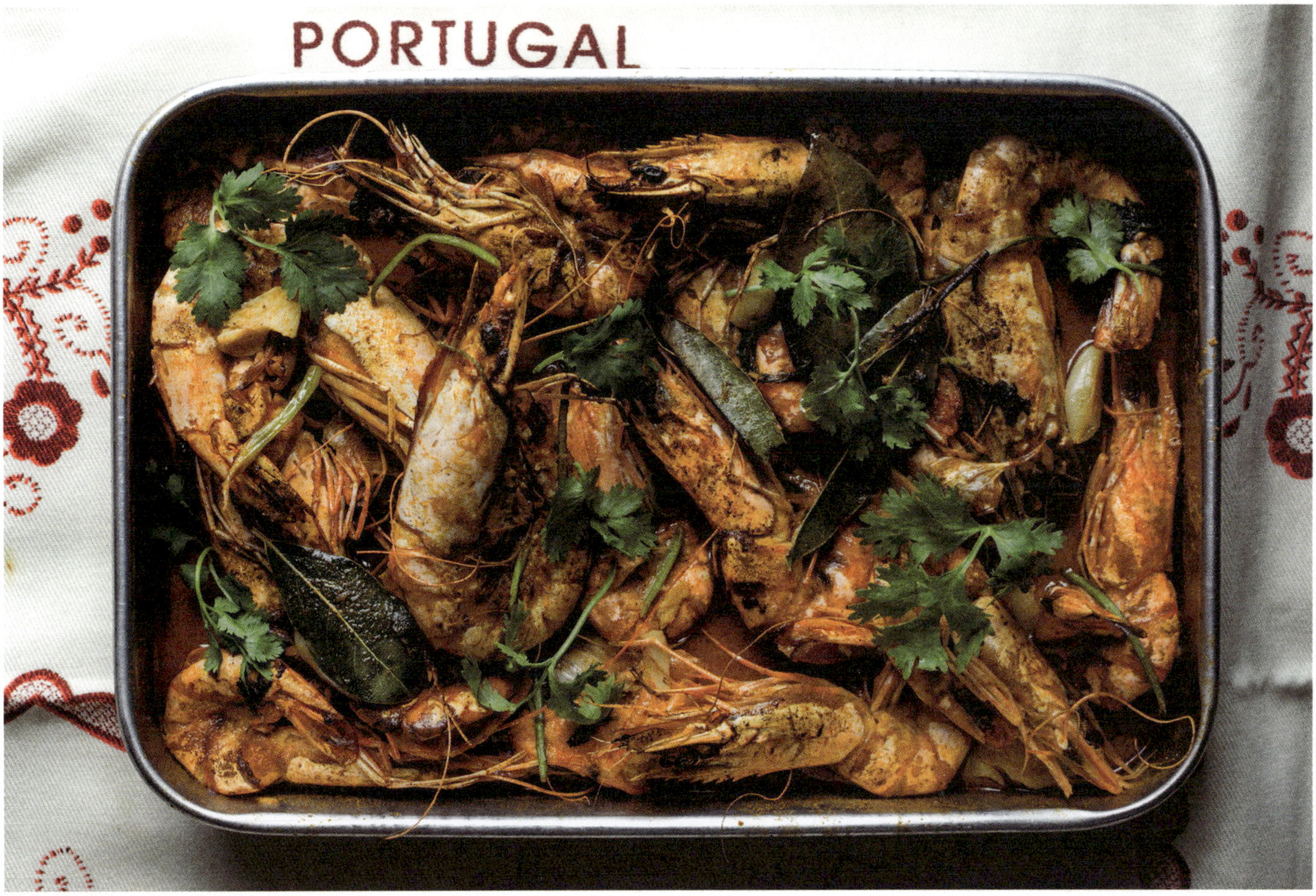
PORTUGAL

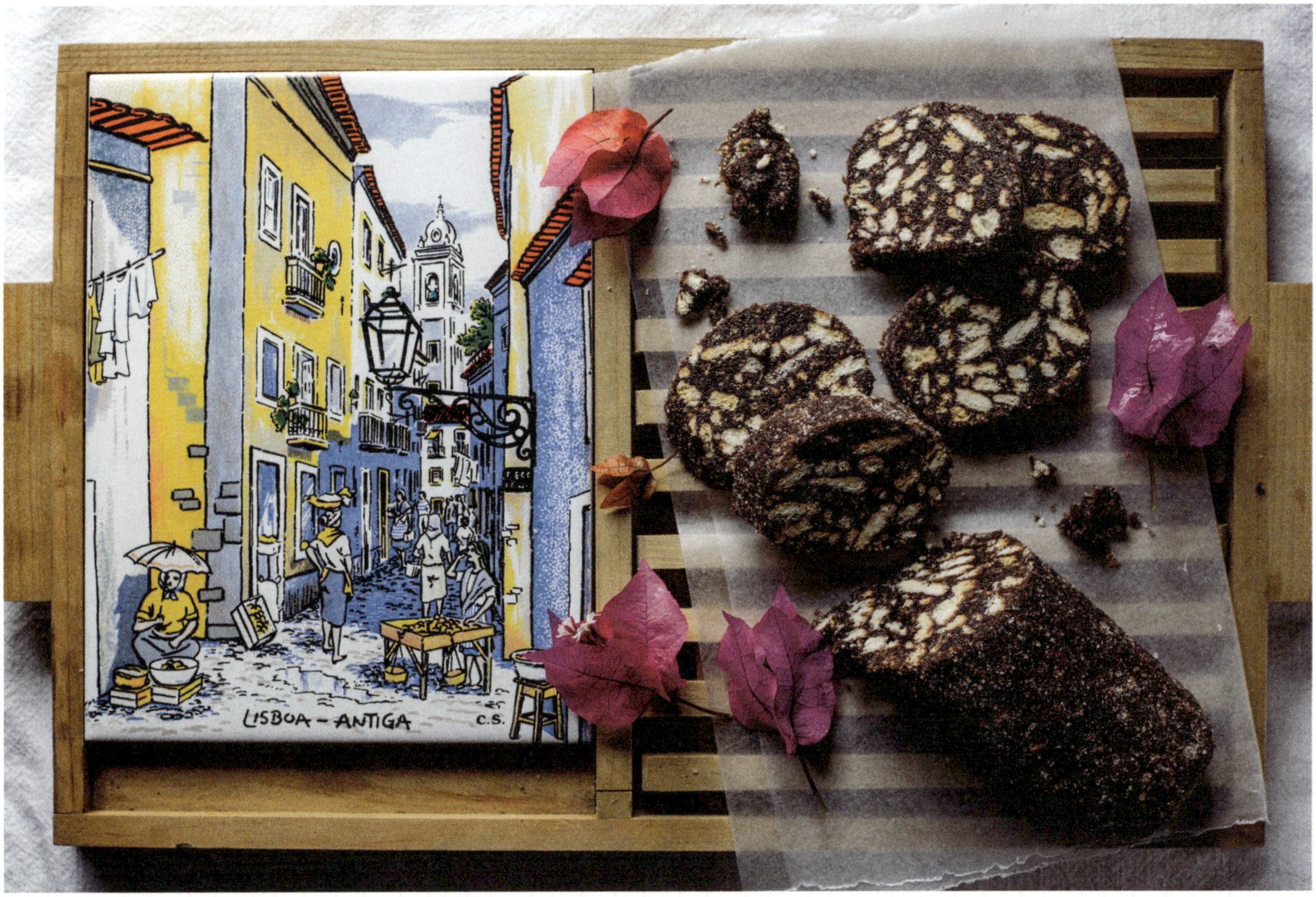
LISBOA - ANTIGA
C.S.

Our family absolutely loves strawberries – 'nature's candy' as they are often called. We believe they are the undisputed super fruit. They are probably one of the most popular fruits among the little ones. There is nothing more glorious than seeing a toddler with red, strawberry-coloured lips...

Yolisua

XOLANI & YOLISWA GUMEDE
CAPPENY ESTATES

GREEN SALAD WITH STRAWBERRIES & STRAWBERRY BALSAMIC VINAIGRETTE
STRAWBERRY COBBLER

*Ballitoville,
KwaZulu-Natal*

GREEN SALAD WITH STRAWBERRIES & STRAWBERRY BALSAMIC VINAIGRETTE

SERVINGS: 4 AS A SIDE DISH | PREP TIME: 10 MINS | SKILL LEVEL: 1 (EASY)

INGREDIENTS

150 g fresh strawberries

120 g baby leaf salad leaves

1 avocado, peeled and sliced

100 g soft goat's milk cheese

Vinaigrette

250 g fresh strawberries, hulled

60 ml olive oil

60 ml balsamic vinegar

½ tsp salt

¼ tsp ground pepper

¼ tsp dried tarragon

¼ tsp honey

METHOD

To make the vinaigrette, place all the ingredients in a blender or food processor. Blend until smooth. Adjust vinegar and honey until you get your preferred balance of sour and sweet.

To make the salad, hull and slice the strawberries. Pile the baby salad leaves in a bowl and add the avocado, goat's milk cheese and sliced strawberries. Dress the salad with the strawberry balsamic vinaigrette and serve immediately.

STRAWBERRY COBBLER

SERVINGS: 4 | PREP TIME: 10 MINS | COOK TIME: 15 MINS | SKILL LEVEL: 1 (EASY)

INGREDIENTS

15 g melted butter
2 cups (500 g)
  strawberries, hulled
60 g unsalted butter,
  at room temperature
110 g sugar
150 g cake flour
125 ml milk
2 tsp baking powder
1 tsp vanilla extract
65 g sugar
125 ml warm water
whipped cream or vanilla
  ice cream, to serve

METHOD

Pre-heat the oven to 180°C. With a pastry brush, coat the bottom of a 13 cm x 9 cm rectangular or large oval ovenproof dish with 15 g melted butter. Spread strawberries evenly on the bottom of the dish. Place dish on a lined baking sheet and set aside. In a medium bowl, mix 60 g unsalted butter, 110 g sugar, cake flour, milk, baking powder and vanilla extract together with a wooden spoon. Spoon batter over the fruit in the dish and spread evenly.

Mix 65 g sugar and warm water together. Pour evenly over the top of the batter. (This gives the cobbler a golden brown crust and makes the strawberries more soft and sweet.)

Bake for 25–30 minutes, until topping is golden brown and fruit is bubbling. Enjoy warm as is, or with whipped cream or vanilla ice cream.

ADI BADENHORST
A. A. BADENHORST FAMILY WINES

RAÚL'S SPANISH TORTILLA
SWARTLAND EGGS BENEDICT

Raúl Perez and his beard come to the Swartland every year. He has a fine beard indeed, a Lord of the Rings-ish kind of beard. Each year he brings his Spanish wine and the finest sherry, and he makes this simple, delicious tortilla. When it comes to buying eggs, don't believe all the boxes that say 'farm fresh' or 'just laid'. Buy your eggs directly from the farm or from your hippie neighbours who still think it's nice to hear a rooster crowing at 4 a.m.

Adi

*Swartland,
Western Cape*

RAÚL'S SPANISH TORTILLA

SERVINGS: 6 | PREP TIME: 15 MINS | COOK TIME: 15–20 MINS | SKILL LEVEL: 1 (EASY)

INGREDIENTS

8 eggs
100 ml milk
200 ml olive oil
3 medium onions, finely chopped
4 medium potatoes, peeled and roughly chopped into small pieces
cayenne pepper, to garnish (optional)
chopped parsley, to garnish (optional)
sliced spring onions, to garnish (optional)

METHOD

Beat the eggs in a bowl and stir in the milk. In a frying pan, heat the oil and when hot, add the onion. Turn down the heat and cook until soft and translucent. When onion is cooked, spoon it out of the pan and directly into the raw beaten egg mixture. Stir gently into the eggs. Cook the potato pieces in the same oil as the onion until soft. (You're not making chips, so make sure the oil isn't too hot.) Add to the eggs and stir in. Pour off the oil, reserving 3 tablespoons of it, and wipe the pan clean. Add the 3 tablespoons of oil back to the pan and heat almost to smoking point (if it's not hot enough, the egg will stick to the pan). Add the egg mixture to the pan and as it cooks, pull it away from the sides of the pan with a spatula, like you would when cooking an omelette. Season with salt and pepper. Turn down the heat, cover and cook gently, being careful not to burn it. After 5 minutes or so, flip the whole thing over and cook the other side for 2 minutes. Slide the tortilla onto a wooden serving board and sprinkle with cayenne pepper, parsley, chopped spring onions or whatever else you fancy to make it look pretty. Can be eaten hot or cold.

SWARTLAND EGGS BENEDICT
POACHED EGGS WITH SKILPADJIES

SERVINGS: 2 | PREP TIME: 10 MINS | COOK TIME: 10 MINS | SKILL LEVEL: 1 (EASY)

INGREDIENTS

4 skilpadjies (portions of lamb's liver wrapped in netvet, which is the fatty membrane that surrounds the kidneys) from your local butcher
olive oil
1 onion, finely sliced
2 glugs wine (A. A. Badenhorst of course!)
1 tbsp vinegar
4 of the freshest eggs you can find
hot buttered toast, to serve

METHOD

Fry the skilpadjies in a little olive oil with the onion until they are cooked through and the onion is soft. Add wine to the pan and allow to reduce and form a gravy. Set aside and make the eggs. Heat a saucepan of water with the vinegar until just below simmering point. Drop the eggs in one at a time and poach to your liking. Serve the poached eggs with the skilpadjies and gravy, buttered toast and lots of salt and pepper.

TIP

Variations on this dish include poached eggs with boerewors and toast, poached eggs and boerewors with spinach, kale or asparagus and toast, and any of the above with tomatoes and new-season, extra virgin olive oil.

MARIE LOMBARD
WITH GERHARD, MARIE- LOUISE, HELEN-JOAN, MELANIE MOOLMAN & MEERKAT FAMILY

DE OUDE KRAAL COUNTRY ESTATE & SPA

MERINO LAMB CARPACCIO

RHEBUCK LOIN STUFFED WITH MARROW & SHIITAKE MUSHROOMS

We've had five generations of women sheep farmers on our land, and luckily I was interested in cooking sheep as well as farming them! My grandfather used to throw grand silver-service dinner parties. As a child, I was in awe of the delicately plated food that was served. I want to continue that inspirational theme and surprise people with what we can serve out here.

Bloemfontein, Free State

MERINO LAMB CARPACCIO

SERVINGS: 8 | PREP TIME: 30 MINS | COOK TIME: 30 MINS | SKILL LEVEL: 1 (EASY)

INGREDIENTS

2 Merino lamb loins

olive oil

fresh figs and mulberries
   (any fresh fruit or berries
   of your choice), to serve

sheep's milk labneh
   cheese, to serve

fig-infused balsamic
   reduction, to garnish

fresh herbs of your choice,
   to garnish

METHOD

Prepare smoker with wood chips (add a few peach-tree leaves, if available, for an extra dimension of flavour). Rub the loins with olive oil. Smoke first loin for 7 minutes. Smoke second loin for 15 minutes. Set aside to cool.

Cut small medallions of both loins and arrange on serving plates. Add fresh fruit, lime zest and labneh cheese. Drizzle with fig-infused balsamic reduction, garnish with fresh herbs and serve.

TIP

Any seasonal fruits, herbs and soft cheese can be used to your taste; what is essential is that the dish features both sweet and sour/tart elements, as these will complement the rich flavour of the lamb.

RHEBUCK LOIN STUFFED WITH MARROW & SHIITAKE MUSHROOMS

SERVINGS: 6 | PREP TIME: 1 HOUR | COOK TIME: 1½ HOURS | SKILL LEVEL: 1 (EASY)

INGREDIENTS

6 marrow bones, plus
  6 extra for serving
  (optional)
1 medium onion, chopped
butter for frying
200 g fresh shiitake
  mushroom, sliced
½ cup grated Cheddar
½ cup Danish feta
1 bunch spring onions,
  chopped
2 slices ciabatta bread,
  processed to form soft
  breadcrumbs
125 g butter
1 rhebuck loin, all sinew
  removed
a few grilled shiitake
  mushrooms, to serve

METHOD

Pre-heat the oven to 200°C. Season the marrow bones and place on a baking sheet. Place in the oven and cook for 50 minutes to 1 hour until just cooked. Cool slightly, then take the marrow out of 6 of the bones and season with salt and black pepper.

Fry onion in a little butter till translucent, season and fry till golden brown. Fry 200 g shiitake mushrooms in a very hot pan with a little butter to ensure moisture evaporates and mushrooms caramelise. Season to taste. Mix together the marrow, fried onion, fried mushrooms, cheeses, spring onions, breadcrumbs and 125 g butter to make the stuffing.

Pre-heat the oven to 160°C or prepare an open braai fire. Make an incision in the rhebuck loin for stuffing without cutting open the sides completely. Fill the loin with the stuffing and close off with toothpicks. Roast the loin in the oven or on the fire on slow heat or roast it until rare or medium rare, about 20 minutes, so the marrow melts and is incorporated into the meat. Rest for 5 minutes. Slice and serve with additional marrow bones, if using, and grilled shiitake mushrooms. We serve the dish with a mushroom sauce for added flavour.

TIPS

Venison is best when obtained from a female animal and when the loin is aged before use.

Venison needs additional fat when cooking, to ensure that the meat does not become dry.

RICHARD HAIGH
ENALENI FARM

AUBERGINES WITH HONEY & MINT
KOLBROEK PORK RIBS
BEETROOT CAKE

I try to cook with everything on the farm. My favourite recipes are also our guests' favourites – simple and delicious. When you cook with such great ingredients, it shows in the end result. We like the concept of abundance, which is why we called our nine-hectare farm Enaleni. It's a Zulu word that implies a place of agricultural abundance; a place where there is more than enough.

Richard

Midlands,
KwaZulu-Natal

AUBERGINES WITH HONEY & MINT

SERVINGS: 4 | PREP TIME: 10 MINS | COOK TIME: 10 MINS | SKILL LEVEL: 1 (EASY)

INGREDIENTS

2 medium-sized firm
  aubergines, topped
  and tailed

oil for frying

½ cup olive oil

a handful of fresh mint
  leaves

1 clove garlic, crushed

zest and juice of 1
  medium-sized lemon

2 tsp coriander seeds,
  lightly cracked

1 tsp honey

METHOD

Cut each aubergine in half lengthways and thinly slice the halves. Fry until lightly brown on each side and soft (a few minutes if the pan is hot enough). While frying the aubergine, put the olive oil, mint leaves and garlic in a pestle and mortar and pound together. Season and add the lemon zest, lemon juice and coriander seeds and mix again. Lastly, add the honey.

When the aubergines are cooked, put them in a bowl and while they are still hot, pour the dressing over. Gently mix for a few minutes to combine the dressing and seal the flavour into the aubergines – this final step is very important.

TIP

This versatile dish is a favourite on the farm; it's excellent combined with haloumi, in a salad, on a baguette or rolled up with figs or cheese as a snack.

KOLBROEK PORK RIBS

SERVINGS: 4 | PREP TIME: 10 MINS PLUS MARINATING | COOK TIME: 55 MINS | SKILL LEVEL: 1 (EASY)

INGREDIENTS

1 kg rack Kolbroek pork ribs

Marinade

1 x 70 g can tomato paste

1 tsp honey

4 tsp soy sauce

¼ tsp sesame oil

2 tsp coriander seeds,
  lightly cracked

½ tsp ground black pepper

½ lemon, juiced

thumb-sized piece of fresh
  ginger, finely grated

1 clove garlic, crushed

½ chilli, finely chopped
  (optional)

METHOD

Mix the marinade ingredients together and smear over the ribs. Place in a ziplock bag and seal. Place in the fridge for 2 days and turn daily.

Pre-heat the oven to 160°C. Place ribs in an ovenproof baking dish and cover. Cook for about 45 minutes, depending on the size of the ribs. When cooked, brown the ribs slightly under the grill, basting them once or twice so they do not dry out.

Serve with a fresh garden salad.

BEETROOT CAKE

SERVINGS: 8–10 | PREP TIME: 15 MINS | COOK TIME: 50 MINS | SKILL LEVEL: 1 (EASY)

INGREDIENTS

1 cup white sugar

4 large free-range eggs

225 ml sunflower oil

2 cups cake flour

3 tsp baking powder

½ tsp mixed spice

½ tsp freshly grated
  nutmeg

3 tsp mixed seeds (linseed,
  poppy, sunflower,
  sesame, pumpkin)

1 cup desiccated coconut

4 medium beetroot, grated
  (about 400 g)

Topping

½ cup double-thick
  yoghurt

1 tsp icing sugar

ground cinnamon or sifted
  icing sugar, for sprinkling

METHOD

Pre-heat the oven to 180°C and lightly grease a round spring-form cake tin with a diameter of about 25 cm. Beat sugar, eggs and oil together until fluffy. Add the flour, baking powder, mixed spice and nutmeg, and mix with a wooden spoon. Add the mixed seeds, coconut and grated beetroot. Pour into the baking tin and bake three-quarters from the top of the oven for about 50 minutes. Test with a skewer to be sure it has cooked through. Remove from the oven, cool and remove from the tin.

Mix the yoghurt and icing sugar together and spread on top of the cooled cake. Sprinkle a little cinnamon over and serve. Or, for a dairy-free version, simply sift icing sugar over the top just before serving.

TIP

Use the same cup for the sugar, flour and coconut; the one I use is roughly 300 ml.

VERA ANN SLUIS-CREMER
KARMA JAMS

SHREDDED ORANGE & PINEAPPLE MARMALADE
PEAR, PINOTAGE & ROSEMARY JAM

I get ideas for the numerous mixtures that I use for my jams by reading as many jam recipe books as I can and by stealing with my eyes at all sorts of fancy delis all over the world. Making jam is very soothing, and the jams are so pretty — like little jewels. The colour of the pear jam is such a gentle pink, it reminds me of Kestell sunsets.

Vera

Kestell, Free State

SHREDDED ORANGE & PINEAPPLE MARMALADE

SERVINGS: ABOUT 2½ LITRES | PREP TIME: 60 MINS | COOK TIME: 1½ HOURS | SKILL LEVEL: 2 (MODERATE)

INGREDIENTS

Pectin soup
10 Granny Smith apples

Marmalade
about 8–10 small oranges
  (use fewer oranges if they
  are large)
1 pineapple, peeled and
  cut into small cubes
1 cup pectin soup
  (see above)
4 cups sugar

METHOD

First make the pectin soup. Peel, core and slice the apples and place them in a pot. Cover with water, bring to the boil and simmer until they are mushy. Strain the apple mixture through cheesecloth and a colander into a large pot or bucket: the liquid (there will be about 1 litre) is pectin soup. It can be used in all jams and helps them to jell.

Peel the oranges with a vegetable peeler and cut the peels into fine shreds with a pair of scissors. Place shreds in a bowl and add the pineapple. Squeeze the oranges and add the juice to the orange peel shreds and pineapple. Add the pectin soup. Measure 4 large cups of the fruit mixture into a large pot and add the sugar. Bring to the boil, slowly stirring until the sugar has completely melted. Turn up the heat and boil the marmalade until setting point has been reached. Setting point is measured when at least 2 drops of the marmalade stick together. Allow the marmalade to cool. Put into sterilised jars and seal.

TIPS

Sourer apples such as Granny Smith are better for the pectin soup, but you can use any variety.

To sterilise the jars, place them in a large pot, cover with water and boil for 10 minutes.

PEAR, PINOTAGE & ROSEMARY JAM

SERVINGS: ABOUT 2½ LITRES | PREP TIME: 30 MINS | COOK TIME: 45 MINS | SKILL LEVEL: 2 (MODERATE)

INGREDIENTS

about 10 pears, peeled and
  cut into small cubes
a handful of rosemary
  leaves (chopped up but
  not too finely; you don't
  want sticks in the jam but
  you do want to see the
  rosemary)
about ½ bottle of Pinotage
  (or other red wine)
1 cup pectin soup
  (see above)
4 cups sugar

METHOD

Mix the pear cubes, rosemary and Pinotage together in a bowl. Add the pectin soup. Measure 4 large cups of the fruit mixture into a large pot and add the sugar. Bring to the boil, slowly stirring until the sugar has completely melted. Also make sure the jam doesn't stick to or burn on the bottom of the pot. Turn the heat up slightly (not to full blast) and keep stirring regularly until the mixture thickens. Put into sterilised jars and seal.

NOTE

Experiment with your own fun flavours: once you have mastered the basic recipes, throw in different fruits and herbs and see what happens.

Karma
Home Products
Pear
Pinotage
and Rosemary
Jam

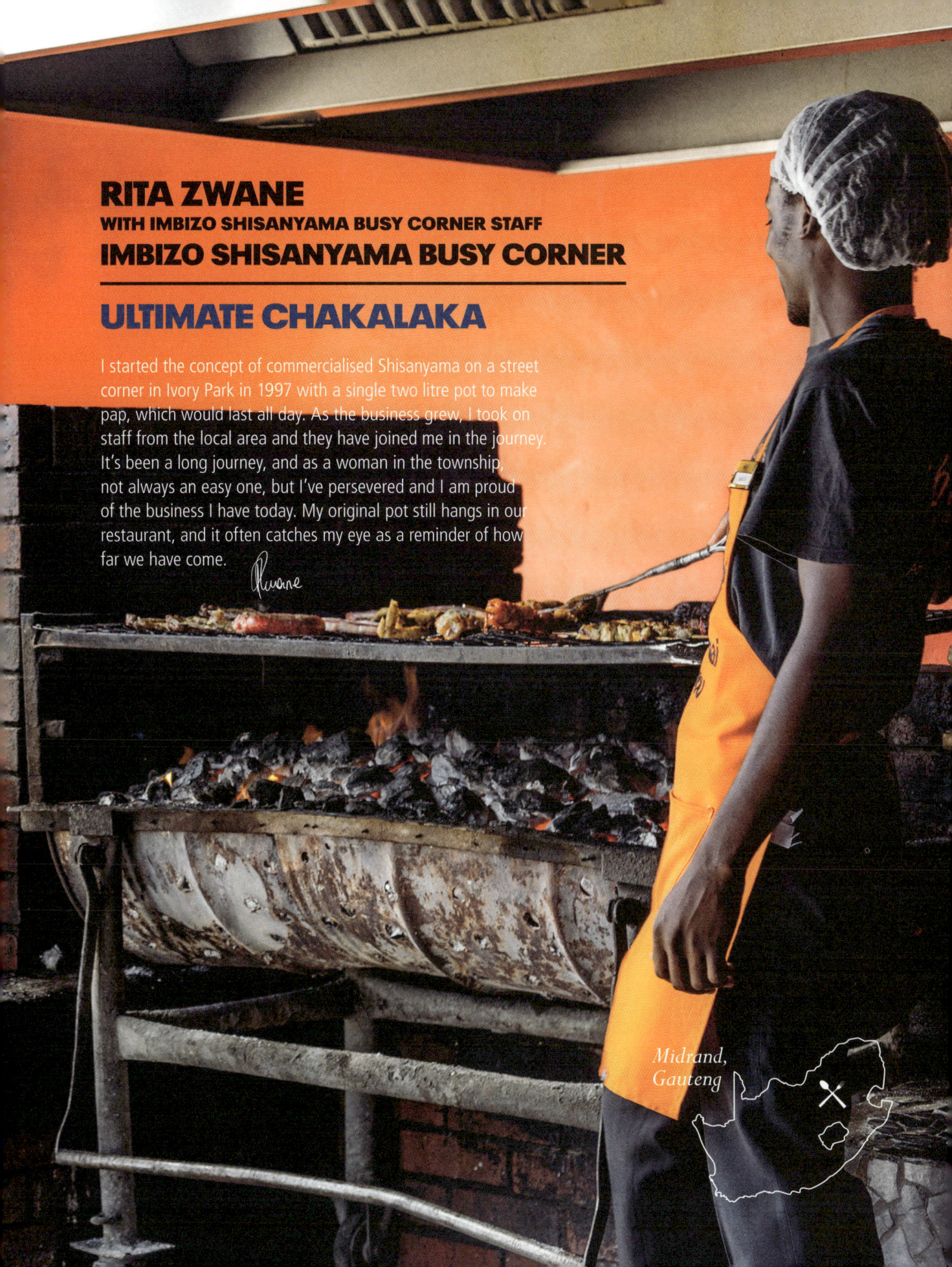

RITA ZWANE
WITH IMBIZO SHISANYAMA BUSY CORNER STAFF
IMBIZO SHISANYAMA BUSY CORNER

ULTIMATE CHAKALAKA

I started the concept of commercialised Shisanyama on a street corner in Ivory Park in 1997 with a single two litre pot to make pap, which would last all day. As the business grew, I took on staff from the local area and they have joined me in the journey. It's been a long journey, and as a woman in the township, not always an easy one, but I've persevered and I am proud of the business I have today. My original pot still hangs in our restaurant, and it often catches my eye as a reminder of how far we have come.

Zwane

Midrand, Gauteng

ULTIMATE CHAKALAKA

SERVINGS: 4–6 | PREP TIME: 5 MINS | COOK TIME: 1¼ HOURS | SKILL LEVEL: 1 (EASY)

INGREDIENTS

150 ml sunflower oil

1 large onion, finely chopped

2 green peppers, de-seeded and diced

2 green chillies, chopped

4 tsp hot curry powder

4 carrots, grated

1 x 410 g can baked beans

1 tsp hot peri-peri sauce

METHOD

Heat a large pan over medium-high heat. Add the oil and sauté the onion, green pepper and chillies until the onions are translucent. Add half of the curry powder and continue to sauté until golden brown in colour. Add the grated carrot and keep stirring and turning the ingredients until the carrots are soft, then add the rest of the curry powder. Turn the heat down to very low, cover and cook slowly for 30–40 minutes, stirring regularly. Add the baked beans and hot peri-peri sauce. Mix thoroughly and simmer gently for a final 15 minutes. Serve hot or cold as part of any good traditional South African meal.

NOTE

At Imbizo Shisanyama, our signature dish is the Original African Braai Mix, which is all about celebrating traditional South African braai food with family and friends. It serves 5–7 people and consists of 280 g of this delicious, spicy chakalaka, as well as 600 g of short rib, 600 g of our special-recipe boerewors, 600 g of chicken wings and drumsticks and 800 g of perfectly roasted lamb chops. The braaied meat is all seasoned with barbecue spice before it's put onto the braai to cook. We serve it all with a generous helping of traditional home-made African dumpling (steamed bread) and iPapa (pap), all accompanied by spinach and coleslaw.

"The concept of shisa nyama comes from our African identity, culture and heritage – simple food cooked on open coals for maximum flavour. Customers come in, pick the meat of their choice, and our braai masters cook it to perfection. I'm always around to help out – this restaurant is my second home and I love being a part of it."

Woodstock,
Western Cape

LUKE DALE-ROBERTS
NATURALIS, POT LUCK CLUB & THE TEST KITCHEN

BARBECUED BROCCOLI MOPS WITH BLUE CHEESE

DUCK BREAST WITH NAARTJIE & YUZU DRESSING

My son and I were eating broccolini one evening, when he picked a piece up by its long stem and shouted, 'Dad, this stuff is exactly the same shape as a mop!' Since then they've been known as broccoli mops in our house, and so I created a nice sauce to mop them up with. *Luke*

BARBECUED BROCCOLI MOPS
WITH BLUE CHEESE SAUCE

SERVINGS: 4–6 | PREP TIME: 10 MINS | COOK TIME: 10 MINS | SKILL LEVEL: 1 (EASY)

INGREDIENTS

250g broccolini or
  tenderstem broccoli
olive oil
sea salt (I use Maldon)
40 g toasted walnuts,
  chopped
40 g toasted flaked
  almonds

Dressing
2½ tbsp honey
2½ tbsp Dijon mustard
150 ml white wine vinegar
375 ml vegetable oil
pinch of salt
2½ tbsp wholegrain
  mustard

Blue cheese sauce
300 ml cream
100 g blue cheese

METHOD

Light a fire and allow to burn until the flames die and the coals are hot. Clean the broccolini stems and set aside until ready to use.

To make the honey-mustard dressing, place the honey, Dijon mustard and vinegar in a blender. With the blender running, slowly add the vegetable oil to emulsify the dressing. Season with a pinch of salt and stir in the wholegrain mustard at the end.

To make the blue cheese sauce, heat the cream and melt in the blue cheese. Use a stick blender to emulsify the sauce, and then reduce to a thick consistency.

Dress the broccolini with olive oil and season with salt. Place them on a grid over the fire. Cook for about 2 minutes until they are golden on the one side. Turn the broccolini and cook for another 2 minutes. Place in a bowl and lightly dress with the honey-mustard dressing and chopped walnuts.

To serve the dish, place a 20 ml ladle of the blue cheese sauce into each serving bowl. Plate the broccolini in each bowl with the heads in the sauce and the stems sticking up. Finish off with a sprinkle of toasted almonds and a drizzle of olive oil.

DUCK BREAST
WITH NAARTJIE & YUZU DRESSING

SERVINGS: 4–6 | PREP TIME: 15 MINS | COOK TIME: 40 MINS | SKILL LEVEL: 2 (MODERATE)

INGREDIENTS

4 duck breasts, skin on
3 parsnips
2 tbsp white sesame
  seeds, toasted
micro coriander leaves,
  to garnish
edible flowers, to garnish

Dressing
100 ml naartjie juice
50 ml yuzu juice
50 ml soy sauce
50 ml olive oil
½ tsp naartjie zest
½ thumb fresh ginger,
  finely grated
1 clove garlic, finely grated
1 tbsp maple syrup

Salad
1 naartjie
10 g fresh coriander
1 spring onion

METHOD

Light a fire and allow the coals to burn for about 10 minutes. Lay the duck breasts, skin sides up, on a tray and salt the skins generously. Once the fire flames have died and the coals are hot, place a grid above the coals and place the duck breasts on the grill, skin sides down. Cook for about 8–10 minutes until the duck fat has rendered and the skins are crisp and golden. Turn the duck breasts over and cook for about 5 minutes more; remove from the fire when the internal temperature of the breasts is 55°C. Place the duck breasts on a clean tray and allow them to cool completely in the fridge.

To make the dressing, mix all of the ingredients together and set aside until ready to use.

To prepare the salad, remove the peel from the naartjie and break it into 2–3 segments. Slice the segments horizontally and set aside until ready to use. Pick the coriander leaves from the stems and very finely slice the spring onion at an angle.

Set a deep fryer to 180°C. Peel the parsnips and slice them very thinly lengthways, either on a slicer or a mandolin. Very finely slice the parsnip slices into thin strips. Once the fryer has come to temperature, fry the parsnips in batches until they are lightly golden. Drain them on a tray with paper towel and season with fine salt.

To serve, slice the duck breasts horizontally into thin slices. Layer slices of duck down the centre of each serving plate. Sprinkle the duck with toasted white sesame seeds. Place 3 slices of naartjie on each plate and generously dress the duck with the naartjie and yuzu dressing. Add a few coriander sprigs and sliced spring onion to each portion. Top with a handful of parsnip crisps. Garnish with micro coriander leaves and edible flowers, and serve.

INA PAARMAN
INA PAARMAN'S KITCHEN

ROASTED BUTTERNUT SOUP
SLOW-COOKED OXTAIL WITH GREMOLATA & CREAMY POLENTA
MILK TART WITH APPLES

I love everything about food. My food career has involved working with so many people, which has given me such joy and satisfaction over the years. These are some of my favourite South African classics. My grandmother would be proud of the milk tart – hers was an incredible recipe, which we believe we've perfected. That one's for you, Ouma!

ina

Cape Town,
Western Cape

ROASTED BUTTERNUT SOUP

SERVINGS: 6 | PREP TIME: 15 MINS | COOK TIME: 45 MINS | SKILL LEVEL: 1 (EASY)

INGREDIENTS

2 onions, chopped

2 cups (700 g) butternut, peeled and diced

1 apple, peeled and diced

1 tsp (5 ml) vegetable spice (I use Ina Paarman's Vegetable Spice)

3 tbsp (45 ml) olive oil

3 tbsp (45 ml) flour

2 tsp (10 ml) curry powder

1 tsp (5 ml) ground cumin

1 tsp (5 ml) seasoned sea salt (I use Ina Paarman's Seasoned Sea Salt)

¼ tsp (1¼ ml) freshly grated nutmeg

4 cups (1 litre) water

3 tbsp (45 ml) chicken stock powder (I use Ina Paarman's Chicken Stock Powder)

grated zest and juice of 1 orange

½ cup (125 ml) fresh cream

butternut crisps, to garnish (see Tip)

orange zest, to garnish

METHOD

Pre-heat the oven to 200°C. Toss the onions, butternut and apple with the vegetable spice and olive oil. Spread out in a single layer on a baking sheet. Bake for 30 minutes (you can also sauté the ingredients in a frying pan). Remove from the oven and stir in the flour, curry powder, cumin, seasoned sea salt and nutmeg, blending them with the vegetables.

In a large saucepan, bring the water to the boil. Add chicken stock powder, orange zest and juice and roasted vegetables. Simmer slowly for 10 minutes. Liquidise the soup with a hand-held blender or in a food processor. Add the cream and check seasoning.

To serve, ladle the soup into bowls and garnish with butternut crisps and orange zest.

TIP

To make butternut crisps, use a potato peeler to shave off long strips of butternut. Deep-fry until crisp and drain on paper towel.

SLOW-COOKED OXTAIL WITH GREMOLATA & CREAMY POLENTA

SERVINGS: 4–5 | PREP TIME: 25 MINS | COOK TIME: 6½ HOURS | SKILL LEVEL: 2 (MODERATE)

INGREDIENTS

2 tbsp (30 ml) flour

1 tbsp (15 ml) garlic and pepper seasoning (I use Ina Paarman's Garlic Pepper Seasoning)

1 tsp (5 ml) meat spice (I use Ina Paarman's Meat Spice)

1¼ kg oxtail, trimmed of excess fat

2 tbsp (30 ml) canola oil

1 tbsp (15 ml) butter

2 onions, chopped

½ tsp (2½ ml) green onion seasoning (I use Ina Paarman's Green Onion Seasoning)

1 large carrot, peeled and sliced into rings

2 sticks celery, finely sliced

½ cup (125 ml) red wine

1 cup (250 ml) water

1 x 25 g sachet liquid beef stock (I use Ina Paarman's Liquid Beef Stock)

1 x 400 g can chopped tomatoes

4 tbsp (60 ml) tomato pesto (I use Ina Paarman's Tomato Pesto)

1 tbsp (15 ml) orange marmalade (optional)

Polenta

4 cups (1 litre) water

2 tbsp (30 ml) chicken stock powder (I use Ina Paarman's Chicken Stock Powder)

1 cup (250 ml) coarse yellow polenta

2 tbsp (30 ml) butter

½ cup (125 ml) grated hard Italian cheese

Gremolata

grated zest of ½ orange

grated zest of 1 lemon

¼ cup (60 ml) finely chopped parsley

3 cloves garlic, finely chopped

METHOD

Place the oven rack one slot below the middle position and pre-heat the oven to 120°C. Measure flour, garlic and pepper seasoning and meat spice into a plastic bag, add oxtail and shake to coat.

Heat a heavy frying pan, add oil and butter. When the butter is brown and bubbly, add half the oxtail and brown it on all sides. Remove from the pan and add to the raw oxtail. It is not necessary to brown all the oxtail. Season the onions with green onion seasoning, add to the pan and brown. Add the carrot and celery and stir-fry with the onions for 2 minutes. Add red wine and boil for 1 minute to reduce it a little. Add water, beef stock, tomatoes, tomato pesto, marmalade (if using), all the oxtail and any leftover seasoned flour.

Transfer the stew to a cast-iron pot with a lid for oven cooking, or to a slow cooker. Cook for 5–6 hours until the meat is very tender and beginning to fall off the bone. At this stage it is best to leave the meat to cool down completely, preferably overnight. Skim off excess fat when completely cooled.

To make the polenta, bring the water to the boil and add the chicken stock powder. Add the polenta in a thin stream while whisking with a wire whisk. Cook slowly with the lid on for 15 minutes, stirring occasionally. Stir in the butter and cheese.

To serve, reheat the oxtail and check seasoning. Mix all the gremolata ingredients together and sprinkle over the oxtail just before serving with the polenta.

TIP

You can either make the polenta just before serving, or make it in advance and pour into a pie dish. Brush the top with a little oil or butter to prevent a skin from forming. Cover with plastic wrap. Reheat it in the microwave (remove the plastic wrap first) for serving.

MILK TART WITH APPLES

SERVINGS: 6–8 | PREP TIME: 25 MINS | COOK TIME: 1 HOUR PLUS COOLING | SKILL LEVEL: 2 (MODERATE)

INGREDIENTS

2 cups (500 ml) full cream milk

1 stick cinnamon, broken up into long splinters

4 tbsp (60 ml) butter

3 extra-large eggs, separated

1 cup (250 ml) vanilla cake mix (I use Ina Paarman's Vanilla Cake Mix)

1 tsp (5 ml) almond essence

Apple base

5–6 Pink Lady or Golden Delicious apples, peeled and cut into small wedges

½ cup (125 ml) apple juice

Cinnamon-sugar topping

3 tbsp (45 ml) sugar

1 tsp (5 ml) ground cinnamon

Garnish (optional)

dried apple slices

¼ cup (50 g) sugar

¼ cup (60 ml) water

10 paper-thin centre slices of apple

METHOD

Bring the milk and broken cinnamon just to the boil. Cover, remove from heat, add the butter and leave to infuse for 20 minutes.

Meanwhile, adjust the oven rack to one slot below the middle position and pre-heat oven to 180°C. In a saucepan, cook the apples in the apple juice for about 15 minutes. Place cooked apples into a buttered deep 22 cm or regular 24 cm pie dish and leave to cool.

To make the cinnamon-sugar topping, mix the sugar and cinnamon together, and sprinkle 1 tablespoon of the cinnamon sugar over the apples.

Remove the cinnamon pieces from the milk. Add a little of the warm milk to the egg yolks while beating with a balloon whisk. Return egg mixture to the pot and then beat in the vanilla cake mix. Add almond essence. Keep stirring over medium heat with a whisk until the mixture starts to thicken on the bottom of the pot. Immediately remove it from the heat and keep stirring, away from any heat, until the consistency is like a thickish yoghurt: it may form lumps, just keep beating with the whisk away from heat to disperse them. Leave to cool slightly.

Whip the egg whites to soft-peak stage. Add one-third of the beaten egg whites to the milk-tart mixture and stir through with the whisk. Add the remaining egg whites and gently fold in. Place into the pie dish on top of the cooked apples. Sprinkle the remaining cinnamon-sugar topping evenly over the top of the milk tart. Bake for 25–30 minutes until puffy. Switch off the oven (leave the door slightly ajar) and leave milk tart in the oven to cool for 15 minutes. Remove and cool to room temperature before slicing.

TIP

If you want to make the milk tart without the apple (this recipe makes a lovely plain crustless milk tart) use a slightly smaller 22 cm pie dish. Bake it for the same length of time.

Permaculture gardens can do many things to uplift the community. I would like to address the issues the community faces in a practical and sustainable way – show them how to recycle, save water, eat healthily, make money and improve the environment. We are here to do magic. I am humbled and very excited. My dream is coming true.

NTOMBENHLE

Mpophomeni,
KwaZulu-Natal

NTOMBENHLE MTAMBO
MPOPHOMENI
CONSERVATION GROUP

VETKOEK
BOM BOM BEANS

VETKOEK

SERVINGS: 12 | PREP TIME: 10 MINS PLUS PROVING | COOK TIME: 20 MINS | SKILL LEVEL: 1 (EASY)

INGREDIENTS

1 kg flour
120 g sugar
10 g sachet instant yeast
2 tbsp oil
1 tbsp salt
1 litre warm water, plus
  up to 1 cup extra if
  dough is too stiff
flour for dusting
oil for deep-frying

METHOD

Mix 1 kg flour, sugar, yeast, 2 tablespoons oil, salt and warm water together. Add extra water only if needed. Knead thoroughly, then prove for 30 minutes until well risen (this will take longer on a cold day). Dust a tray with flour. Scoop up handfuls of dough and roll into balls. Place vetkoek on the tray and leave to rise until doubled in size.

Heat oil in a deep pot. Fry a few vetkoek at a time: drop in a few dough balls and put on the lid. Check the vetkoek after 10 minutes – they should have risen to the top of the oil. Turn over to brown on the other side. Drain and set aside until ready to serve. Serve with a fresh green salad.

NOTE

We make our salad from whatever there is in the garden – carrots, fennel, spinach, spring onions, cabbage, beetroot, lettuce – all grated or chopped finely, and topped with herbs and edible flowers.

BOM BOM BEANS

SERVINGS: 8 | PREP TIME: 10 MINS PLUS SOAKING | COOK TIME: 1 DAY | SKILL LEVEL: 1 (EASY)

INGREDIENTS

1 cup dried white beans
(bom bom beans)
2 onions, chopped
2 carrots, chopped
1 medium butternut,
peeled and chopped into
small pieces
2 potatoes, chopped
vegetable oil
1 tsp curry powder
stock (optional) or water

METHOD

Soak beans overnight in cold water. Place in a pot, cover with water and bring to the boil on the stove. Simmer for 20 minutes, then put into a Wonderbag (see note) to finish cooking for the rest of the day. When the beans are cooked, fry the onion, carrot, butternut and potato until the onions have softened. Add the cooked beans, curry powder and some water or stock, simmer for 15 minutes and serve.

NOTE

A Wonderbag is a non-electric, portable slow cooker that continues to cook food that has been brought to the boil by conventional methods for up to 8 hours without the use of additional electricity or fuel. For more information visit wonderbag.co.za.

Stellenbosch,
Western Cape

BERTUS BASSON
WITH CHARLTON DE RUITER,
MARELI BASSON & ALISTAIRE LAWRENCE

**BERTUS BASSON FOOD
TRUCK & OVERTURE**

LAMB BOER-RITO

When it comes to cooking lamb on the spit, I'm a purist: lamb and salt only. There's something about the South African spit braai that brings people to food like bees to honey. The taste and quality of South African lamb definitely makes it my choice of beast for the boer-rito (our take on the classic Mexican burrito).

bertus

LAMB BOER-RITO

SERVINGS: 6–8 | PREP TIME: 25 MINS PLUS DRAINING & INFUSING | COOK TIME: 15 MINS PLUS ROASTING
SKILL LEVEL: 2 (MODERATE)

INGREDIENTS

1.8–2 kg shoulder of lamb
plenty of coarse salt
8 fresh rotis (see recipes on
  pages 343 and 346)

Hummus
500 g cooked chickpeas
100 ml plain yoghurt
5 ml smoked paprika
5 g toasted, crushed cumin seeds
1 clove garlic, crushed
1 tbsp sesame oil
juice of 1 lemon

Tomato salsa
250 g baby tomatoes, quartered
2 baby onions, thinly shaved

30 g coriander leaves
1 chilli, finely chopped
juice of 1 lemon
60 ml olive oil

Rocket paste
200 g rocket
15 ml wholegrain mustard
40 ml oil
10 g grated Parmesan

Cucumber salad
1 cucumber, cut into small cubes
500 ml plain yoghurt
zest of 1 lemon
5 g toasted, crushed cumin seeds

Beans
1 onion, finely chopped
1 clove garlic, crushed
1 chilli, chopped
a big knob of butter
500 ml (2 cups) cooked butter
  beans
1 tbsp chopped parsley

Gremolata oil
zest of 3 lemons
60 g finely chopped parsley
3 cloves garlic, finely chopped
150 ml olive oil

METHOD

Start the day before. To make the cucumber salad, lightly salt the cucumber and leave overnight in a sieve hanging over a container, to remove any excess liquid. The next day, press out excess liquid and mix cucumber with the remaining ingredients. Season to taste and refrigerate until ready to use.

To make the gremolata oil, mix all the ingredients together and allow to infuse overnight. (Stir it before using as the bits sink to the bottom.)

Pre-heat the oven to 90°C. Lightly season the lamb, rubbing the salt into the meat. Cover and roast overnight. Remove and pull the meat apart into large shreds. Set aside until ready to use.

To make the hummus, place all the ingredients in a food processor and blend thoroughly. Set aside until ready to use.

To make the tomato salsa, mix all the ingredients together and refrigerate until ready to use.

To make the rocket paste, place all the ingredients in a blender and blend until you get a smooth paste. Season to taste and set aside until ready to use.

To cook the beans, sweat the onion, garlic and chilli in the butter in a heavy-based pot. Add the beans and cook slowly until they become very soft and a little mushy. Sprinkle with parsley and check seasoning. Set aside until ready to use.

To assemble the dish, lightly toast the rotis and spread each one with a generous amount of hummus. Place some of the pulled lamb on each roti. Add some tomato salsa, a few dollops of rocket paste, some cucumber salad and beans. To finish, drizzle with some gremolata oil. Roll up and enjoy.

We run our cookery school the same way a top restaurant is run: teaching the classical basics and then adding our modern touch. These dishes show how you can have a bit of fun with classic breakfast recipes.

Jackie

JACKIE CAMERON
WITH CARLA SCHULZE, CARA CONWAY, ELAINE BOSHOFF & KATE COUSINS

JACKIE CAMERON SCHOOL OF FOOD & WINE

BRIOCHE FRENCH TOAST WITH MORNAY SAUCE

SAVOURY PORK PIES WITH WALDORF SALAD

Hilton, KwaZulu-Natal

BRIOCHE FRENCH TOAST WITH MORNAY SAUCE

SERVINGS: 4 | PREP TIME: ABOUT 60 MINS PLUS RESTING | COOK TIME: ABOUT 60 MINS
SKILL LEVEL: 2 (MODERATE)

INGREDIENTS

Brioche

30 ml lukewarm water

10 ml (8 g) instant dry yeast

125 g cold salted butter

90 g white sugar

1 litre (517 g) cake flour (we use Champagne Valley Stonemill flour)

1¾ ml (2 g) fine salt

175 ml lukewarm full-cream milk

2 whole eggs

7½ ml (9 g) white sugar

5 ml vanilla extract

1 egg, beaten

50 g salted butter

French toast

20 g salted butter

8 slices brioche (see above)

35 g Parmesan shavings

60 g thinly sliced Parma ham

2 whole eggs

30 ml cream

15 ml salted butter

15 ml sunflower oil (we use Sunfoil)

Mornay sauce

500 ml full cream milk

3 whole black peppercorns

1 bay leaf

100 g sliced onion

10 g crushed garlic

1 sprig fresh thyme

30 g salted butter

30 g cake flour

50 g Cheddar, grated (we use Chrissie Beetroot and Sage Cheddar Cheese, but any type of Cheddar can be used)

To serve

2 limes, halved

METHOD

Start making the brioche the day before. Mix water and yeast together and allow to stand for 10 minutes. Mix 125 g butter and sugar together and place in the fridge to get cold. Combine flour and salt. Whisk milk, whole eggs, sugar and vanilla together. Make a well in the centre of the flour and add the milk mixture. Work together to form a dough. Add the yeast mixture. Then work the chilled butter and sugar mixture into the dough using the 'pinch and pull' method: take a small piece of dough (pull it, don't break it off) and add a small piece of butter-sugar mixture, then close it and work it into the dough. If making by machine, place the dough in a mixer fitted with a dough hook and add the butter and sugar, little by little, to ensure incorporation. If kneading by hand, to ensure incorporation while kneading, you should almost throw or slam the dough onto the countertop as this helps to bring it together (slamming the dough on the countertop becomes the kneading process). Place dough in a buttered bowl, cover and refrigerate overnight.

The following day, take the dough out of the fridge and bring to room temperature. (This will take about an hour, depending on the weather.) Pre-heat the oven to 160°C. An easy home-style way to make brioche is to grease a muffin tray with large cups very well, divide the dough between the muffin cups, place the dough in the muffin tray and allow to prove in a warm spot – it should double in size. Brush the tops with beaten egg. Bake for 30 minutes.

Remove the brioche from the oven, spread the 50 g butter around the brioche rounds, place them on a cooling rack and allow to cool. You will not use all the brioche for the French toast, but they freeze really well (to defrost, leave overnight in the fridge and then heat up in the oven at 180°C until crisp).

To make the French toast, butter the brioche slices well. Sandwich the Parmesan and ham between slices. Whisk eggs and cream together and season, then soak the brioche sandwiches in the mixture. Heat a frying pan and add the butter and oil for frying. Cook the sandwiches side by side, slowly, to ensure the cheese melts.

To make the Mornay sauce, bring the milk, peppercorns, bay leaf, onion, garlic and thyme to the boil, allowing the flavours to infuse. Strain and set aside. Next make a blonde roux: place a small pot on the heat and add the butter. When melted, add the flour and cook until golden brown. Slowly add the warm strained milk while whisking continuously so no lumps form. Bring to the boil and simmer until the correct consistency is reached. Add the cheese and season to taste. If not using immediately, cover with plastic wrap that touches the sauce so no skin forms.

Serve the French toast sandwiches with Mornay sauce drizzled over or in ramekins on the side. Serve with the lime halves for squeezing over, and freshly ground black pepper.

SAVOURY PORK PIES WITH WALDORF SALAD

SERVINGS: 4 | PREP TIME: 30 MINS PLUS RESTING | COOK TIME: 45 MINS | SKILL LEVEL: 2 (MODERATE)

INGREDIENTS

Pastry

200 g cake flour

125 g cold salted butter, cut into cubes

5 ml freshly squeezed lemon juice

62½ ml cream, whipped

Filling

250 g pork sausages

1 clove garlic, crushed

1 sprig fresh rosemary, stalk removed and leaves finely chopped

2 egg yolks

To assemble pies

50 g cake flour for dusting and rolling the pastry

1 egg

15 ml water

Purée

500 ml water

125 ml white sugar

5 (750 g) Granny Smith apples, cored and quartered

50 g celery leaves (use the top leaves, as these are really nice and green, and often just get thrown away)

To serve

60 ml Greek yoghurt

60 g walnuts, roasted and roughly broken

1 Granny Smith apple, cored and cut into little cubes

METHOD

To make the pastry, sift the flour into a bowl. Rub in the butter cubes using your fingertips until the mixture resembles breadcrumbs. Whisk the lemon juice and cream together. Cut the whipped cream and lemon juice mixture into the flour mixture. Bring the pastry mixture together with your hands. Cover in plastic wrap and rest for at least 20 minutes in the refrigerator.

To make the pie filling, squeeze the sausage meat out of the skins. Add the garlic, rosemary, egg yolks and salt and pepper to taste. Weigh out four 60 g balls and roll them in some of the extra flour. Place in the refrigerator.

Roll out the pastry, in batches, on a floured surface and cut out four 4 cm x 10 cm and four 4 cm x 11 cm rounds. Place these in the refrigerator on a board or tray covered with plastic wrap and rest for 20 minutes.

To assemble and bake the pies, pre-heat the oven to 160°C. Lightly brush egg glaze (1 egg whisked with 15 ml water) onto the 10 cm rounds. Top each with a pork mince ball and mould the 11 cm pastry rounds over the mince balls to close the pies. Very lightly, mark a cross on the top of each pie with the back of a knife. Brush with egg glaze and finish the edges off with the back of a fork (dipped into extra flour as you go) to imprint and to ensure the pastry layers are stuck together. To neaten up the pies, finish with a 9½ cm cutter, which you place over each entire pie. Bake for 30 minutes or until golden brown.

While the pies are baking, make the apple purée. In a small saucepan on a medium heat, bring the water and sugar to the boil, stirring continuously until the sugar crystals are dissolved. Add the apples and cook until soft. Remove from the heat and strain all the liquid off. In a food processor, blend the apples with the celery leaves to a smooth purée and strain. Season to taste with salt and freshly ground black pepper. Place in a piping bag and set aside.

Serve the pork pies with Greek yoghurt and apple purée. Sprinkle over the walnuts and garnish with the fresh apple cubes.

The secret to preparing, cooking and serving delicious food is keep it fresh and simple, but more importantly to do it with love… that way all the enjoyment you get when making the dish is magically transmitted to the eaters. Works every time!

Justne

JUSTINE DRAKE
WITH NZWAKAZI SPAYIRE, TRIXIE-ROSE & MARC MURRAY
FOOD EDITOR & TV PERSONALITY

ROAST CHICKEN IN HERBS & VERJUICE
GREEK SALAD WITH A TWIST

Cape Town, Western Cape

ROAST CHICKEN IN HERBS & VERJUICE

SERVINGS: 4 | PREP TIME: 15 MINS | COOK TIME: 1½ HOURS | SKILL LEVEL: 1 (EASY)

INGREDIENTS

1 large free-range chicken
½ cup (125 ml) verjuice
½ cup (125 ml) chicken stock
½ cup (125 ml) finely chopped fresh herbs (rosemary, sage, parsley, thyme)
zest of 1 large lemon
juice of ½ lemon
3 fat cloves garlic, crushed
2 heaped tsp (20 ml) Dijon mustard

METHOD

Pre-heat the oven to 200°C. Wash the chicken, pat dry and place in a roasting pan. Mix together the verjuice, chicken stock, herbs, lemon zest and juice, garlic and mustard, and season to taste with sea salt and freshly ground black pepper. Pour the verjuice mixture over the chicken – and don't forget to pour some into the cavity (this ensures that it steams inside, keeping the chicken extra moist). Cover with foil and roast for 30 minutes, then remove foil and roast for about 1 more hour until it's cooked through.

TIP

I often add leeks, shallots, carrots and celery to the pan – then they roast in the gravy and there's no need to cook extra vegetables.

166

GREEK SALAD WITH A TWIST

SERVINGS: 4 | PREP TIME: 15 MINS | COOK TIME: 4 MINS PLUS INFUSING | SKILL LEVEL: 1 (EASY)

INGREDIENTS

⅓ cup (80 ml) olive oil

1 clove garlic, sliced

leaves from 2 sprigs fresh origanum

juice of 1 lemon

pinch of sugar

8 baby cucumbers

16 vine tomatoes

1 red onion, cut into thin crescents

handful of Kalamata-style olives

4–6 thick slices feta cheese

olive oil

METHOD

Heat olive oil with garlic and origanum. Set aside to infuse for 10 minutes. Mix in lemon juice, sugar and some sea salt and freshly ground black pepper, and set aside.

Arrange salad vegetables and olives on a platter. Brush feta with a little olive oil and fry in a non-stick pan for about 1–2 minutes per side.

Drizzle dressing over salad and top with feta. Serve immediately with hot, crusty bread.

ANGUS MCINTOSH
FARMER ANGUS

BONE BROTH
BILTONG
PASTURE BURGER
WITH FRIED EGG

Although I grew up on a farm, I never intended to become a farmer. Michael Pollan's book *The Omnivore's Dilemma* changed all that. Our methods of farming here are very different to those on the farm on which I grew up. These recipes are celebrations of our pastures: a grilled beef patty topped with a fried egg from our outdoor hens, bone broth (a tonic that has been linked with helping to cure myriad diseases) and, of course, biltong – one of South Africa's most iconic food products.

Angus

*Stellenbosch,
Western Cape*

BONE BROTH

MAKES: ABOUT 4 LITRES | PREP TIME: 15 MINS PLUS SOAKING | COOK TIME: APPROX. 30 HOURS
SKILL LEVEL: 1 (EASY)

INGREDIENTS

2 kg grass-fed beef bones
6 litres filtered rainwater
2 tbsp vinegar
2 carrots, roughly chopped
1 onion, cut in half
1 sprig rosemary
1 celery stalk
1 clove garlic
2 tsp turmeric
1 tsp black peppercorns
2 bay leaves

METHOD

Cover the bones in rainwater and vinegar and leave to soak for 2 hours. Bring to a slow simmer, just below boiling point. Scoop off any scum that rises to the top. Add carrots, onion, rosemary, celery, garlic, turmeric, peppercorns and bay leaves. Simmer slowly for 26–28 hours. Allow to cool with the bones in the broth (about another 3 hours). Remove bones and scoop off any fat from the top, then bottle and keep in the fridge. Drink it neat or use as a base for soups or risottos.

BILTONG

MAKES: ABOUT 1KG | PREP TIME: 5 MINS PLUS SOAKING AND DRYING | SKILL LEVEL: 1 (EASY)

INGREDIENTS

2 kg grass-fed beef
  (preferably silverside)
150 ml very good vinegar
2 tbsp coarse salt
2 tbsp coriander seeds, roasted
  and crushed

METHOD

The drying process can take anything from 24 hours to 5 days, depending on where you hang the meat, so start at least 1–2 days before. Cut the meat into 2 cm slices (about 20 cm in length, depending on your cut of meat). Mix together the vinegar, salt and coriander seeds in a glass or non-metallic dish. Soak the beef overnight in the vinegar mixture, in the fridge. Remove meat from the vinegar mixture and hang to dry in a space free of flies and ideally with a fan moving the air. It's important to keep the biltong free from humidity.

PASTURE BURGER WITH FRIED EGG

SERVINGS: 6 | PREP TIME: 10 MINS | COOK TIME: 5–10 MINS | SKILL LEVEL: 1 (EASY)

INGREDIENTS

1¼ kg best quality pasture-
  raised mince, forequarter trim
3 tsp coarse salt
  (we use Khoisan)
a few tbsp butter, to fry
6 free-range eggs
  (we use our own)

METHOD

Mix the mince with the salt and divide into 6 x 200 g pieces. Shape into 6 chunky burgers. Either braai or fry for a few minutes on each side until cooked to your liking. Heat the butter in a pan and fry the eggs until crispy on the base but with soft yolks. Serve the eggs on top of the burgers.

KHANYA MZONGWANA
OFF THE WALL POP-UP RESTAURANT

ULTIMATE ROAST CHICKEN IN A CREAMY LEEK & FENNEL SAUCE
WARM LENTIL SALAD WITH COUSCOUS & VEGGIES

I believe that being able to cook is definitely like possessing a type of magic — especially when you're trying to figure out what to make with the last can of beans and an onion at the end of the month. I grew up around a lot of abject poverty in the Eastern Cape, and that environment taught me plenty about what enjoying food really means and how powerful the ability to cook a meal with next to nothing can make you.

KHANYA

*Pretoria,
Gauteng*

ULTIMATE ROAST CHICKEN
IN A CREAMY LEEK & FENNEL SAUCE

SERVINGS: 4–6 | PREP TIME: 15 MINS | COOK TIME: 1 HOUR 15 MINS | SKILL LEVEL: 1 (EASY)

INGREDIENTS

1 whole free-range
 chicken

80 ml extra virgin olive oil

200 g leeks, washed and
 sliced

100 g baby fennel bulbs,
 washed and halved
 lengthways

30 g chicken stock powder

400 ml cream

sprig of fresh thyme

¼ cup fennel fronds,
 chopped

150 g French beans,
 tops removed

extra virgin olive oil

¼ cup flat-leaf parsley,
 to garnish

METHOD

Pre-heat the oven to 200°C. Rub chicken with salt, pepper and half the olive oil. Roast in the oven for about 1 hour or until golden and crispy.

Meanwhile, heat a pan and add the rest of the olive oil. Gently fry the leeks and fennel. Season with chicken stock powder and add cream, stirring frequently. Add sprig of thyme and simmer for about 6–10 minutes. Remove from heat and remove thyme sprig. Add the chopped fennel fronds and stir through. Set aside until ready to serve.

Blanch the beans for 2 minutes. Drain and toss in some olive oil, salt and pepper.

Once the chicken is cooked, remove from the oven and allow to rest and cool slightly. Roughly pull meat (with skin on) away from the carcass. Arrange on a serving platter and spoon creamy leek and fennel sauce on top. Top with the French beans and garnish with chopped parsley.

WARM LENTIL SALAD WITH COUSCOUS & VEGGIES

SERVINGS: 6 | PREP TIME: 15 MINS | COOK TIME: 45 MINS | SKILL LEVEL: 1 (EASY)

INGREDIENTS

100 g dried brown lentils

30 ml extra virgin olive oil

1 sweet red pepper,
de-seeded and diced

1 sweet yellow pepper,
de-seeded and diced

1 medium aubergine,
cubed

1 red onion, diced

1 clove garlic, finely
chopped

10 g fresh ginger, minced

1 bird's eye chilli, finely
chopped

1 tsp cumin seeds

1 tsp red masala curry

100 g tomato paste

1 x 400 g can chopped
tomatoes

1 tsp brown sugar

500 g couscous, steamed

METHOD

Boil the lentils in water for 25–30 minutes or until tender but firm. Drain and set aside. Heat a pan and add olive oil. Fry the peppers, aubergine and onion with the garlic, ginger and chilli until onions are soft, sweet and translucent and the ginger is fragrant. Add cumin seeds and red masala curry and continue frying for another 5 minutes. Add tomato paste and stir it in, followed by the canned tomatoes and sugar. Simmer gently for five minutes, stirring often. Season. Remove sauce from heat and stir into the steamed couscous thoroughly.

Serve as a main dish or a perfect side to a roast.

"Learn about ingredients so that you can always enjoy what you eat, no matter what you eat."

ZAYAAN KHAN
INDIGENOUS
FOOD REVIVALIST

HONEY SORGHUM SALAD

Khoekhoe (Khoi) food is gathered on the journey: berries picked here and there, medicine foraged from the veld. Snacking becomes a way to sustain oneself between meals. This honey sorghum salad is an ode to the foragers' way of life, using local ingredients – from the salt to the fruit – and understanding the need to transform foods.

Zayaan

*Cape Town,
Western Cape*

HONEY SORGHUM SALAD

SERVINGS: 6 | PREP TIME: 10 MINS PLUS SOAKING | COOK TIME: 45 MINS PLUS COOLING
SKILL LEVEL: 1 (EASY)

INGREDIENTS

1½ cups wholegrain sorghum

4½ cups strong rooibos tea

3 tbsp fynbos honey

1 cup dried sea lettuce (seaweed)

a few springs of fynbos herbs such as *Salvia* and aasbos (see Foraging Notes)

2 cups sliced Kei apples

2 tbsp dune crowberry seeds (optional)

a few sour fig (*Carpobrotus edulis*) leaves, to garnish (optional)

METHOD

Soak sorghum in water overnight. Add the rooibos tea to the pre-soaked sorghum, bring to a simmer and cook until all the tea is absorbed, about 40 minutes. Allow to cool. Add the honey, mix through and add the sea lettuce and herbs. Stir through and top with the sliced Kei apples. Garnish with dune crowberry seeds and a few sour fig leaves, if using.

FORAGING NOTES

Veldkos (field or bush food) has been part of South African diets since the country's first peoples gathered it. It's not a good idea to simply pick and eat plants from the bush at will – both in terms of potentially eating something that is not edible, and also with regard to the impact your picking may have on the plants' sustainability. In short, foraging should only be undertaken by experts. Here are some notes about the foraged veldkos featured here:

Seaweed: once dried, seaweeds have a very long shelf life and are easily reconstituted. The sea lettuce used here is a mix of species from the *Ulva* genus and was foraged in St Helena Bay, rinsed and sundried. It adds an umami flavour to the sweet salad.

Salvia africana-lutea (grey leaves): one of the many indigenous sages, it is used as a herb and medicinally.

Coleonema alba or aasbos: a common plant that is a member of the buchu family; it is highly fragrant and works very well in herb blends.

Muraltia spinosa or tortoise berry: the berries of these spiny plants can have a tomato-sweet, slightly bitter flavour often referred to as a medicinal taste. It fruits in abundance, is high in vitamin C and provides nourishment and hydration in times of scarcity.

A mix of berries from the genus *Searsia* or crowberries, our own African sumac: these berries can be eaten fresh or dried. This is a typical veldkos ingredient as the bushes fruit in huge quantities and if stored well, the flavoursome, dried spice may be eaten all year round.

Carpobrotus edulis a.k.a. sour fig or vygies: this plant is famous for its dried fruits. Khoekhoe people have been eating it for generations, both fresh and dried. Easy to transport and store, the fruit acts as a laxative if too much of it is eaten. The leaves are eaten as an astringent, as a source of water, and can be cooked too, as well as being used topically for skin ailments.

Kei apples (*Dovyalis caffra*) are native to the Eastern Cape and have a flavour similar to apricots – sweet, sour and tangy. This juicy fruit may be eaten whole, seeds and all.

RUSSELL ARMSTRONG
WITH EB SOCIAL KITCHEN & BAR STAFF
EB SOCIAL KITCHEN & BAR

GRILLED MUSHROOM RISOTTO WITH TRUFFLE CREAM

Cooking with incredible local produce is what I find so exciting here in South Africa. That's the ethos I work with at home and what I've tried to bring into the kitchen at Social, so the menu is totally SA-inspired and, we feel, has the best produce elements from all over the country.

Russell

Hyde Park, Gauteng

GRILLED MUSHROOM RISOTTO
WITH TRUFFLE CREAM

SERVINGS: 4 | PREP TIME: 5 MINS | COOK TIME: 35 MINS | SKILL LEVEL: 1 (EASY)

INGREDIENTS

350 g mushrooms,
  cleaned and trimmed
  (use any or a mix of
  portobello, shiitake, cep
  [a.k.a. porcini], shimeji
  or button mushrooms)

knob of butter for frying

60 g unsalted butter

4 cloves garlic, finely diced

50 g French shallots,
  finely diced

250 g carnaroli rice

80 ml dry sherry

approx. 1½ litres chicken
  stock

160 g mascarpone

splash of sherry

80 g Parmesan

100 ml cream, lightly
  whipped, seasoned
  and scented with white
  truffle oil, to serve

sprigs of chervil, to garnish

METHOD

In a heavy-based pan, fry the mushrooms in a knob of butter. Set aside until ready to use.

Place a knob of the 60 g of butter in a clean, large heavy-based pan and sweat the garlic and shallots without allowing them to colour. Add the rice and turn up the heat to allow the butter to seal the grains of rice. Add the sherry and cook until it is absorbed. Add ladles of stock in increments of approximately 150 ml, while vigorously stirring the rice, allowing it to simmer and absorb the stock.

When the risotto is cooked (see Tip), add the fried mushrooms. Remove the pot from the heat and fold in the mascarpone, the remaining butter and a splash of sherry. Adjust the seasoning using grated Parmesan and freshly ground pepper. Spoon into bowls and serve topped with a quenelle of truffle cream and a sprig of chervil.

TIP

Stirring the pot frequently prevents the rice from settling at the bottom and allows the stock to be evenly absorbed. The motion also reveals the exact amount of broth that will be required, and how close you are to that wonderful moment when all the elements combine into a union of flavour, texture and consistency.

CHANELLE & FRITZ SCHOON
SCHOON DE COMPANJE

POTBROOD
WILD MUSHROOMS ON TOAST WITH SOUR CREAM & SAGE SPREAD

*Stellenbosch,
Western Cape*

We naturally ferment our doughs to develop the full flavour of the grain we are using and for easy digestion. Baking as authentically as we do, we are forced, by nature, to be very aware of the life in our bread: the temperature, humidity, wild yeast organisms and quality of our grain are monitored constantly. And our wood oven (aptly named Black Betty) has proven herself to be the grande dame of our bakery, producing perfect dark, crusty loaves for the community daily.

Chanelle

POTBROOD
POT BREAD COUNTRY LOAF

MAKES: 1 LOAF | PREP TIME: 15 MINS PLUS PROVING | COOK TIME: 1 HOUR | SKILL LEVEL: 2 (MODERATE)

INGREDIENTS

Starter
1 g yeast
240 g water
270 g wholegrain flour
   (we use Highland Hard
   Red)
5 g salt

Loaf
515 g starter
225 g water
340 g white bread flour
80 g salt

METHOD

To make the starter, mix the yeast and water together in a bowl, then add flour and salt. Mix until smooth and then cover. Let the dough ferment for 5 hours at 24°C.

To make the loaf, dissolve 515 g starter in the water. Add the flour and salt and mix until smooth, cover the dough and put it in the fridge for 30 minutes. After 30 minutes, fold the dough over, cover and and leave in the fridge for another 2 hours. After 2 hours give the dough another fold and cover. Leave the dough in the fridge overnight.

Next morning, take the dough out of the fridge, fold it over neatly and place in a round container lined with a clean, lightly floured cloth. Leave the dough to rise to 1½ times its original size.

Pre-heat your oven to 260°C with the pot in which you are going to bake the loaf in the oven. (You will need a pot with a lid.)

Carefully take the pot out the oven and gently tip your dough into the pot. Score the top of the loaf, put the lid on and put the pot in the oven to bake for 20 minutes.

After 20 minutes, take off the lid and lower the heat to 230°C. Bake for a further 20 minutes. If you have a food thermometer on hand place the end in the centre of the loaf. You are aiming for 98°C. Otherwise, stick a knife into the centre of the loaf, remove it slowly and inspect for any wet dough. If it comes out dry, it should be baked.

Once the top of the loaf is a deep golden colour, carefully tip the bread out of the pot and place it on a cooling rack to cool completely. Have real farm butter on standby.

WILD MUSHROOMS ON TOAST WITH SOUR CREAM & SAGE SPREAD

SERVINGS: 4 | PREP TIME: 15 MINS | COOK TIME: 15 MINS | SKILL LEVEL: 1 (EASY)

INGREDIENTS

4 slices potbrood (see recipe on page 190), toasted

wild rocket leaves, to serve

Sour cream & sage spread

1 cup sour cream

2 tbsp flour

2 tbsp butter

½ red onion, finely chopped

500 ml cream

50 g finely chopped sage

¾ cup grated Parmesan

squeeze of lemon juice, if required

Mushrooms

4 tbsp butter

1 tbsp olive oil

3–4 cups mixed wild mushrooms

50 ml vegetable or mushroom stock

METHOD

To make the spread, mix sour cream and flour in a bowl. Heat butter in pan, add onion and fry until soft, then add cream and reduce a little. Remove from heat and mix in sage, sour cream mix and Parmesan. Season with salt and pepper to taste. A squeeze of lemon juice can be added if it is required. Store in the fridge to thicken; the spread will keep for 3 days when refrigerated.

To prepare the mushrooms, heat butter in a frying pan until slightly browned, add olive oil and fry mushrooms until they soften. Add stock and allow to reduce slightly: the mushrooms should be moist from the stock. Season to taste.

To serve, spread sour cream spread on 4 slices toasted potbrood and grill under a hot grill until the spread bubbles and browns slightly. Pile mushrooms onto each slice of toast and top with wild rocket leaves.

SIBA MTONGANA
AUTHOR & CELEBRITY CHEF

SPICY CORN RUB
PAPIZZA

Growing up in Mdantsane, we cooked traditional food —
always rice or samp and beans, meat, gravy and at least
three vegetables. But don't be fooled — these simple
ingredients saw so many new variations that it was
possible to believe that my mother was a magician. This
is really the crux of it: food is all about family and friends,
and putting your heart into preparing a meal is the same
as presenting them with a wonderful gift. Food prepared
with care says, 'I love you.'

Siba

Cape Town,
Western Cape

SPICY CORN RUB

SERVINGS: 6 | PREP TIME: 5 MINS | COOK TIME: 10 MINS | SKILL LEVEL: 1 (EASY)

INGREDIENTS

6 fresh corn cobs

30 ml butter, to serve

Spice mix

30 ml smoked salt (you'll find it at good delis)

15 ml cayenne pepper

30 ml dried chilli flakes

30 ml dried mixed herbs

30 ml smoked paprika

2 ml lime zest (optional)

METHOD

Combine the spice mix ingredients and set aside. Prepare medium-hot braai coals. Meanwhile, soak the corn cobs in a bowl of cold water until ready to cook – this will prevent them from burning and popping while braaiing. Braai the corn cobs for 10 minutes or so until cooked, making sure you turn them every few minutes. Once cooked with a bit of charring here and there, remove from the braai grill.

To serve, brush with the butter and sprinkle generously with the spice mix.

TIP

Store the spice mix in a sterilised jar – just make sure the jar is completely dry before putting it in. To use as a meat rub, add a little olive oil to make it easier to brush over the meat before braaiing.

PAPIZZA

SERVINGS: 4 | PREP TIME: 10 MINS | COOK TIME: 40 MINS | SKILL LEVEL: 1 (EASY)

INGREDIENTS

750 ml water

pinch of salt

530 ml maize meal

30 ml butter

125 ml basil or rocket pesto

30 ml sweet chilli sauce

225 g chorizo, sliced

½ red onion, sliced

150 g broccolini, blanched (see Tip)

300 ml shaved Parmesan

rocket, to garnish (optional)

METHOD

Pre-heat the oven to 220°C. In a medium-sized saucepan, bring the water and salt to a rapid boil. Add half the maize meal and whisk to remove lumps. Reduce heat to medium, stir with a wooden spoon and cook, covered, for 8 minutes. Stir again and add the remaining maize meal, a little at a time, stirring and repeatedly mashing it against the sides of the saucepan with the back of the wooden spoon to prevent lumps from forming. This will take about 5 minutes. Reduce heat further and cook for 15–20 minutes until the pap has thickened to a stiff consistency and is cooked. Add butter and mix. Cool slightly. Flatten into a pizza pan to create a pizza base.

Smear the papizza base with half the pesto and all the sweet chilli sauce. Scatter with chorizo, onion, broccolini, the remaining pesto and Parmesan. Season and bake for 10 minutes, or until cheese has melted. Remove from the oven and garnish with rocket, if using. Slice and serve warm.

TIPS

Broccolini is often sold as tenderstem broccoli. To blanch it, bring a pot of salted water to the boil, add the broccolini, cook for 2 minutes and remove to a colander. Rinse with cold water and drain.

You'll need a pizza lifter or fish slice to lift the pizza slices, as the papizza will be soft when warm.

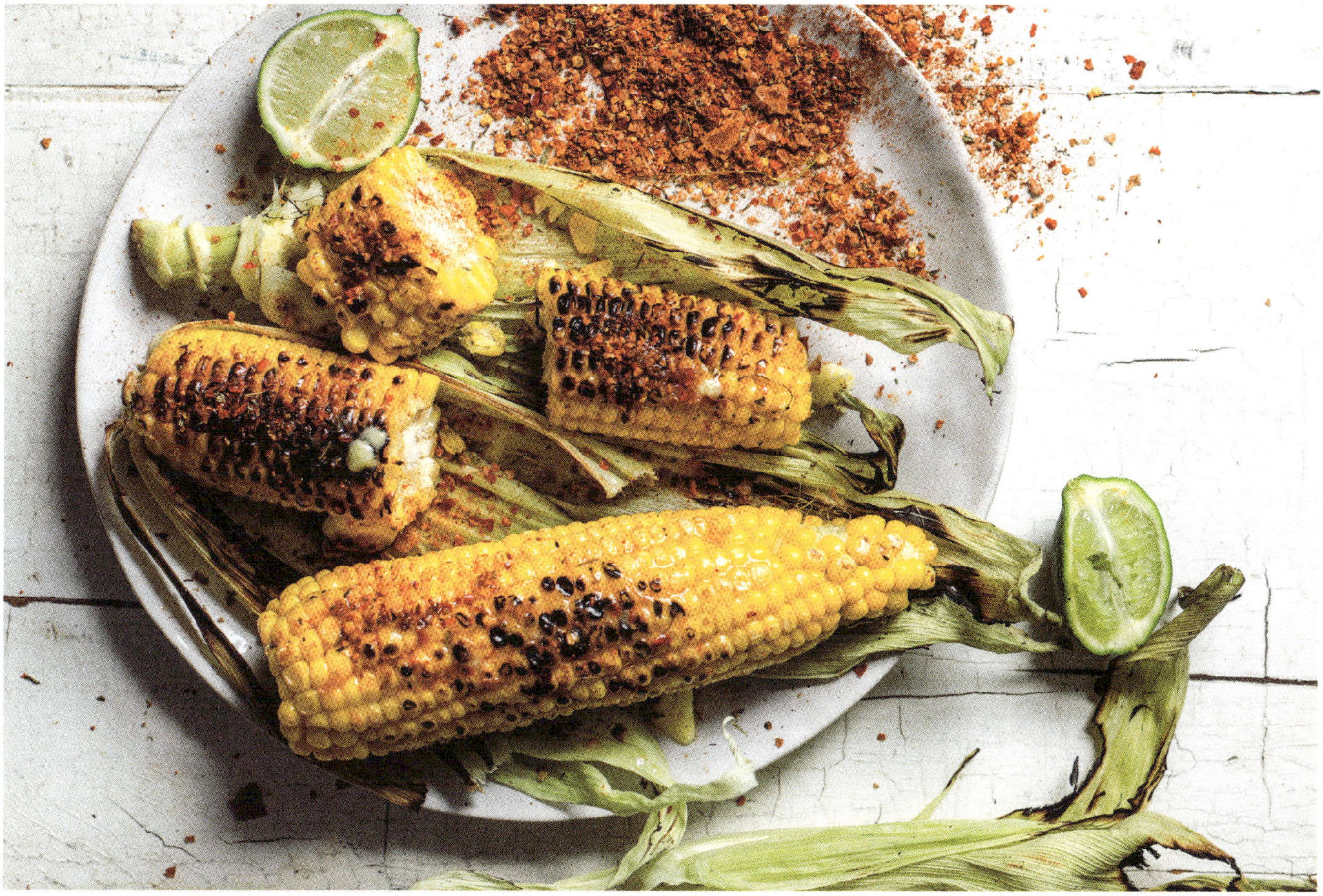

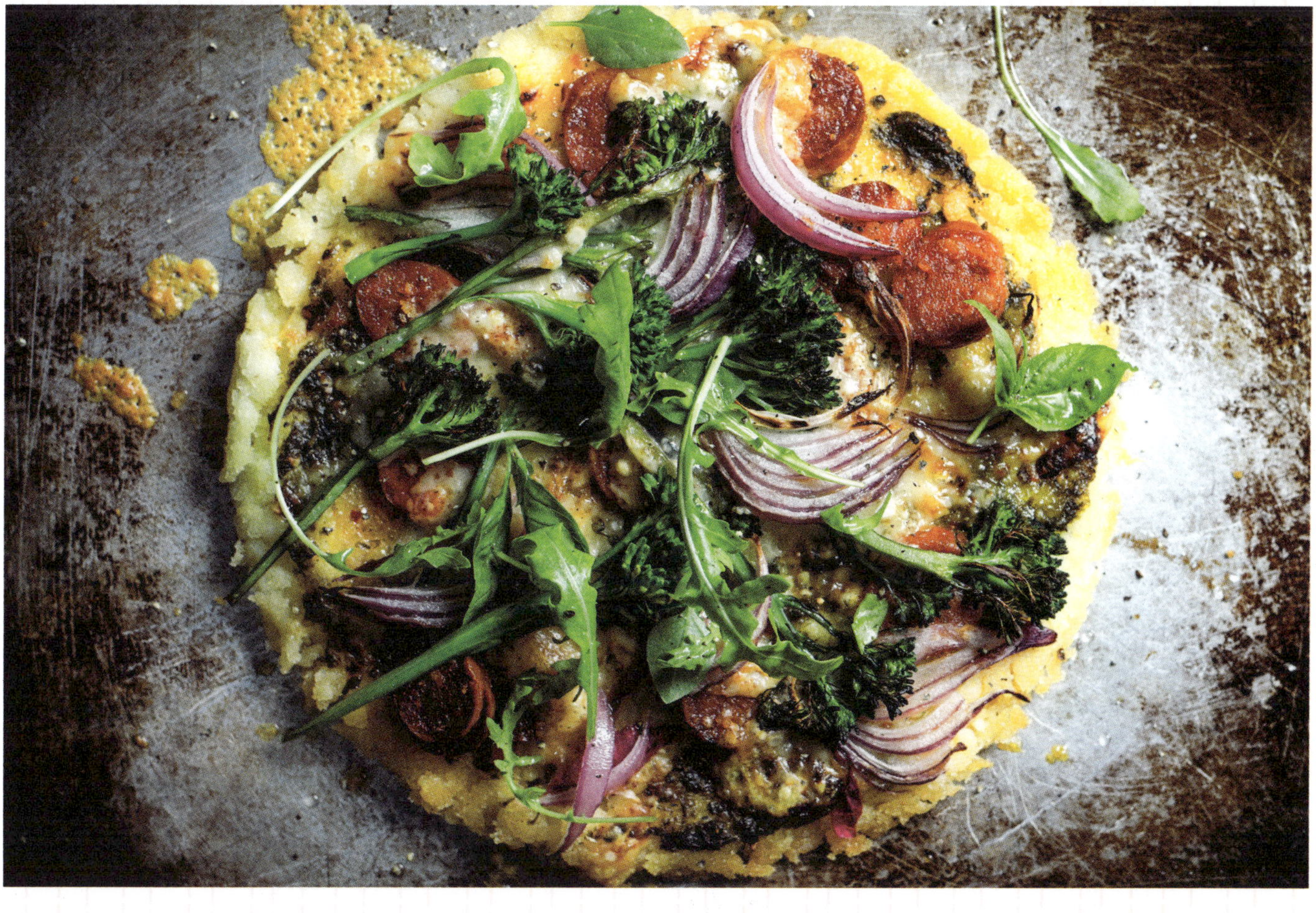

NATASHA SIDERIS
TASHAS

SCRAMBLED SWEETCORN
POLENTA PORRIDGE
HONEYBUSH-POACHED PEAR
& BILTONG SALAD
BREAD & BUTTER PUDDING

As much as I love cooking, I don't enjoy complicated recipes and fussy food. I value simple, beautiful food. I want the ingredients to stand out. I try to make sure our food is comforting, unpretentious and honest.

Natasha

Johannesburg, Gauteng

SCRAMBLED SWEETCORN

SERVINGS: 4 | PREP TIME: 10 MINS | COOK TIME: 10 MINS | SKILL LEVEL: 1 (EASY)

INGREDIENTS

12 rashers streaky bacon

30 g butter

1 x 400 g can corn kernels

12 eggs

1 tbsp chopped parsley

4 tsp chopped spring
  onion, to garnish

micro greens, to garnish

24 Parmesan shavings,
  to garnish

METHOD

Cook the streaky bacon until crisp and chop into pieces. Melt the butter in a non-stick pan and sauté the corn kernels briefly. Add the eggs and scramble together with the corn. Add the parsley and some salt and pepper. Serve topped with the bacon, chopped spring onion, micro greens and Parmesan.

TIP

Be sure not to overcook the eggs. They may appear runny because of the addition of the corn.

POLENTA PORRIDGE

SERVINGS: 4 | PREP TIME: 20 MINS | COOK TIME: 1 HOUR | SKILL LEVEL: 1 (EASY)

INGREDIENTS

1 litre water

5 ml salt

5 ml chicken stock powder

5 ml dried thyme

150 g polenta

60 g butter

60 g grated Parmesan

200 ml cream

4 pinches of chilli flakes,
  to garnish

4 pinches of chopped
  parsley, to garnish

24 Parmesan shavings,
  to garnish

Toppings

8 button mushrooms,
  sliced

12 rashers streaky bacon

4 eggs

METHOD

Prepare the toppings: fry the mushrooms and cook the bacon until crispy. Poach the eggs. Set them all aside and keep warm, or reheat briefly just before serving.

To make the porridge, bring the water to the boil with the salt, chicken stock powder and thyme. Add the polenta and whisk to ensure that no lumps form. Continue whisking until the polenta thickens, then cook for 30–40 minutes. Add the butter and 60 g Parmesan and allow to melt into the polenta. Slowly add the cream just before serving.

Serve the polenta in 4 bowls, topped with the bacon, mushrooms and a poached egg. Sprinkle with chilli flakes and parsley, and garnish with Parmesan shavings.

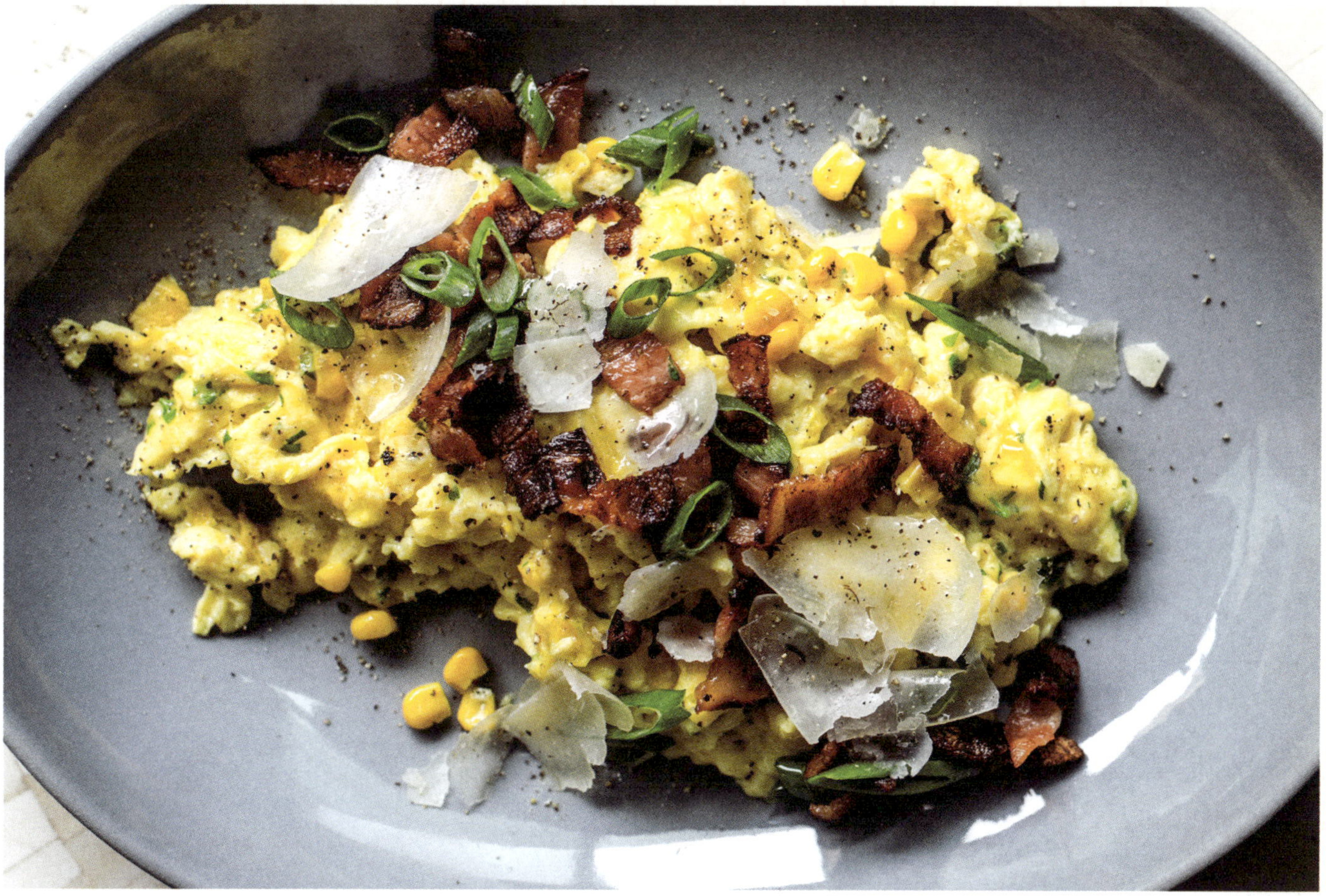

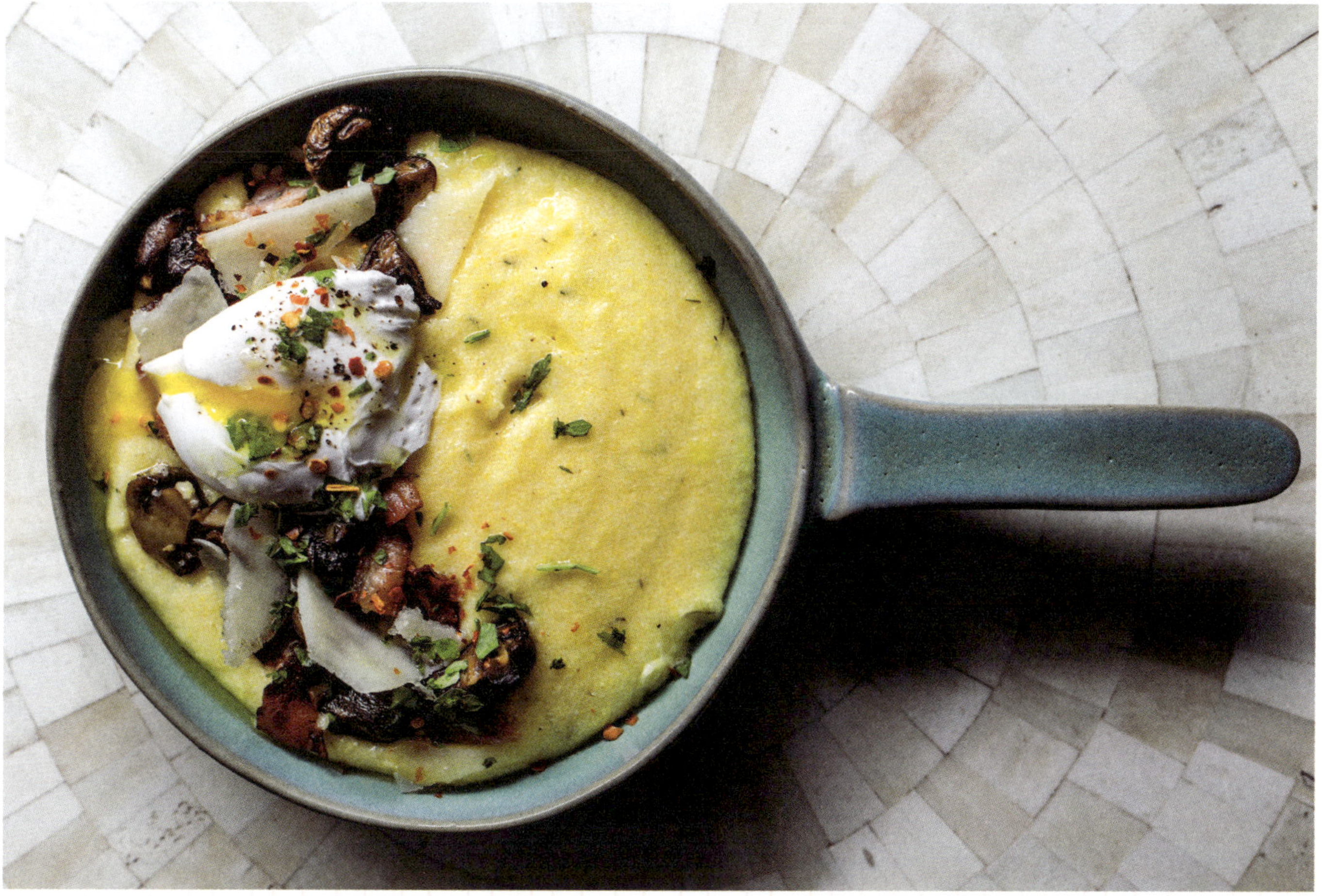

HONEYBUSH-POACHED PEAR & BILTONG SALAD

SERVINGS: 4 | PREP TIME: 20 MINS | COOK TIME: 45 MINS PLUS COOLING | SKILL LEVEL: 2 (MODERATE)

INGREDIENTS

Biltong
25 ml wholegrain mustard
300 ml olive oil
75 ml balsamic vinegar
70 g treacle sugar
200 g moist biltong, thinly
  sliced

Pears
750 ml white wine
2 honeybush teabags
2 rooibos teabags
200 g sugar
1 star anise
1 cinnamon stick
10 peppercorns
5 cloves
4 whole pears, peeled
60 g crushed walnuts
20 ml biltong powder
120 g Gorgonzola
20 ml caster sugar

Salad
20 baby spinach leaves,
  shredded
60 g walnuts, roasted and
  salted
20 g micro greens
20 ml biltong powder,
  to garnish

METHOD

To make the marinated biltong, mix the mustard, olive oil, balsamic vinegar and treacle sugar together in a bottle with a lid and shake well. Pour over the biltong to marinate and set aside until ready to use.

To poach the pears, place the wine, teabags, sugar, spices and pears in a saucepan and simmer over medium heat for 20 minutes. Remove the pears from the saucepan and increase the heat to high to reduce the liquid to a light syrup. Once syrup is reduced, place the pears back into the syrup, cool and store in the fridge. Once cooled, use a melon baller to core the pear from the bottom to be able to fill them with the gorgonzola mix.

Pre-heat the oven to 180°C. Mix the crushed walnuts with the biltong powder. Fill the poached pears with Gorgonzola and create a 'stopper' at the bottoms of the pears with the walnut and biltong mixture. Place the filled pears on a non-stick oven tray and bake until well heated and the cheese has started to melt, about 5–10 minutes. Remove the pears from the oven and sprinkle with caster sugar. Caramelise with a kitchen blowtorch.

To serve, make a salad with the marinated biltong, baby spinach, walnuts and micro greens. Dress with about 60 ml of the biltong marinade. Place the pears on top of the salad and sprinkle with biltong powder.

BREAD & BUTTER PUDDING

SERVINGS: 4 | PREP TIME: 25 MINS | COOK TIME: 40 MINS | SKILL LEVEL: 2 (MODERATE)

INGREDIENTS

4 croissants

20 ml caster sugar

5 ml ground cinnamon,
  to garnish

60 ml mascarpone,
  to serve

Apples

4 Golden Delicious apples,
  peeled and cut into
  eighths

80 g butter

120 g caster sugar

20 ml lemon juice

Crème anglaise

560 ml cream

1 vanilla pod, split

3 egg yolks

1 whole egg

75 g caster sugar

METHOD

To bake the apples, pre-heat the oven to 200°C. Place apple pieces in an ovenproof dish and add the butter, sugar and lemon juice. Bake for 15 minutes, turning each piece after 8 minutes. Remove from the oven and set aside until ready to use. Reduce the oven temperature to 180°C.

Meanwhile, make the crème anglaise. In a medium saucepan, bring the cream and vanilla pod just to the boil. In a separate bowl, whisk the egg yolks, egg and sugar together. Slowly pour the hot cream over the eggs, whisking continuously, and leave to cool in the bowl.

To assemble the pudding, cut the croissants in half and then into 8 fingers. Layer the apples and croissants in an ovenproof bowl or dish, pour the crème anglaise over, sprinkle with caster sugar and bake for 15 minutes. Remove from the oven and sprinkle with cinnamon. Serve with mascarpone.

Cape Town,
Western Cape

PETE GOFFE-WOOD
MASTERCHEF SOUTH AFRICA JUDGE, RESTAURATEUR & TV PERSONALITY

HOT-SMOKED YELLOWTAIL WITH FENNEL & ORANGE SALAD & TARRAGON CREAM

GRILLED PRIME RIB STEAKS WITH ROASTED SHALLOTS, FINGERLING POTATOES & MASALA BUTTER

SLOW-ROASTED PORK BELLY

I love cooking over hot coals. Elize and I can sit outside and enjoy a bevvy or two while the food cooks in our inevitable Weber. We are seriously big on food sustainability in our household, so we always use SASSI-approved fish for the hot-smoked fish recipe. Most of all, food is about sharing, so enjoy these recipes with special friends and family. *Peter*

HOT-SMOKED YELLOWTAIL
WITH FENNEL & ORANGE SALAD & TARRAGON CREAM

SERVINGS: 6–8 | PREP TIME: 15 MINS PLUS MARINATING | COOK TIME: 30 MINS PLUS COOLING
SKILL LEVEL: 2 (MODERATE)

INGREDIENTS

1 side yellowtail
2 bulbs fennel
50 ml extra virgin olive oil
juice of 2 lemons
1 tsp caster sugar
2 oranges

Brine
1 litre water
125 g salt
125 g brown sugar
1 tsp juniper berries
1 tsp black peppercorns
4 whole cloves

Tarragon cream
3 eggs
120 ml white wine vinegar
120 g sugar
200 ml cream
2 tbsp chopped fresh
  tarragon (or, if using
  dried tarragon, add to
  the vinegar)

METHOD

To make the brine, combine all the ingredients together in a small saucepan. Bring to the boil and then remove from the heat. Leave to cool.

Put the yellowtail into the brine and leave in the fridge to marinate for 1 hour. Remove the fish from the brine and place in a smoker, season with salt and pepper and smoke over a gentle heat for about 20 minutes. Remove from heat and leave to cool in the smoker.

Meanwhile, make the tarragon cream. Put eggs, vinegar and sugar together in a stainless steel bowl and whisk over boiling water. Whisk until thick ribbon stage is reached. Remove from the double boiler and allow to cool. When cooled, whisk the cream into the egg base. Add the chopped fresh tarragon and season to taste with salt and pepper.

Thinly slice the fennel and dress with the olive oil and lemon juice. Season with salt, pepper and caster sugar. Segment the oranges and add to the dressed fennel. Serve the cooled, smoked side of yellowtail topped with the fennel and oranges, with tarragon cream on the side.

GRILLED PRIME RIB STEAKS WITH ROASTED SHALLOTS, FINGERLING POTATOES & MASALA BUTTER

SERVINGS: 4 | PREP TIME: 10 MINS PLUS MARINATING | COOK TIME: 1 HOUR | SKILL LEVEL: 1 (EASY)

INGREDIENTS

100 ml extra virgin olive oil

50 ml Worcestershire sauce

1¼ kg prime rib steak on the bone, about 2 slices

600 g shallots

600 g fingerling potatoes

30 ml extra virgin olive oil

4 cloves garlic

10 g thyme

Masala butter

½ onion, finely chopped

1 clove garlic, finely chopped

extra virgin olive oil

2 tbsp curry powder

1 tbsp lemon juice

1 tbsp Worcestershire sauce

4 anchovy fillets

1 tbsp baby capers

1 tsp salt

1 tsp pepper

10 g flat-leaf parsley

10 g basil

10 g thyme

1 tsp ground ginger

1 egg yolk

200 g unsalted butter

METHOD

Mix 100 ml olive oil and 50 ml Worcestershire sauce together and use to marinate the steaks for 30 minutes to 1 hour.

To make the masala butter, fry the chopped onion and garlic in a little olive oil until soft and translucent. Add the curry powder and fry for a couple of minutes. Place the onion mix with the rest of the ingredients, other than the butter, in a blender. Blend to a rough paste. Add the butter and blend until evenly mixed. Check seasoning and refrigerate until ready to serve.

Pre-heat the oven to 200°C. Peel the shallots and cut them in half lengthways. Cut the fingerling potatoes in half lengthways and combine with the shallots in a roasting pan. Drizzle the vegetables with 30 ml olive oil and add the cloves of garlic and thyme. Season with salt and pepper and roast in the oven for about 30 minutes or until the vegetables are soft and begin to colour. Remove the vegetables from the oven and keep warm until ready to serve.

Season the steak liberally with salt and pepper and place it on the grill over hot coals. Cook to your preference: assuming this is average prime rib and each steak is about 600–700 g, I'd say 8–12 minutes per side. Remove the steaks from the heat and leave to rest for a few minutes.

Slice the steak and arrange on a platter with the roasted shallots and potatoes. Add a hefty dollop of masala butter on top of the steak and serve.

SLOW-ROASTED PORK BELLY

SERVINGS: 4–6 | PREP TIME: 15 MINS PLUS MACERATING | COOK TIME: 2 HOURS | SKILL LEVEL: 1 (EASY)

INGREDIENTS

1¾ kg pork belly, skin on

Dijon mustard, to serve

METHOD

Score the skin of the pork belly. Rub sea salt and freshly ground black pepper into the skin. Place the pork over indirect coals in an enclosed barbecue (I use a Weber) and roast for about 2 hours, turning it once or twice. The pork is ready when the skin is very crisp and clear juices run from it when a skewer is inserted. The meat should also start coming loose from the bone. Serve the pork belly in slices – I serve with a cabbage salad (see recipe on page 286) and plenty of Dijon mustard.

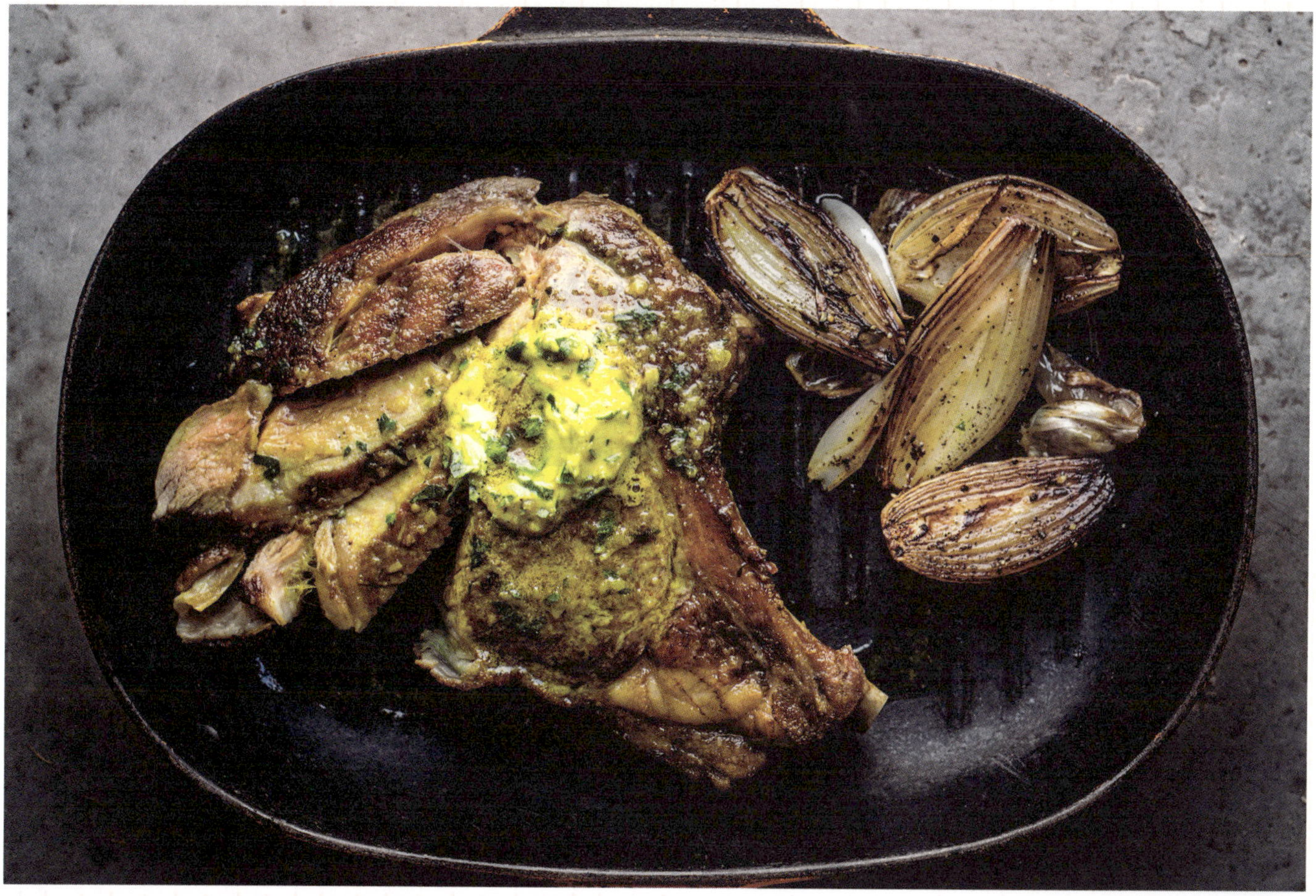
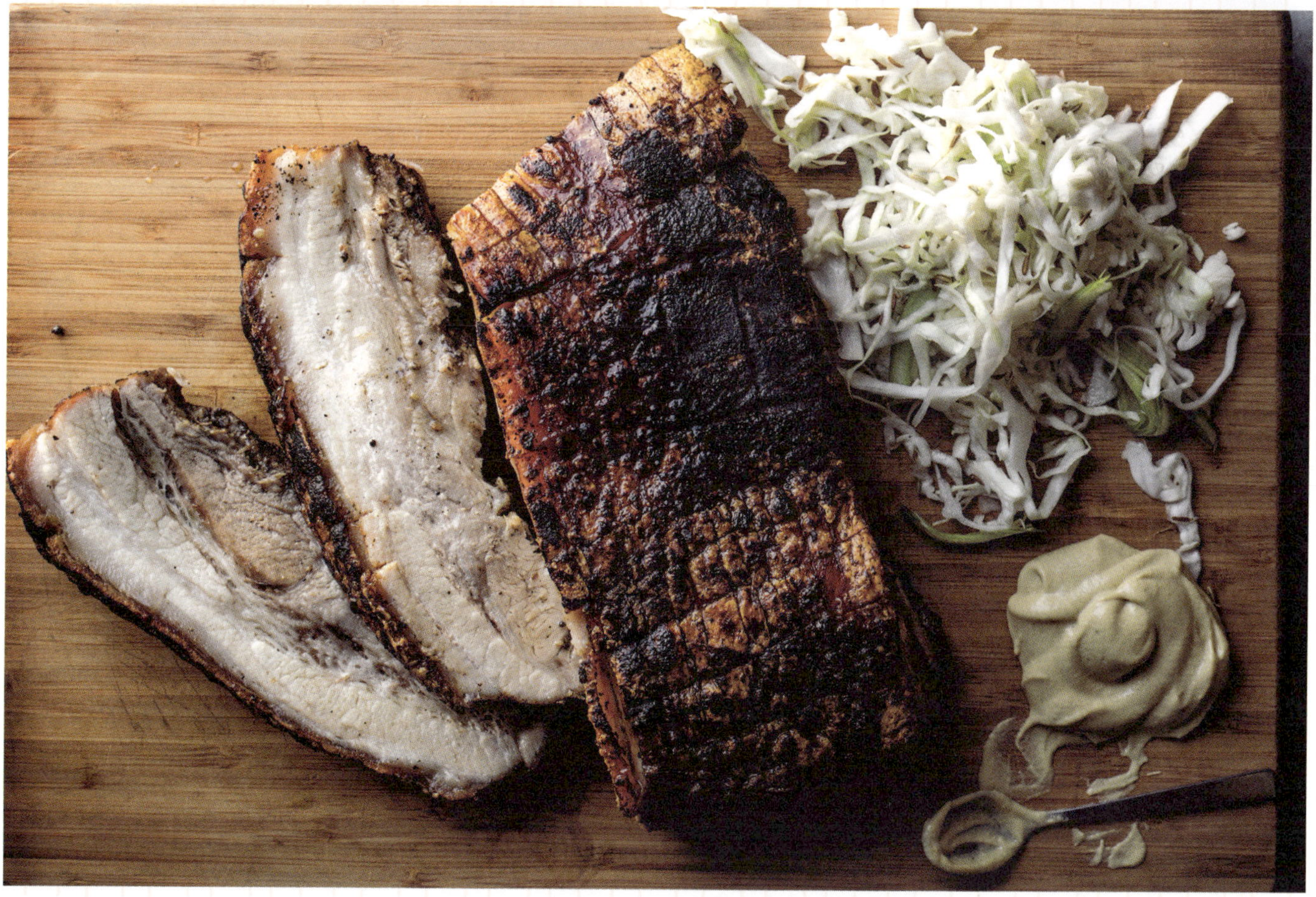

LIAM TOMLIN
CHEFS WAREHOUSE

BEETROOT-CURED SALMON WITH HORSERADISH CREAM

VEGETABLE SPRING ROLLS WITH PEANUT SAUCE

Tapas is the ideal illustration of the style of food I like to cook and the way I like to eat, with lots of different tastes, textures and cooking styles. Food, for me, is about the enjoyment of the whole process, from the sourcing of the ingredients to their preparation and cooking. And above all – the eating!

LIAM

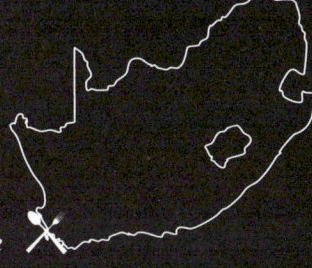

Cape Town,
Western Cape

BEETROOT-CURED SALMON WITH HORSERADISH CREAM

SERVINGS: 4–6 | PREP TIME: 10 MINS PLUS CURING | SKILL LEVEL: 2 (MODERATE)

INGREDIENTS

1 kg raw beetroot, peeled and grated

240 g treacle sugar

240 g sea salt

15 g crushed black peppercorns

35 g crushed juniper berries

80 ml dark rum

50 g dill, including stalks, chopped

zest of 3 lemons, pared with a potato peeler

1 kg side of salmon, trimmed and pin boned

micro herbs, to garnish

balsamic reduction, to garnish

Horseradish cream

100 ml whipping cream

50 g freshly grated horseradish

1 tsp Dijon mustard

1 tbsp white wine vinegar

pinch of sugar

METHOD

Start 3–4 days before you wish to serve. Mix together the beetroot, treacle sugar, sea salt, crushed black peppercorns, crushed juniper berries, dark rum, dill and lemon zest.

Spread a sheet of aluminium foil large enough to wrap the salmon in on your work surface. Cover the foil with plastic wrap. Place the salmon with the flesh side facing up onto the plastic wrap. Evenly spread the salmon with the beetroot mixture. Wrap the fish tightly in the plastic wrap and again in the aluminium foil. Place the salmon parcel on a tray and refrigerate for 3–4 days, draining off excess juice from the salmon daily.

After 4 days, scrape off the beetroot cure and discard it. Wipe the flesh with a clean, damp tea towel. Cut into cubes to serve as shown, or carve thin slices of salmon the same thickness as you would for smoked salmon.

To make the horseradish cream, whip the cream to ribbon stage. Add horseradish, mustard, vinegar, sugar, and salt and freshly ground pepper to taste. Gently fold the ingredients through the cream. Refrigerate until ready to use.

To serve, arrange the salmon on a chilled plate and serve with horseradish cream, garnished with micro herbs and balsamic reduction.

TIP

If you cannot find fresh horseradish, buy a good-quality horseradish sauce. To 2 parts horseradish sauce, add 1 part whipped cream for a mild-flavoured sauce.

VEGETABLE SPRING ROLLS WITH PEANUT SAUCE

SERVINGS: 10 | PREP TIME: 25 MINS | COOK TIME: 10 MINS | SKILL LEVEL: 1 (EASY)

INGREDIENTS

1 x 500 g packet rice vermicelli

3 drops sesame oil

selection of vegetables such as pickled carrot, pak choi, broccolini, enoki mushrooms, asparagus spears, bean sprouts, cos lettuce

mint, finely chopped

basil, shredded

coriander, roughly chopped

fresh lime juice

10 rice paper rounds

25 g peanuts, roasted and roughly chopped

Peanut sauce

2 tbsp vegetable oil

2 large shallots, peeled and finely chopped

2 cloves garlic, peeled and finely chopped

2 cm piece fresh ginger, peeled and finely chopped

1 red chilli, de-seeded and finely chopped

5 ml soy sauce

1 tbsp caster sugar

250 ml coconut cream

100 g peanut butter

15 g roasted peanuts, roughly chopped

fresh lime juice

small bunch coriander, roughly chopped

METHOD

Place the rice vermicelli in a large bowl and cover with boiling water. Cover the bowl with plastic wrap and leave to stand for 4–5 minutes until tender but still with some bite. Drain the vermicelli, then rinse under cold running water until cool, then under hot, running water, then under cold running water again. (This cold-hot rinse prevents the vermicelli from sticking together and breaking.) Drain well and mix sesame oil through the vermicelli. Set aside until ready to use.

Place the prepared vegetables in a bowl and season with salt and freshly ground pepper. Add mint, basil, coriander and lime juice to taste. Set aside until ready to use.

To make the peanut sauce, heat the vegetable oil in a heavy-based saucepan over a medium heat. Add the shallots and sweat without allowing them to colour for 3 minutes. Then stir in the garlic, ginger and chilli and cook for a further 4 minutes. Add the soy sauce and sugar and let it reduce slightly before adding the coconut cream. Cook for 2 minutes, and then stir in the peanut butter and half of the chopped peanuts until fully incorporated into the sauce. Remove the sauce from the heat and add a squeeze of lime juice to taste. Set sauce aside until ready to use. Just before serving the peanut sauce, stir in the chopped coriander.

Fill a deep bowl with 2 parts boiling water and 1 part cold water. Take a rice paper sheet and briefly dip it in the water, removing it as soon as your fingers touch the water. Allow any excess water to drain off. Lay the softened rice paper sheet on a plate. Brush a little peanut sauce on the top of the sheet, half an inch away from the sides. Sprinkle some chopped peanuts over the sauce. Place some of the vegetable mix on the peanut sauce and top with some noodles. Holding the rice paper edge closest to you, fold it over the mixture to enclose it tightly, then fold over the sides and continue to roll it as tightly as possible until you have formed a compact cylinder. Place the spring roll on a tray and cover with a damp tea towel to keep it moist. Repeat with the remaining rice paper and filling ingredients.

The rolls can be made up to 2 hours in advance. Refrigerate them, covered with a damp tea towel, until ready to serve. Serve the spring rolls with bowls of peanut sauce for dipping.

XOLISWA NDOYIYA
NELSON MANDELA'S PRIVATE CHEF

UMLEQWA

This chicken dish reminds you of who you are and where you grew up. It was Mr Mandela's favourite and he always asked for his gravy on the side. If it wasn't there, he would call me and say, 'Xoli, where is my gravy? Wasn't the bird drinking anything?'

Xoliswa

Queenstown,
Eastern Cape

UMLEQWA
FARM CHICKEN

SERVINGS: 4 | PREP TIME: 15 MINS | COOK TIME: 35 MINS | SKILL LEVEL: 1 (EASY)

INGREDIENTS

1½ kg chicken (farm is best but otherwise free range), cut into pieces

1 onion, chopped

1 tbsp flour

3 cups (750 ml) chicken stock

chopped fresh parsley, to serve

METHOD

Season the chicken with salt and pepper. Boil the chicken in 1 cup water for 10 minutes with the lid off; the water will evaporate. Allow the chicken to slightly fry in its own fat for a further 5 minutes. Add the onion and flour, and cook for another few minutes. Stir in the stock, bring to the boil and cover. Cook for 20–25 minutes until the chicken has cooked through.

Scatter with parsley, and serve with the sauce on the side.

SAMMY PHALANE
WITH MBUYISELO XABA
GREEN-BUDS FRESH PRODUCE MARKET

BAKED BUTTERNUT
CINNAMON APPLE BREAD

Cooking with our fresh produce from the local area is obviously a favourite with us. We are very lucky to have this great produce at hand, and eat it ourselves as well as offer it to the trade in the area. Luckily my wife is a great cook, and I am able to get away with being the veg supplier. *Sammy*

Rustenburg,
North West

BAKED BUTTERNUT

SERVINGS: 6 | PREP TIME: 10 MINS | COOK TIME: 1 HOUR | SKILL LEVEL: 1 (EASY)

INGREDIENTS

1 kg peeled butternut,
  cut into 1 cm slices

250 ml fresh cream

125 ml milk

2 cloves garlic, crushed

1 x 60 g packet white
  onion soup mix

ground black pepper,
  to taste

chopped chives,
  to garnish

METHOD

Pre-heat the oven to 180°C. Layer half the butternut slices in a greased 2-litre casserole dish. Mix together remaining ingredients, except the chives, and pour half the mixture over the butternut. Repeat with another layer using the rest of the butternut and sauce. Cover and bake for 30 minutes. Remove lid and bake for a further 30 minutes. Garnish with chopped chives.

CINNAMON APPLE BREAD

SERVINGS: 8 | PREP TIME: 10 MINS | COOK TIME: 50 MINS | SKILL LEVEL: 1 (EASY)

INGREDIENTS

½ packed cup brown
  sugar

1½ tsp ground cinnamon

⅔ cup white sugar

½ cup butter, softened

2 eggs

2 tsp vanilla essence

1½ cups all-purpose flour

1½ tsp baking powder

½ cup milk

1 large apple, peeled,
  cored and finely chopped

METHOD

Pre-heat the oven to 180°C. Grease and flour a standard 23 cm x 13 cm loaf tin. Mix brown sugar and cinnamon together in a bowl and set aside. In a stand mixer, cream white sugar and butter until smooth. Add eggs and vanilla essence and continue to beat on medium speed until combined. Add flour and baking powder, and then add milk. Pour half the batter into the prepared tin. Cover with half of the apple. Pat the apple into the batter with the back of a spoon. Sprinkle with half of the brown sugar and cinnamon mixture. Pour the remaining batter over the apple layer and top with the remaining apple and the rest of the brown sugar and cinnamon mixture. Pat the topping into the batter with the back of a spoon. Bake for 50 minutes or until a toothpick inserted in the middle of the loaf comes out clean. Cool in the pan for 10 minutes before transferring to a cooling rack.

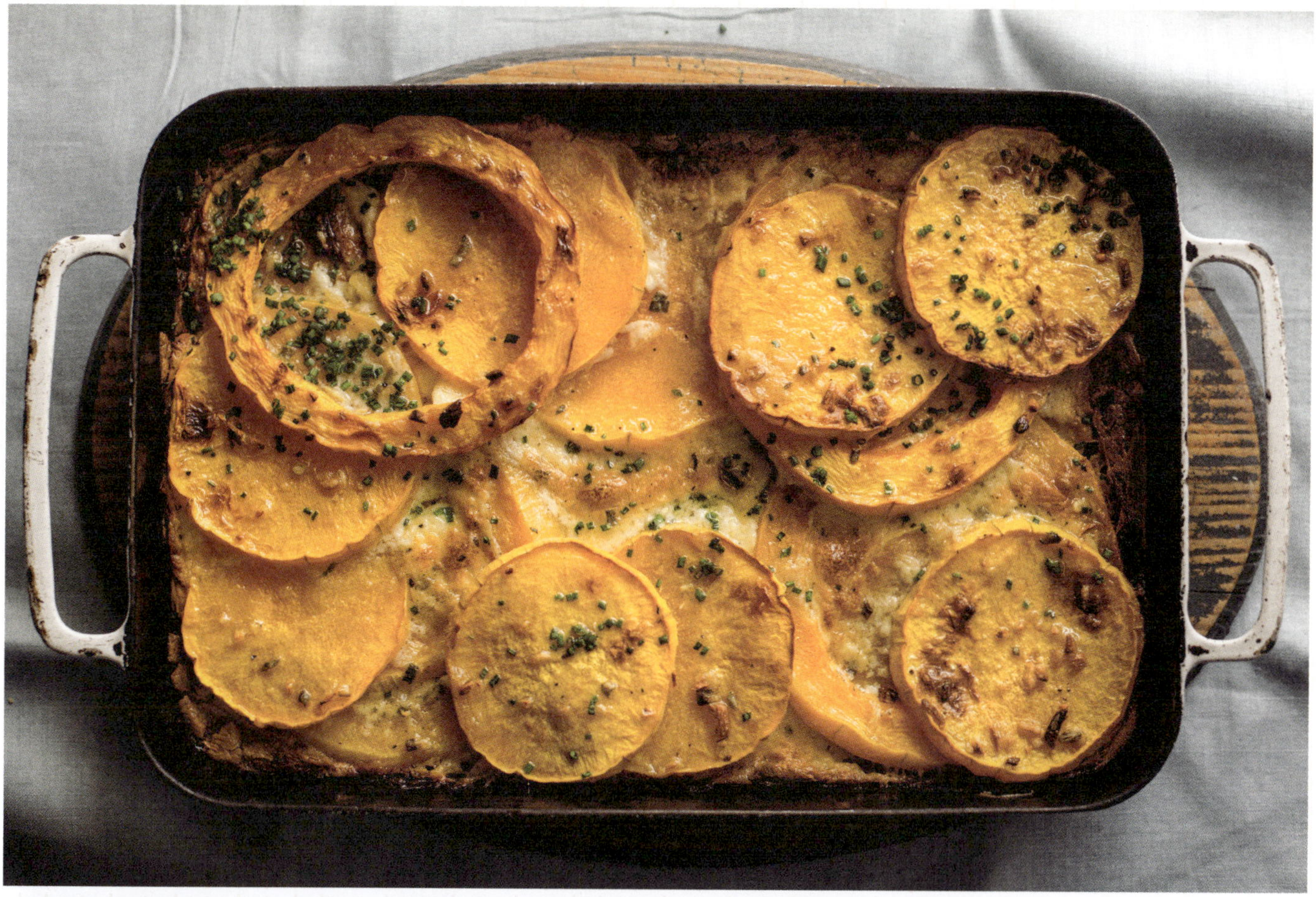

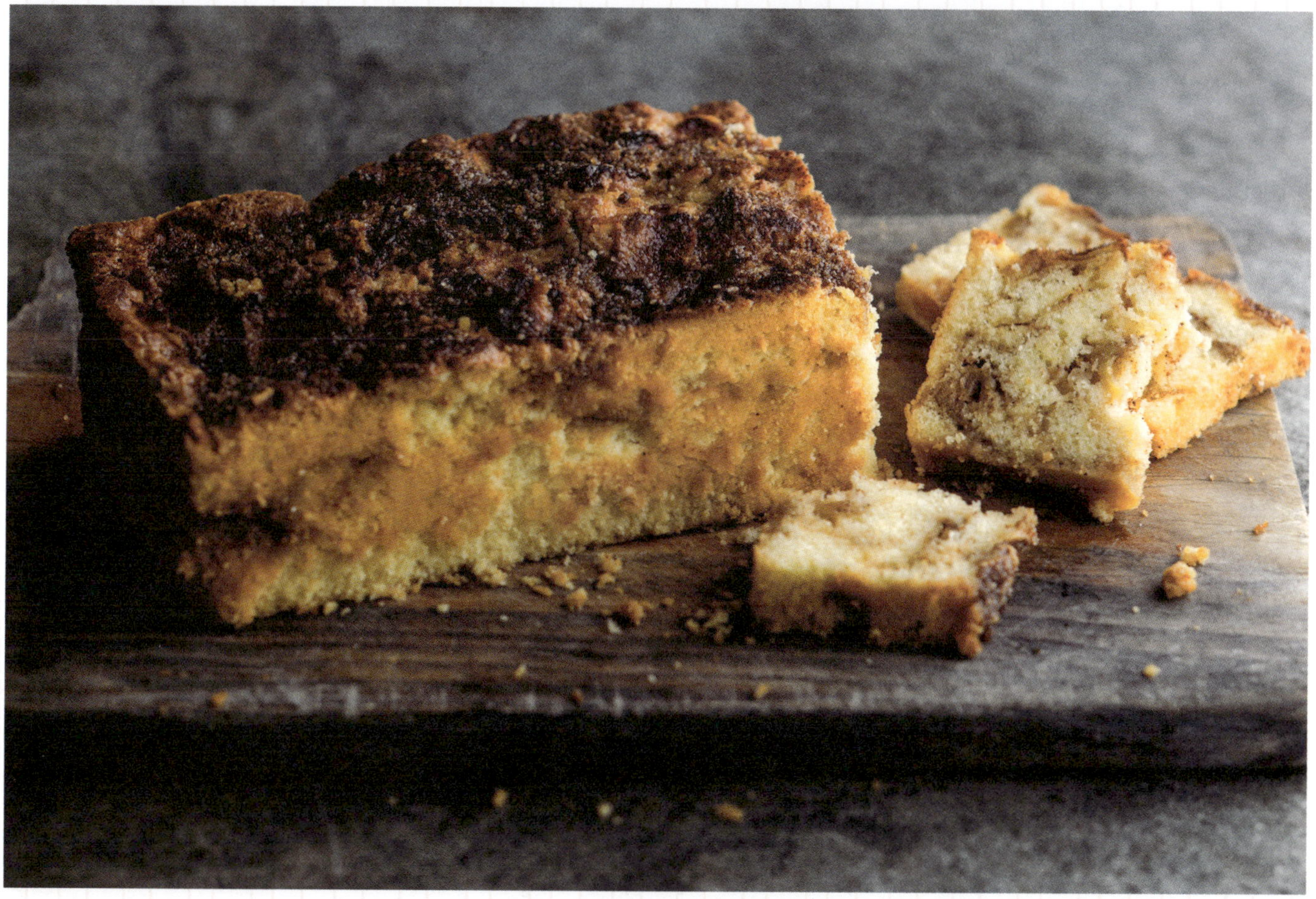

JULES MERCER
**WITH FRIK OOSTHUIZEN, SANTA ANNA'S;
AND CHARLIE & JULIE CROWTHER, GLEN OAKES FARM**
OUTLANDISH KITCHEN

JULIE CROWTHER'S STICKY PORK KNUCKLES

BARBECUED PULLED PORK TORTILLAS

RINA'S CUCUMBER PICKLE

I love bringing people closer to their food source. We all work together to create a long table heaving with innovative and sustainable produce. Charlie and Julie raise pigs in the most pukka way possible, Frik and the team from Santa Anna's smoke it all up in their genius smokers, and I provide the table, gees (atmosphere) and guests. It's great to see people understand more about what it takes to grow our food, and to raise a glass with the producers.

Jules

Hemel-en-Aarde Valley,
Western Cape

JULIE CROWTHER'S
STICKY PORK KNUCKLES

SERVINGS: 4 | PREP TIME: 15 MINS | COOK TIME: 1 HOUR 30 MINS | SKILL LEVEL: 1 (EASY)

INGREDIENTS

2 large unsmoked pork knuckles
  or hocks

2 carrots, roughly chopped

2 onions, roughly chopped

2 sticks celery (stalks and leaves),
  roughly chopped

2 bay leaves

1 tsp black peppercorns

1 tsp salt

2 star anise

Glaze

⅓ cup soy sauce

⅓ cup tomato sauce

⅓ cup chutney

⅓ cup brown sugar

2 tbsp Worcestershire sauce

1 tsp cumin

2–3 cloves garlic, finely chopped

1 knob ginger, peeled and finely
  chopped

splash of balsamic vinegar

2 tbsp honey

METHOD

Put the pork joints in a large pot with the carrots, onions, celery, bay leaves, peppercorns, salt and star anise. Cover with water, bring to the boil and simmer very gently for 1 hour. Allow to cool in the stock. Once cooled, remove from stock and gently remove the skin, keeping as much of the fat layer as possible on the meat.

Pre-heat the oven to 180°C. Mix all the ingredients for the glaze together. Put the pork joints into an oven dish and cover with glaze mixture. Roast in the oven until the glaze has reduced to a sticky brown coating, about 45 minutes in total. You might need to turn the joints over during roasting to allow the glaze to cover them as much as possible.

In winter, serve the joints with mashed potato or pumpkin, and lemon courgettes. In summer, serve with coleslaw or green leaves and plenty of lemon juice – the lemon juice definitely complements the richness of the sticky meat.

BARBECUED PULLED PORK TORTILLAS

SERVINGS: 6–8 | PREP TIME: 10 MINS PLUS MARINATING | COOK TIME: 4–8 HOURS | SKILL LEVEL: 1 (EASY)

INGREDIENTS

1 pork shoulder, skin on and
  bone in
20 ml olive oil
1 tsp salt
1 tsp brown sugar
1 tsp white sugar
1 tbsp paprika
½ tbsp garlic powder
½ tsp black pepper
½ tsp ground ginger
½ tsp onion powder or flakes
½ tsp dried rosemary
12 corn tortillas, to serve
  (we use Santa Anna's Organic
  Corn Tortillas)
barbecue or braai sauce, to serve
fresh coriander leaves, to garnish

METHOD

Rub the pork shoulder on the meat side with an even coating of oil. Combine the flavourings, herbs and spices and use the mixture to coat the shoulder evenly on the meat side. Wrap in plastic wrap and refrigerate for 1 hour. Pre-heat a smoker to 100°C and smoke the shoulder for 4–8 hours, until the internal temperature reaches 95°C. Rest for 30 minutes, then pull apart with two forks, removing the skin and bone. Serve with corn tortillas and your favourite barbecue or braai sauce and garnish with coriander.

RINA'S CUCUMBER PICKLE

SERVINGS: 1 LARGE (1¼ LITRE) JAR | PREP TIME: 10 MINS | COOK TIME: 5 MINS PLUS CURING
SKILL LEVEL: 1 (EASY)

INGREDIENTS

1 large cucumber
1 cup vinegar
110 g sugar
2 tbsp salt
1 tsp mustard seeds
2 star anise
1 tsp coriander seeds
handful of fresh dill leaves

METHOD

Start at least 1 day before you wish to serve. Slice the cucumber whichever way you like – either long strips or rounds. Pack tightly into a large jar. In a saucepan, heat the vinegar, sugar, salt, spices and dill leaves. Simmer until the sugar has dissolved. Turn off the heat, pour the mixture over the cucumber and place the lid on the jar while still hot. Once cooled, leave the pickle to stand for anything from 1 day to 1 month, stored in the fridge. Serve with absolutely anything – cheese, smoked meats, tortillas, frittatas, the list goes on…

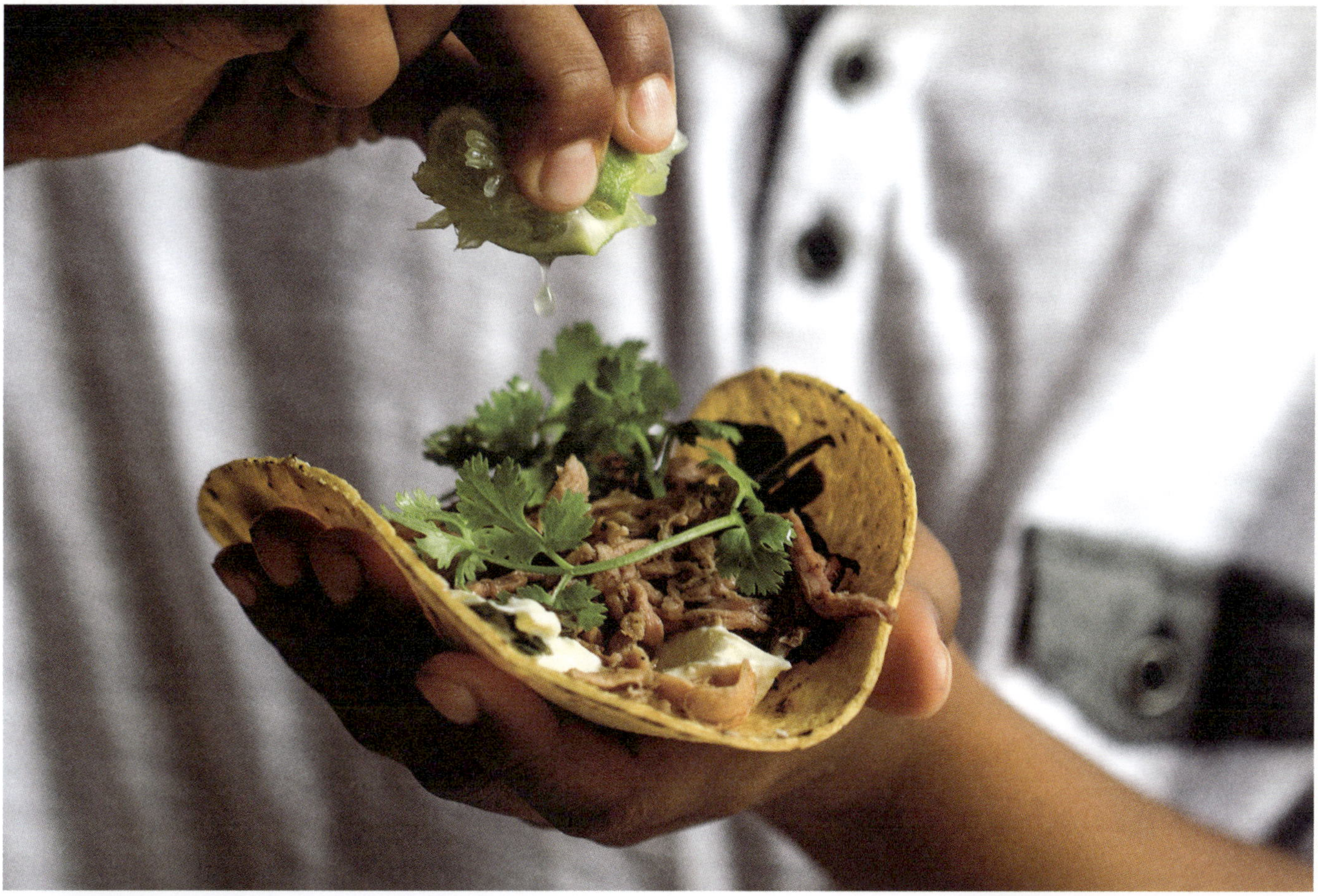

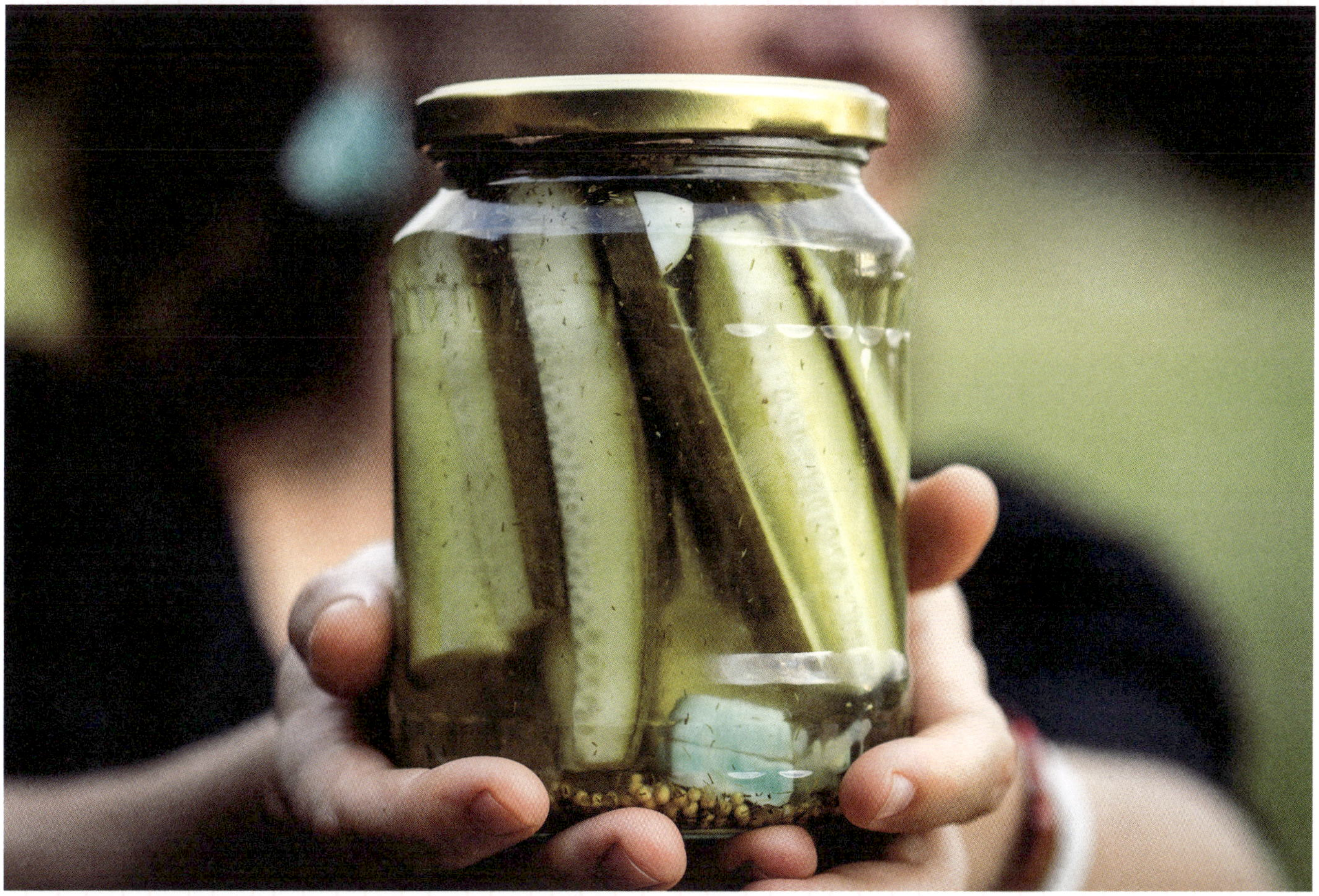

ALEX LAVARIS
WITH THE CAME FAMILY
THE PIG AND WHISTLE INN

HEARTY GUINNESS SPRINGBOK SHANKS
MALVA PUDDING

The Pig and Whistle has been serving food for over 100 years. We source from local farmers and suppliers, and create a menu based on whatever the community wants. There are no airs and graces about our food – it's home cooking at its best. Shanks are a Sunday favourite at our Roast Table, which has become an institution in Bathurst. Malva pudding is a great favourite too. Don't look at the calories or the sugar – our portion sizes are for farmers who need their grub.

Alexander

*Bathurst,
Eastern Cape*

HEARTY GUINNESS SPRINGBOK SHANKS

SERVINGS: 10 | PREP TIME: 15 MINS | COOK TIME: 4 HOURS | SKILL LEVEL: 1 (EASY)

INGREDIENTS

olive oil

10 sprigs of rosemary

10 springbok shanks

3 large red onions, roughly chopped

2 handfuls of raisins

2 tbsp tomato sauce

2 tbsp Worcestershire sauce

2 tbsp pineapple marmalade

1 x 340 ml can Guinness

1½ litres chicken stock

METHOD

Heat a large pan to medium and add two glugs of olive oil, then add the sprigs of rosemary and the springbok shanks. Fry, turning regularly, until they are golden brown in colour on all sides. Remove from heat and set aside.

Add two glugs of olive oil to a separate large pot, then fry the onions until they are transparent. Add raisins, tomato sauce, Worcestershire sauce, marmalade and Guinness and bring to the boil. Add the browned shanks and chicken stock.

Make sure the shanks are completely submerged, lower the heat to a gentle simmer and cook for 3½ hours until the meat is falling off the bone. Serve with creamy mashed potato.

MALVA PUDDING

SERVINGS: 6 | PREP TIME: 15 MINS | COOK TIME: 45 MINS | SKILL LEVEL: 1 (EASY)

INGREDIENTS

4 eggs

2 cups sugar

150 g butter

2 tbsp apricot jam

4 cups flour

4 tsp baking powder

4 tsp bicarbonate of soda

½ tsp salt

2 tbsp vinegar

Sauce

2 cups sugar

2 cups milk

2 cups cream

1 cup water

125 g butter

1 tsp vanilla essence

METHOD

Pre-heat the oven to 180°C. In a large bowl, mix together eggs, sugar, butter and jam. Slowly add dry ingredients and then mix in vinegar. Pour into a buttered baking dish and bake for 45 minutes.

Meanwhile, bring all the ingredients for the sauce to the boil, stir and remove from heat. Set aside.

When the pudding is cooked, remove from the oven and pour sauce over. Serve the pudding hot with homemade custard, or drown it in fresh farm cream. Enjoy!

Clifton,
Western Cape

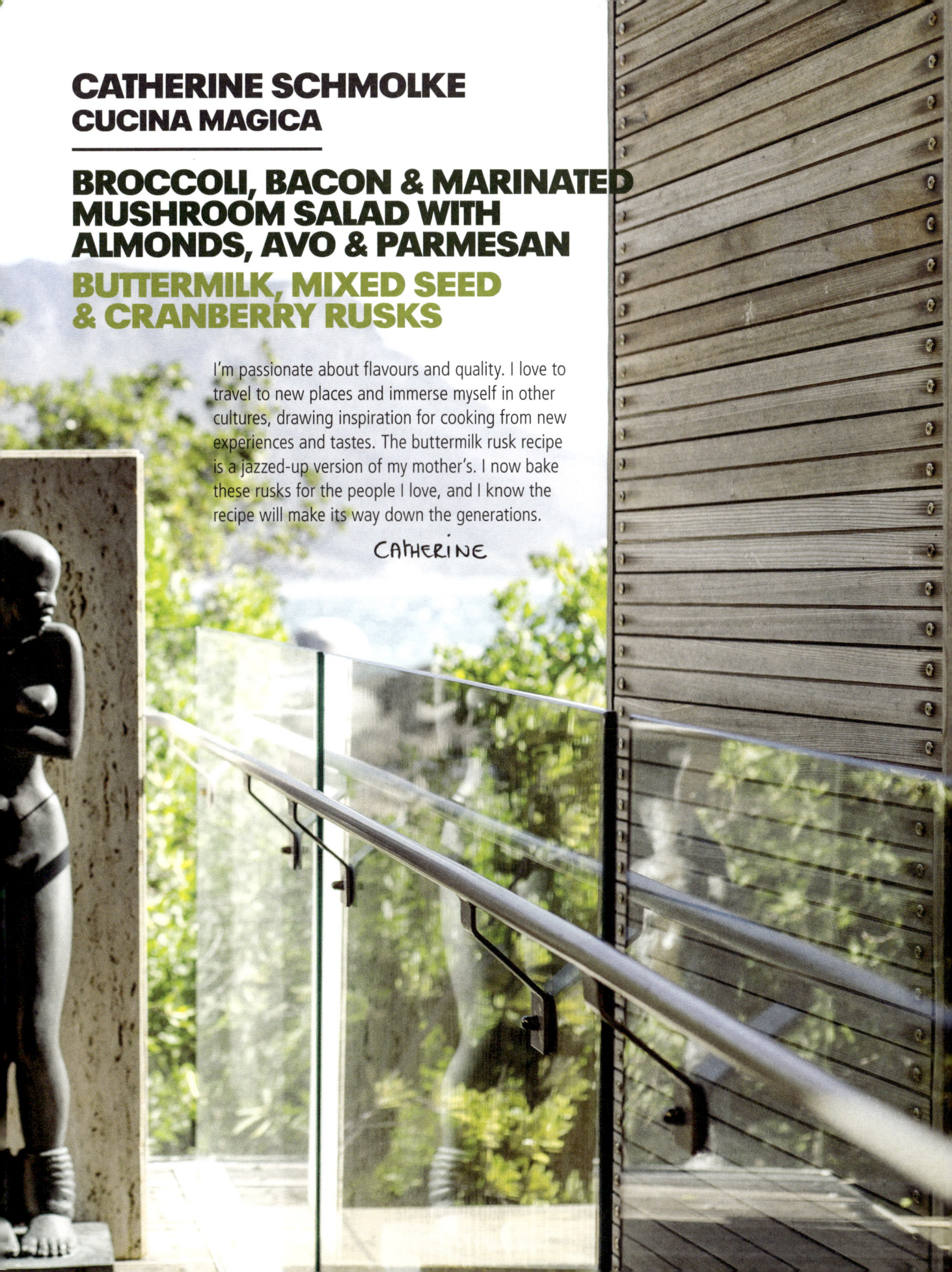

CATHERINE SCHMOLKE
CUCINA MAGICA

BROCCOLI, BACON & MARINATED MUSHROOM SALAD WITH ALMONDS, AVO & PARMESAN
BUTTERMILK, MIXED SEED & CRANBERRY RUSKS

I'm passionate about flavours and quality. I love to travel to new places and immerse myself in other cultures, drawing inspiration for cooking from new experiences and tastes. The buttermilk rusk recipe is a jazzed-up version of my mother's. I now bake these rusks for the people I love, and I know the recipe will make its way down the generations.

CATHERINE

BROCCOLI, BACON & MARINATED MUSHROOM SALAD WITH ALMONDS, AVO & PARMESAN

SERVINGS: 4 | PREP TIME: 20 MINS | COOK TIME: 10 MINS | SKILL LEVEL: 1 (EASY)

INGREDIENTS

300 g mixed mushrooms (I like to use exotic mushrooms like enoki and shiitake too)

2 tbsp vegetable oil

1 tsp chopped fresh thyme

2 cloves garlic, crushed

30 ml balsamic vinegar

60 ml olive oil

15 ml soy sauce

300 g broccoli florets (or tenderstem broccoli)

250 g streaky bacon

70 g flaked almonds

1 avocado

zest of 1 lemon

about 60 g mixed salad leaves

Dressing

½ cup mayonnaise

1 clove garlic, crushed

¼ cup grated Parmesan

2 tsp wholegrain mustard

1–2 tbsp water

METHOD

Make the dressing by whisking together all the ingredients. Season to taste with salt and pepper, and set aside.

Pre-heat the oven to 180°C. Sauté mushrooms in vegetable oil till soft and browned (about 5 minutes) and then turn off the heat. Mix the thyme, garlic, balsamic vinegar, olive oil and soy sauce together and add to the mushrooms. Set the mixture aside to marinate for about 20 minutes.

While the mushrooms are marinating, blanch the broccoli in boiling water for 2 minutes, drain and refresh in a bowl of iced water. Dice bacon and fry over a medium heat until crisp. Toast flaked almonds in the oven for 5 minutes until light brown. Peel the avocado and cut it into cubes.

Arrange the salad leaves on a platter and top with the marinated mushrooms, broccoli, avocado, bacon, almonds and lemon zest and serve with the dressing.

"This salad helps me get some greens into my family's weekday meals, but it's got loads of flavour too."

BUTTERMILK, MIXED SEED & CRANBERRY RUSKS

MAKES: ABOUT 48 | PREP TIME: 20 MINS | COOK TIME: 45 MINS PLUS DRYING | SKILL LEVEL: 1 (EASY)

INGREDIENTS

butter for greasing
2½ cups cake flour
5 tsp baking powder
2 tsp bicarbonate of soda
1 tsp fine salt
1½ cups wholewheat flour
75 g digestive bran
1 cup brown sugar
¼ cup sunflower seeds
¼ cup sesame seeds
¼ cup pumpkin seeds
¼ cup flaxseeds
½ cup dried cranberries
  or raisins
250 g melted butter
300 ml buttermilk
5 ml white vinegar
1 egg

METHOD

Pre-heat the oven to 180°C. Grease 2 loaf tins and line with baking paper. Sift dry ingredients into a mixing bowl. Add sunflower, sesame and pumpkin seeds, flaxseeds and dried cranberries or raisins, to the dry ingredients and stir through. In a separate bowl, mix together the melted butter, buttermilk, vinegar and egg. Add wet ingredients to dry ingredients and mix until a soft dough forms. Divide the mixture between the prepared loaf tins and bake for 45 minutes until golden brown. Remove from the oven and cool on a drying rack.

Once completely cooled, pre-heat the oven to 100°C. Cut each loaf into about 8 thick slices and cut each slice into 3 rusks. Put on a baking tray and dry in the oven for about 4 hours until dry and crisp. Store in an airtight container.

NOMPUMELELO MQWEBU
WITH: MAMA REFILOE MOLEFE, BAMBANANI CO-OPERATIVE;
MATAPELO MZIZI & VUSI NENE, DOWNTOWN FARMERS
AFRICA MEETS EUROPE CUISINE

**COURGETTE FLOWERS STUFFED
WITH PUMPKIN LEAVES**

**AMADUMBE, MBUYA
& PURSLANE SALAD**

*Soweto,
Gauteng*

I am very passionate about farmers as they help me navigate my food history. Farmers impart skills and knowledge that talk to our nomadic and hunter-gatherer food culture, which has been almost wiped out. These recipes pay homage to the farmers and their produce, which we are so fortunate to have.

Nompumelelo

COURGETTE FLOWERS
STUFFED WITH PUMPKIN LEAVES

SERVINGS: 4 AS A STARTER | PREP TIME: 35 MINS | COOK TIME: 15 MINS | SKILL LEVEL: 1 (EASY)

INGREDIENTS

1 medium courgette
500 g pumpkin leaves
250 g sweet potato leaves
1 tbsp peanut oil
2 spring onions, sliced
1 small onion, diced
½ tsp cumin
1 tsp salt
8 courgette flowers

METHOD

Wash the courgette, slice and cook for 2 minutes in salted water. Remove from heat and set aside in a clean bowl.

Prepare the pumpkin leaves by using a small paring knife to remove prickles from the backs of the leaves. Finely chop the pumpkin and sweet potato leaves. In a pan, heat peanut oil and sweat spring onion and onion. When soft, add cumin and stir while adding the leaves. Season with 1 teaspoon salt and some pepper, then add a little water and cook for 5 minutes. Remove from heat and set aside.

To prepare the courgette flowers, gently open the flowers and use a small pair of scissors to cut the stamens off (handle the delicate flowers with great care). Also remove the stalks. Rinse flowers inside and out and leave to dry on a dry paper towel. Do not pat them dry: they will wilt if you do so. Heat a pot of salted water to steam the stuffed flowers, making sure water is shallow so as not to touch the flowers.

To stuff the flowers, gently open them and stuff with the pumpkin leaves mixture using a teaspoon or piping bag. Do not overfill; add just enough stuffing so that you can twist the petals together to close them. Set aside leftover leaves mixture. Steam the stuffed flowers for 2 minutes and set aside.

Place the courgettes around a serving plate and top with the reserved leaves mixture. Arrange the stuffed flowers on the plate and serve.

TIP

Pick the courgette flowers on the day you will use them and keep refrigerated until you start preparing them.

AMADUMBE, MBUYA & PURSLANE SALAD

SERVINGS: 4 | PREP TIME: 15 MINS | COOK TIME: 50 MINS | SKILL LEVEL: 1 (EASY)

INGREDIENTS

200 g mbuya (amaranth)
  leaves
50 g young blackjack
  leaves
50 g purslane
100 g amadumbe, well
  washed but unpeeled

METHOD

Wash all the greens and dry well. In a pot on medium heat with enough water to cover, boil the amadumbe in salted water (depending on their size, this will take 40–50 minutes). When amadumbe are cooked, cool and then peel them. Steam the mbuya leaves until cooked (I prefer to blanch them and refresh in cold water, but some people prefer them steamed). In a bowl, mix all the leaves together and season with salt and pepper, then slice amadumbe into the salad. Serve the salad in a large bowl or individual portions, and add a salad dressing of your choice if you like.

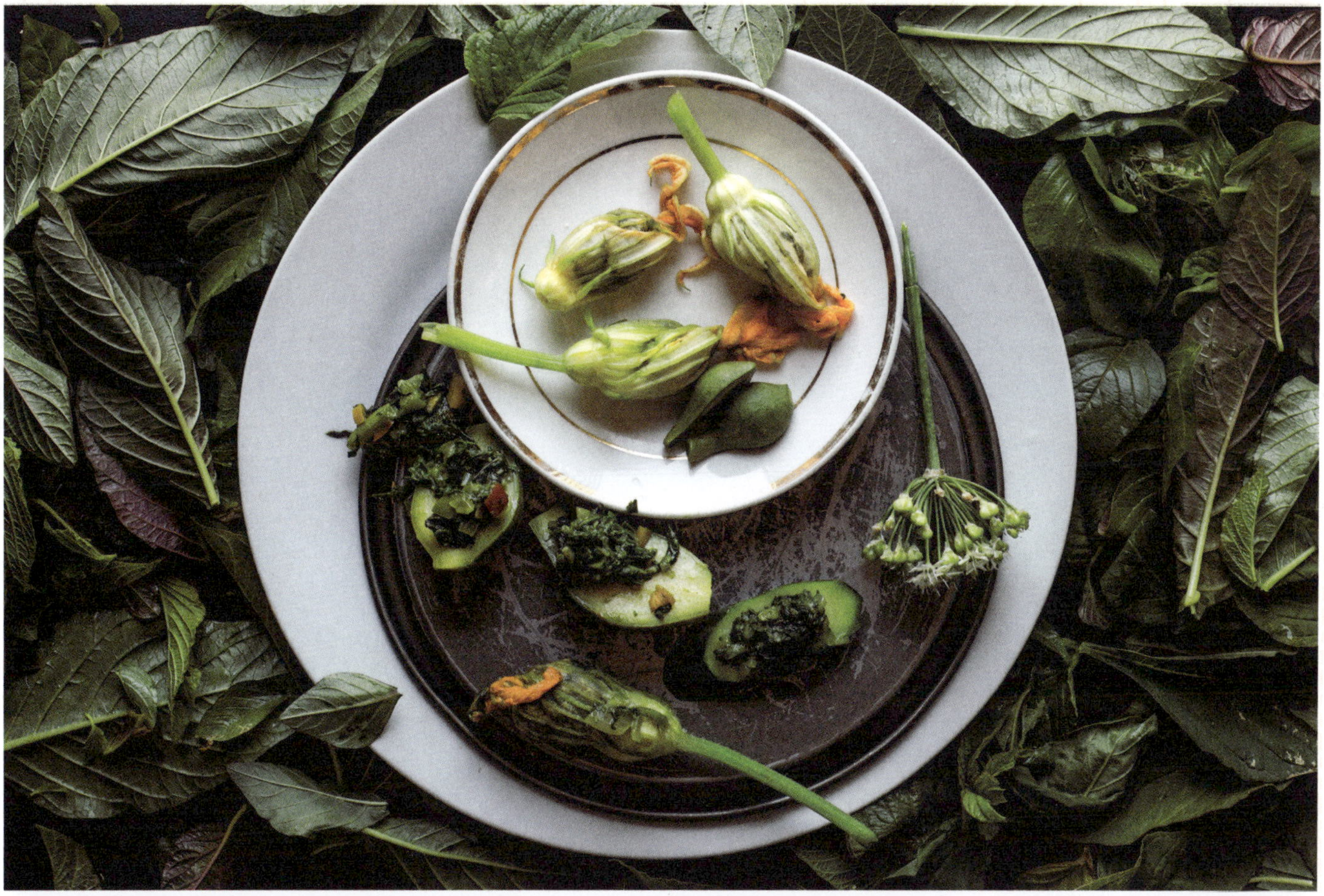

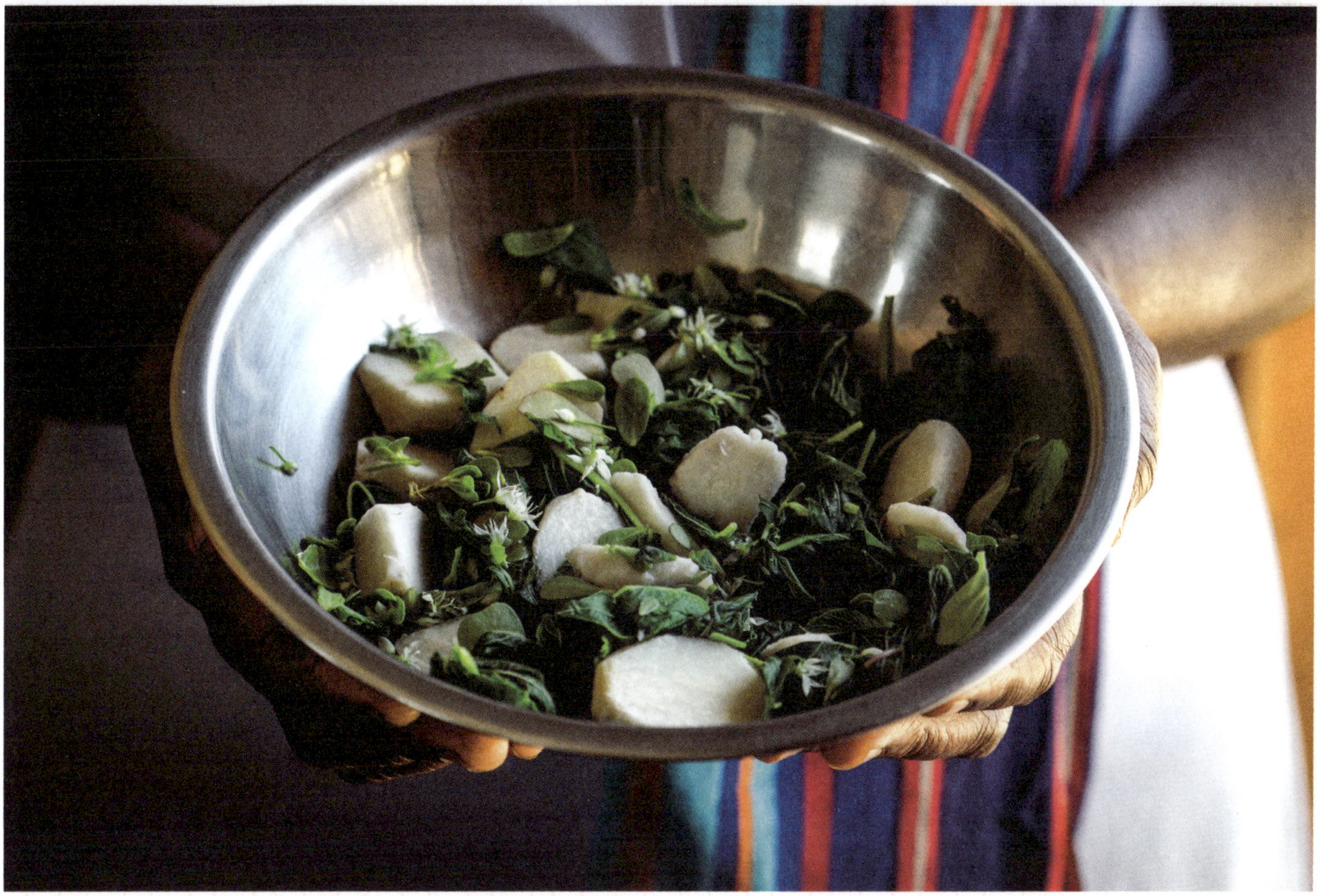

DARIO SORESI
WITH ADELIA, ARIANNA, MIKAELA, KIARA, FRANCA & BRUNO
LA LOCANDA

SPAGHETTI CARBONARA

*George,
Western Cape*

Spaghetti carbonara used to be the dish prepared by miners in the coal-mining areas of Italy. Perhaps the name carbonara, which loosely means 'in the manner of coal miners', was derived from the practice of sprinkling black pepper over the cooked food – the pepper looked like coal dust, which would have easily been a common topping on food prepared close to the mines!

SPAGHETTI CARBONARA

SERVINGS: 4 | PREP TIME: 10 MINS | COOK TIME: 10 MINS | SKILL LEVEL: 1 (EASY)

INGREDIENTS

400 g spaghetti
1 whole egg
4 egg yolks
300 g coarsely chopped
 bacon or pork lardons
80 g grated Parmesan

METHOD

Bring a large pot of salted water to the boil. Cook the spaghetti according to packet instructions, remove and drain. Meanwhile, beat the egg and yolks together in a small bowl and set aside. Cook the bacon in a large pan for a few minutes until the fat is released and it is partially cooked. Add the drained pasta to the pan and toss to heat the pasta through. Stir continuously so the pasta does not stick to the pan. Remove the pan from the heat and stir through the beaten eggs. The mixture will thicken and turn silky. Divide the pasta between 4 warmed plates, sprinkle with the grated Parmesan and plenty of freshly ground black pepper, and serve immediately.

LIESL VAN DER WALT
HEAD GARDENER, BABYLONSTOREN

ROASTED TOMATO, BASIL & BREAD SALAD
CHORIZO, POTATO & MOZZARELLA FRITTATA WITH ROCKET
WATERMELON & LIME SORBET WITH ELDERFLOWER CORDIAL

Babylonstoren is, and continues to be, a great journey for the team and me. We're all incredibly proud to be part of a truly unique and special food garden in the heart of the Winelands. My go-to favourite for book club suppers is the bread salad – heirloom tomatoes, roasted slowly to bring out their sweetness, tossed with toasted bread and a dressing.

Liesl

Winelands, Western Cape

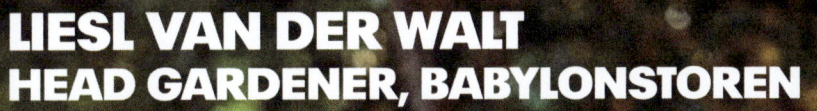

ROASTED TOMATO, BASIL & BREAD SALAD

SERVINGS: 6 | PREP TIME: 20 MINS | COOK TIME: 40 MINS | SKILL LEVEL: 1 (EASY)

INGREDIENTS

500 g ripe cherry or plum tomatoes

olive oil, for roasting

1 loaf ciabatta

handful of fresh basil leaves

juice of ½ lemon

Dressing

½ cup (125 ml) olive oil

2 tbsp (30 ml) red wine vinegar

4 cloves garlic, crushed

handful of fresh basil leaves

juice of ½ lemon

METHOD

Pre-heat the oven to 180°C. Place cherry tomatoes on a baking tray, drizzle with olive oil and season with salt and pepper. Roast for 30–40 minutes until soft. Roughly break the bread into chunks, place on a baking tray and toast in the oven for 5–10 minutes – the exteriors of the chunks must be crispy but the insides soft. Place bread and tomatoes in a salad bowl.

In a separate bowl, mix olive oil, vinegar, garlic, salt and black pepper together to form a salad dressing. Drizzle dressing over bread and tomatoes. Add the basil leaves, lemon juice and more black pepper to taste. Mix gently. Allow the salad to stand for about 15 minutes before serving. Best eaten by hand...

CHORIZO, POTATO & MOZZARELLA FRITTATA WITH ROCKET

SERVINGS: 6–8 | PREP TIME: 15 MINS | COOK TIME: 30–45 MINS | SKILL LEVEL: 1 (EASY)

INGREDIENTS

500 g baby potatoes

350 g chorizo

30 ml olive oil

2 handfuls of rocket leaves

125 g mozzarella, cut into small pieces

10 eggs

2½ ml nutmeg

sweet chilli sauce, to serve

METHOD

Pre-heat the oven to 180°C. Boil the potatoes until soft, drain and allow to cool. Cut potatoes in half. Slice the chorizo. Heat oil and lightly fry chorizo in a pan, add and fry potatoes with another drizzle of oil until golden. Place chorizo, potatoes and 1 handful of rocket leaves in a greased ovenproof dish, and spread out evenly. Place mozzarella pieces on top. Whisk the eggs with the nutmeg, season with salt and freshly ground black pepper and pour over the warm chorizo and potatoes. Bake for 30–45 minutes until golden brown and set. Serve with the rest of the fresh rocket leaves, more freshly ground black pepper and sweet chilli sauce.

WATERMELON & LIME SORBET
WITH ELDERFLOWER CORDIAL

MAKES: 1½ LITRES | PREP TIME: 20 MINS PLUS STANDING | COOK TIME: 2 HOURS PLUS FREEZING
SKILL LEVEL: 1 (EASY)

INGREDIENTS

1 cup water

1 cup sugar

4 cups cubed watermelon, pips removed

5 tbsp lime juice, or to taste

fresh mint leaves, to serve

extra watermelon, to serve

Elderflower cordial

1½ litres water

1 kg sugar

4 lemons

10 big elderflower heads with buds that have opened fully (it's best to cut these in the early morning)

METHOD

Prepare 1–2 days ahead. To make the sorbet, put the water and sugar in a saucepan and bring to the boil, stirring until all the sugar crystals have dissolved. Remove from heat and allow to cool. Blend watermelon roughly in a blender, then mix watermelon, sugar syrup and about 5 tablespoons of lime juice to taste. Place in the freezer until almost frozen solid, take out and liquidise again. Place in the freezer again and freeze overnight. Remove from freezer a short while before serving to allow sorbet to soften a bit. Enjoy with mint leaves and fresh watermelon, and a drizzle of elderflower cordial.

To make the cordial, boil the water and then remove from heat. Add the sugar while water is still hot and stir until dissolved. Allow to cool. Slice the lemons. Cut the elderflowers from their stems and add, with the lemons, to the sugar water. Cover and allow to stand for 48 hours. Remove the lemon slices and elderflowers. Pour the cordial into a sterilised bottle with a lid and keep in the fridge. Enjoy diluted with sparkling water in a ratio of 1:3, or drizzled over sorbet.

"Watermelons are prolific in summer, and sometimes they are so big you can't quite finish them. I always turn the leftovers into sorbet, and just love the delicate pink colour."

MOKGADI ITSWENG
WITH MOTSIRI ITSWENG & FENYANG
LOTSHA FOODS

FISH CURRY WITH TAMARIND

This recipe reflects my culinary influences and is one I learnt from my maternal granny, who was a cook at a hotel in Durban. She was half-Indian and taught me about spices and tamarind – her food was always flavourful and spicy.

Mokgadi

Johannesburg, Gauteng

FISH CURRY WITH TAMARIND

SERVINGS: 4–6 | PREP TIME: 15 MINS | COOK TIME: 20 MINS | SKILL LEVEL: 1 (EASY)

INGREDIENTS

100 ml sunflower oil

1 tbsp mustard seeds

4 curry leaves

2 tbsp curry powder

1 tbsp garam masala

1 onion, chopped

1 tbsp crushed garlic and ginger mix

1 x 400 g can whole peeled tomatoes, chopped

1 tbsp chilli jam (I use Lotsha Sticky Chilli Jam)

1 tsp salt

800 g yellowtail, cut into cubes

30 ml tamarind, soaked in 200 ml warm water

a handful of fresh coriander, chopped

METHOD

Heat oil and add mustard seeds, curry leaves, curry powder and garam masala. Cook at medium heat for 3 minutes to release the flavour of the spices and seeds. Add onion and garlic and ginger mix and cook for a further 5 minutes. Add the tomatoes and the jam, cook at medium heat for 5 minutes and add the salt. Add the fish and cook for 10 minutes, stirring continuously. Add the tamarind and cook for a further 10 minutes, until the sauce has thickened. Add the coriander and cook for a further 5 minutes.

Serve warm with morogo (see recipe on page 34) and sorghum.

DE RUSTICA OLIVE ESTATE

BEN BLOU, MENZEL DRAAI, BAKKAS MEYER, KAREL OLCKERS, JAN MEYER, SIMON STUURMAN & KOBUS SWARTZ

LEMON 'N HEAVEN OLIVE OIL CAKE
OLIVE, BASIL & CHEESE MUFFINS

Olive oil has become a love affair for me, and over the years I have learnt so much. In the beginning I thought it was just expensive oil used for salad dressings and in marinades, but this is not the case. The nutty flavours of the delicate oils add depth to mayonnaise, cake and muffin recipes, and the darker green, more intense oils are perfect for making pestos and pasta dressings.

Angela Frey, wife of Kallie Frey, master oil blender

De Rust,
Western Cape

LEMON 'N HEAVEN OLIVE OIL CAKE

SERVINGS: 8–10 | PREP TIME: 15 MINS | COOK TIME: 40–45 MINS | SKILL LEVEL: 1 (EASY)

INGREDIENTS

2 cups stoneground cake flour

1 tsp baking powder

½ tsp salt (I use Oryx or Himalayan salt)

6 free-range eggs

2 cups caster sugar

1 cup delicately flavoured olive oil (I use De Rustica Extra Virgin Olive Oil)

juice of 3 lemons

zest of 1 organic lemon

Icing

250 ml smooth cream cheese

125 g icing sugar

juice and zest of ½ lemon

edible flowers, to decorate

METHOD

Pre-heat the oven to 180°C. Grease 2 round 23 cm cake tins and line with baking paper. Sift flour, baking powder and salt into a bowl. In a separate bowl, beat the eggs and caster sugar together until thick and creamy. Mix olive oil and lemon juice together and gently stir a stream of the mixture into the sugar and egg mixture with a rubber spatula, taking care not to over-mix. Add this mixture to the flour mixture, adding lemon zest and gently folding it in with the spatula until a smooth batter is created. Pour half the batter into each prepared cake tin and bake for 40 minutes or until a tester inserted comes out clean. Allow to cool slightly, remove from tins and transfer to a cooling rack to cool completely. Mix all the icing ingredients except the flowers together in a bowl. When cakes are completely cool, sandwich together with some icing, cover top and sides with more icing and decorate with edible flowers.

OLIVE, BASIL & CHEESE MUFFINS

MAKES: 12 | PREP TIME: 10 MINS | COOK TIME: 20 MINS | SKILL LEVEL: 1 (EASY)

INGREDIENTS

2 cups flour

2 tsp baking powder

1 tsp bicarbonate of soda

½ tsp ground nutmeg

½ tsp cayenne pepper

1 tsp salt

1 cup finely grated Cheddar

80 g feta, crumbled

1 cup pitted and sliced olives

2 tbsp crushed raw cashew nuts

1 bunch basil leaves, finely chopped

1 cup full-cream milk

½ cup extra virgin olive oil

2 large free-range eggs, beaten

METHOD

Pre-heat the oven to 210°C and grease a 12-hole muffin tin. Sift flour, baking powder, bicarbonate of soda, nutmeg, cayenne and salt into a large bowl. Add Cheddar, feta and olives and mix into flour mixture – coat well. Add cashew nuts and basil and mix through till also covered in flour. Combine the milk, olive oil and beaten egg. Make a well in the dry ingredients and add all the liquid at once. Mix lightly until just combined – the batter should be quite lumpy. Spoon into the muffin tin and bake for 20 minutes or until golden brown. Turn out onto a wire cooling rack. While cooling, cover with a cloth for soft muffins, or let dry uncovered for crispier outsides.

VALERIE ELDER
THE REAL CHEESE

BOCCONCINI & TOMATO SKEWERS
BEST CHEESE TART

Cheese can transform any basic recipe into something exciting. I keep at least one interesting cheese in my fridge so there's always inspiration to cook up a storm. Karoo cheeses are incredibly interesting – all that fynbos makes for fragrant and unique flavours. I love getting to know my cheese suppliers and supporting new people. There is so much variety here – we are indeed lucky.

Valerie

*Observatory,
Western Cape*

BOCCONCINI & TOMATO SKEWERS

SERVINGS: 6 | PREP TIME: 10 MINS | SKILL LEVEL: 1 (EASY)

INGREDIENTS

1 x 150 g tub bocconcini (I use Buffalo Ridge Bocconcini)

200 g cherry tomatoes

a big handful of fresh basil

6 tbsp extra virgin olive oil (I use Foxenburg Estate Extra Virgin Olive Oil)

balsamic vinegar

METHOD

These make a heavenly light supper when you have a glut of summer tomatoes. Thread the bocconcini onto skewers with cherry tomatoes and basil leaves. Serve immediately with glugs of olive oil and balsamic vinegar, seasoned well with salt and pepper.

BEST CHEESE TART

SERVINGS: 4–6 | PREP TIME: 30 MINS PLUS CHILLING | COOK TIME: 35 MINS | SKILL LEVEL: 2 (MODERATE)

INGREDIENTS

1 cup flour

3 cups grated hard goat's milk cheese (I use Foxenburg Estate Foxtail)

125 g melted butter

2 tbsp butter

2 tbsp flour

2 cups warm milk

3 eggs, lightly beaten

1 red onion, chopped and fried until soft, or 1 cup cooked bacon pieces (or use both)

METHOD

To make the pastry, blend 1 cup flour, 1 cup of the grated cheese and melted butter in a food processor until it forms a ball. Chill well.

Pre-heat the oven to 200°C. Use 2 tablespoons butter, 2 tablespoons flour and the milk to make a basic white sauce. Add the eggs, 2 cups of the grated cheese and onion and/or bacon to the sauce and mix. Set aside.

Press chilled pastry into a tart tin with a loose base, pushing it well up the sides and making sure there are no holes. Pour sauce mix into pastry case and bake for 30–35 minutes.

CHEESE TIP

One of the top trends in cheese right now is the cheese tower. They are perfect for parties and gatherings of every kind. Simply take 1 wheel cow's milk semi-soft cheese with a white rind (try Langbaken Alanna) and stack ½ wheel cow's milk blue cheese (such as Gansvlei Blue Moon) and 1 wheel raw cow's milk washed-rind cheese (Langbaken Sunset is a good option) to form a wedding cake-like 'tower'. Decorate with fruit, flowers and nuts in season, and just before serving, drizzle a good amount of local honey over the entire tower. Serve with cheese biscuits or good bread. This will serve 50 people at the end of a celebratory meal.

Bo-Kaap,
Western Cape

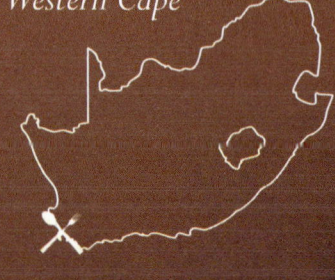

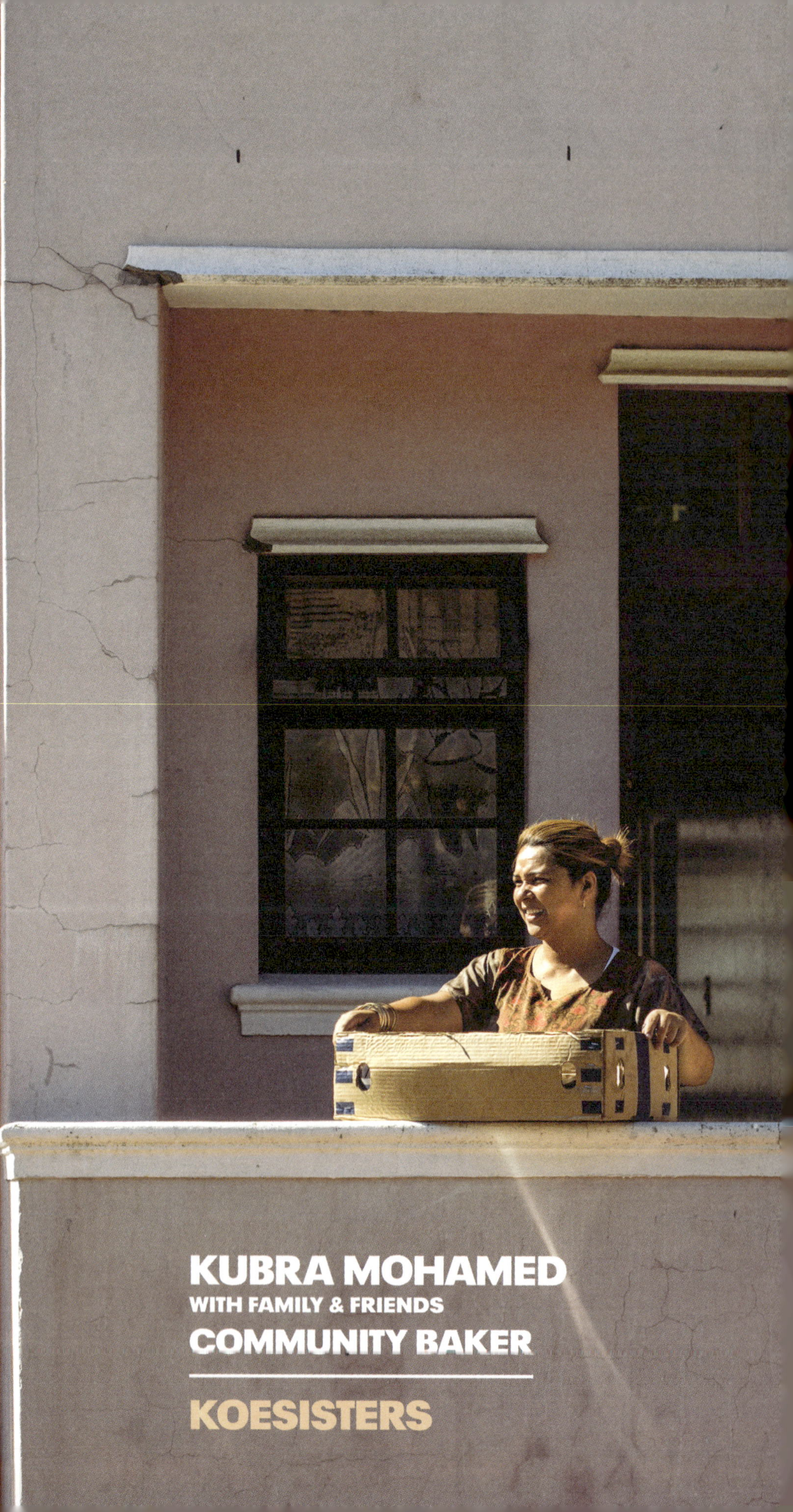

KUBRA MOHAMED
WITH FAMILY & FRIENDS

COMMUNITY BAKER

KOESISTERS

Every Saturday for the past 18 years, I've been cooking koesisters for the people of the Bo-Kaap community in Cape Town. My first customers arrive at about 4 a.m., after mosque, so I have everything prepared and ready. They line up in the street and then in my passageway, bringing along their plates and weekend chatter. Feeding my community on the weekend is incredibly important to me, and I'll carry on as long as I can.

KUBRA

KOESISTERS

MAKES: 70–80 (SMALL) | PREP TIME: 20 MINS PLUS RESTING AND RISING | COOK TIME: 20 MINS
SKILL LEVEL: 2 (MODERATE)

INGREDIENTS

1 cup sugar
125 g soft butter
1½ cups boiling water
1 cup milk
1 tbsp fine cinnamon
1 tbsp elachi (cardamom)
1 tbsp fine dried ginger
1 tbsp mixed spice
1 tsp fine aniseed
2 tsp ground naartjie peel
  (see tip)
20 g instant yeast
1 egg
1 kg flour
vegetable oil for
  deep-frying
2 cups desiccated coconut,
  for sprinkling

Syrup
4 cups water
3 cups sugar
2 strips dried naartjie peel
  (see tip)

METHOD

Place the sugar and butter in a bowl, add rapidly boiling water and milk, and mix well. Add in the spices, yeast and egg, and mix well again. Add the flour to form a dough, then knead it until it's smooth and allow it to rest for an hour.

Make the syrup by combining the ingredients in a pot and bringing the mixture to a slow simmer.

Roll the dough into 'sausages', then cut them into 5 cm pieces and make the ends rounded. Leave the koesisters to rise for 15 minutes.

Deep-fry the koesisters on a medium heat until dark brown on the outside. Prick the koesisters and place in the syrup in the pot. Simmer for 5 minutes on each side, remove and sprinkle with coconut.

TIP

To make dried naartjie powder, sun-dry 10 naartjie peels for 2 days until very dry. Store the dried peel in an airtight container until needed (it must stay totally dry to avoid mould). Grind to a fine powder in a coffee grinder just before using.

NOTE

My recipe is simple and has taken many years to perfect. Naartjies are so prolific towards the end of winter, so that's the best time to buy in bulk. We dry the skins in the hot African sun. Once the skins are totally dried out, I blend them in a coffee grinder to a fine powder. This produces a naartjie flavour that is incredibly sweet and citrusy, and I think this is what I would call my secret ingredient! It adds another depth of flavour to basic bread dough, and lends itself to the other spices we use in the koesisters.

KOBUS VAN DER MERWE
FORAGER & OEP VE KOEP

ASKOEK & BOKKOM BUTTER
AUTUMN OYSTERS

The West Coast Peninsula has a rich history of early civilisation. For these first peoples – herders, foragers and gatherers – the Saldanha Strandveld fynbos kingdom provided edible indigenous bounty, while the Atlantic Ocean supplied them with omega-rich seafood. This landscape inspires me to experiment with simple heritage dishes, incorporating indigenous wild food picked off the land and harvested from the sea.

Kobus

Paternoster,
Western Cape

ASKOEK & BOKKOM BUTTER

SERVINGS: 6 | PREP TIME: 20 MINS PLUS PROVING | COOK TIME: 35 MINS | SKILL LEVEL: 1 (EASY)

INGREDIENTS

1 kg white bread flour
pinch of salt
10 g instant yeast
700 ml lukewarm water

Bokkom butter

250g salted farm butter, cubed
a handful of mixed seasonal wild and garden herbs such as lemon buchu, wild garlic, mint, origanum, thyme and basil, finely chopped
2 fillets of maasbanker (horse mackerel) bokkoms, chopped

METHOD

Sift the flour into an enamel basin. Add the salt and instant yeast and stir through. Make a well in the centre and add the warm water, mixing briskly with your hands until everything comes together in a rough ball. Turn the dough out onto a floured surface. Fold it over on itself 4 times, then leave to rise until doubled in volume, approximately 40 minutes. Knock down by folding the dough over on itself, gently pressing down. Shape into 6 flattened ovals and place directly on recently spent coals and ash. Cover with more coals and ash and leave to cook for approximately 20 minutes or until they sound hollow when knocked with your knuckles. When cooked, use a pastry brush to brush off excess coals and ash that may cling to the bread.

While the askoek are baking, make the bokkom butter. Using a fork, combine the butter, herbs and chopped bokkoms in a mixing bowl until thoroughly mixed. Refrigerate until ready to serve.

To serve, gently melt the bokkom butter in a skillet and serve alongside the freshly baked askoek.

NOTE

Bokkoms are whole, salted and dried fish usually made from maasbanker (horse mackerel) or haarder (southern mullet).

AUTUMN OYSTERS

SERVINGS: 4 | PREP TIME: 10 MINS | COOK TIME: 10 MINS | SKILL LEVEL: 1 (EASY)

INGREDIENTS

12 large oysters (I use Saldanha Bay oysters)
12 fine slices preserved quince
30 ml soutslaai-leaf juice
a mixed handful of Strandveld shoreline herbs such as dune celery, dune spinach, samphire and soutslaai, thoroughly washed

METHOD

Pre-heat the oven to 180°C. Place the oysters in their shells, round side down, in an ovenproof dish. Bake for about 7–10 minutes, until they just start to open. Shuck the oysters, gently loosening them from their shells. Top each oyster with a slice of quince, about ½ teaspoon of soutslaai juice and a scattering of Strandveld herbs. Serve immediately, while still slightly warm.

NOTE

Soutslaai is a succulent plant commonly found in the Saldanha Strandveld coastal region. Its Latin name is *Mesembryanthemum crystallinum* and it is also known in English as ice plant.

Our business is first and foremost about the bees and then about the honey. We consider ourselves custodians of the hives. Keeping the bees happy is our main concern, and we try to harvest the honey in the kindest way possible.

Meagan

OWEN WILLIAMS
& MEAGAN VERMAAS
WITH JULES MERCER
HONEYCHILD HONEY

HONEY CRUNCHIES
HONEY LEMONADE

*Knysna,
Western Cape*

HONEY CRUNCHIES

MAKES: 12–15 | PREP TIME: 15 MINS | COOK TIME: 40 MINS | SKILL LEVEL: 1 (EASY)

INGREDIENTS

2 cups cake flour
2 cups desiccated coconut
2 cups sugar
4 cups rolled oats
8 tbsp raw honey
8 tbsp butter
2 level tsp bicarbonate
  of soda

METHOD

Pre-heat the oven to 110°C and grease a shallow rectangular baking tin. In a large mixing bowl, stir flour, coconut, sugar and rolled oats together with a big wooden spoon. Bring honey and butter to the boil in a pot, add the bicarbonate of soda and stir really quickly. This mixture bubbles up fast, so stir rapidly until it has stopped rising and then pour over dry ingredients. Mix well. Press firmly into the baking tin and bake in the middle of the oven for about 40 minutes until the top is golden brown and risen slightly. Remove from the oven and leave to cool for about 10 minutes, and then cut into squares. Leave to cool completely in the tin.

NOTE

This is Meagan's recipe, which came from her mum. In those days they would have used golden syrup, but honey is a million times better!

HONEY LEMONADE

SERVINGS: 6 | PREP TIME: 5 MINS | SKILL LEVEL: 1 (EASY)

INGREDIENTS

1 cup raw honey
1 cup freshly squeezed
  lemon juice
6 cups cold water
ice, to serve
lemon slices, to serve

METHOD

This is one of the simplest recipes but it's the absolute best on a hot summer's day. Stir honey, lemon juice and water together with a whisk. Pour into a large jug, add ice and lemon slices and serve.

"Always taste your honey before cooking with it – not all honeys are equal, so you want to ensure you are using the best quality you have before cooking with it."

THELMA NTOMBOZI MAGWADI
NANAGA FARM STALL

ROOSTERKOEK
LEMON MERINGUE PIE

*Alexandria,
Eastern Cape*

Our roosterkoek and pies are so popular that we actually had to move our farm stall back from the road in 2008, as the National Roads department thought our road access was so busy that it might be dangerous! Our brilliant roosterkoek maker, Thelma Ntombozi Magwadi, has been making this South African favourite at Nanaga for many years now. Thelma is our food hero here at the farm stall, and we are so excited about sharing her recipe.

The Nanaga team

ROOSTERKOEK
BREAD ROLLS COOKED IN A GRID OVER A BRAAI FIRE

SERVINGS: 10–12 | PREP TIME: 15 MINS PLUS RISING | COOK TIME: 20 MINS | SKILL LEVEL: 1 (EASY)

INGREDIENTS

1 kg white flour
1 tbsp salt
60 g sugar
1 x 10 g packet yeast
about 400–500 ml
lukewarm water

METHOD

Prepare a braai fire. Mix together the flour, salt and sugar in a large bowl. Mix the yeast into the lukewarm water and allow to sit for a few minutes to dissolve. Add the water to the flour mixture until you have a malleable dough (add more water if necessary). Knead for 10 minutes, and then leave in a warm place to double in size (about 40–45 minutes). Knead the dough again and roll it out into a large rectangle or square. Cut into 10–12 rectangles, depending on how large you would like your roosterkoek to be. Lay the dough squares on a braai grid, about 10 cm apart. Cook over a low to medium braai for about 10 minutes on each side. Take care not to burn them. Remove the roosterkoek from the braai when they are cooked through and allow them to cool slightly before slicing in half and filling.

LEMON MERINGUE PIE

SERVINGS: 8 | PREP TIME: 20 MINS PLUS CHILLING AND SETTING | COOK TIME: 10 MINS
SKILL LEVEL: 1 (EASY)

INGREDIENTS

1 x 200 g packet Tennis
biscuits
100 g butter, melted
2 x 385 g cans condensed
milk
¼ cup lemon juice
5 eggs, separated
½ cup caster sugar
½ tsp baking powder

METHOD

Mix together the Tennis biscuits and melted butter, press this mixture into a pie dish or tin and refrigerate for 30–45 minutes to set. Mix together the condensed milk, lemon juice and egg yolks. Beat together well. Pour the lemon filling into the crust and place in the fridge to chill for about 30 minutes.

Pre-heat the oven to 180°C. Whisk the egg whites until thick and fluffy, and slowly pour in the sugar, while whisking, until the meringue forms glossy peaks. Beat in the baking powder. Spread the meringue on top of the pie and place in the oven. Immediately reduce the oven temperature to 140°C. As soon as meringue topping is golden brown (about 10 minutes), switch off the oven and allow to cool with the door slightly open.

VONNI ROMANO
**MARIA'S GREEK CAFÉ
& RESTAURANT**

SPANAKOPITA
SPIRALS
LAHANOSALATA
YIOUVETSI
ME KOTA

Kimon, my first grandchild, who was all of three-and-a-half years old at the time, looked up from tucking into his second helping and announced, 'Vonni, you cannot imagine how much I love chicken yiouvetsi!' I glowed with twofold pride at his advanced vocabulary and the success of my original recipe. My passion for passing on these recipes to my grandchildren makes me so happy.

Yonni

*Kenilworth
Western Cape*

SPANAKOPITA SPIRALS

SERVINGS: 6 | PREP TIME: 40 MINS | COOK TIME: 20 MINS | SKILL LEVEL: 1 (EASY)

INGREDIENTS

125 g phyllo pastry, thawed

olive oil for brushing

Filling

30 ml olive oil

1 medium onion, finely chopped

a generous grating of nutmeg

1 small bunch spring onions, finely chopped

200 g Swiss chard

500 g baby spinach, well rinsed

200 g feta, crumbled

30 ml snipped fresh flat-leaf parsley

30 ml snipped fresh mint

30 ml snipped fresh dill

2 medium eggs, beaten

(V)

METHOD

To make the filling, heat 30 ml oil and cook onion and nutmeg for a few minutes until soft. Add spring onions and cook for a minute. Chop Swiss chard coarsely and add to the onions. Stir-fry briefly until just wilted. Add baby spinach and cook for a minute. Remove pan from the heat and allow to cool before adding the feta, snipped herbs, eggs, and some salt and ground black pepper. Mix well and check seasoning. Cover and store in the fridge until needed.

Pre-heat the oven to 180°C. Remove the phyllo pastry from its packaging, and cover with a dry cloth. Place a damp cloth on top of this to prevent the pastry from drying out. Taking one sheet at a time, brush lightly with oil and fold in half, brushing with oil again.

Spread a line of filling lengthwise along the bottom. Roll up loosely into a sausage shape. Fold into a spiral and place, cut-side down, on a greased oven tray. Brush the tops and sides with oil and bake in the centre of the oven for 15–20 minutes or until crisp and golden brown.

TIP

The wonderful taste of these spinach and feta spirals depends entirely on really fresh garden herbs. No matter how small my home may be, I always make sure that I have the pleasure of picking my own on demand.

LAHANOSALATA
CABBAGE SALAD

SERVINGS: 6 | PREP TIME: 15 MINS | SKILL LEVEL: 1 (EASY)

INGREDIENTS

1 medium cabbage

3 ml coarse salt

pomegranate seeds, to garnish

Dressing

15 ml olive oil

15 ml fresh lemon juice

ground black pepper, to taste

METHOD

Rinse cabbage thoroughly and drain well. Slice very thinly, discarding all coarse stems. Place in a large ziplock bag and sprinkle with salt. Close the bag and squeeze to bruise the cabbage and bring out the flavour. Tip into a salad bowl.

Whisk dressing ingredients until blended and pour over the salad. Toss well and adjust the seasoning if necessary. Chill. Garnish with pomegranate seeds before serving.

YIOUVETSI ME KOTA
CHICKEN GIOUVETSI

SERVINGS: 8–10 | PREP TIME: 5 MINS PLUS MARINATING | COOK TIME: 60 MINS | SKILL LEVEL: 1 (EASY)

INGREDIENTS

1 kg filleted chicken breasts and thighs

30 ml olive oil

2 medium onions, finely chopped

10 ml ground cinnamon

500 ml chopped tomato

500 g large orzo pasta

115 g tomato paste

15 ml olive oil

fresh origanum sprigs, to garnish

100 g grated pecorino, to serve

Marinade

juice of 2–3 lemons (125 ml)

30 ml olive oil

5 fat cloves garlic, crushed with 7 ml salt

3 ml ground white pepper

ground black pepper to taste

10 ml rigani (Greek dried origanum; see Tip)

METHOD

Whisk together the marinade ingredients and pour over the chicken portions. Cover and leave for a minimum of 2 hours but preferably overnight if possible, turning from time to time.

Heat 30 ml olive oil and fry onions until soft and golden. Drain the chicken pieces, reserving the marinade, and turn up the heat. Fry in batches to sear all surfaces before sprinkling with cinnamon and some seasoning. Add the remaining marinade to the chicken and then add the chopped tomato. Stir through, cover, and cook gently over a low heat for about 20 minutes or until the chicken is tender.

Meanwhile, boil the orzo in plenty of salted water for 12 minutes or until al dente. Drain through a colander, keeping aside 500 ml of the pasta water. Return orzo to the saucepan and stir in tomato paste, 15 ml olive oil and a little of the reserved pasta water.

Pour the orzo over the chicken pieces and stir through. Adjust seasoning if necessary. Cover and cook over a very low heat for 10 minutes, adding more of the reserved liquid if the orzo becomes dry. Keep checking with a wooden spatula to make sure that it doesn't stick to the bottom of the pot.

Alternatively, the dish can be finished in the oven, at 180°C for about 10 minutes, once the pasta is added to the chicken. Either way, although the pasta will have absorbed most of the liquid, the dish should still be nice and saucy. Garnish with fresh origanum sprigs and serve with grated pecorino.

NOTE

Rigani (dried Greek origanum) grows on dry, craggy mountains whose slopes are perfumed by its fragrance mingled with wafts of Aegean ozone. Greek food is unimaginable without rigani. It is harvested in late summer; the dried flowers and leaves are crushed and it is sold in the markets. We lug bagsful home whenever we're there as its unique pungency lasts for years. I cannot think of any dish that would not be enhanced by the intense flavour and aroma.

EMMA CHEN
PRON & RED CHAMBER

PORK, PICKLED BAMBOO & LONG BEAN NOODLE CURLS
TOFU 'SKIN' & LEEK SALAD

I believe that cooking should be spontaneous and mood-driven. If you are not in the mood to cook, don't. When you do, start at the fridge and see what is available. Ingredients can be changed, quantities added or decreased. You know what you like. Cooking for people I love is just like cooking for myself – I must absolutely love the dishes so that they come out perfect. *Emma*

Johannesburg, Gauteng

PORK, PICKLED BAMBOO & LONG BEAN NOODLE CURLS

SERVINGS: 4 | PREP TIME: 20 MINS | COOK TIME: 20 MINS | SKILL LEVEL: 2 (MODERATE)

INGREDIENTS

250 g pickled bamboo
240 ml water
500 ml cake flour
200 g pork belly
200 g long beans
2 cm piece fresh ginger
2 cloves garlic
2 spring onions
25 ml soy sauce
25 ml oil

METHOD

Soak pickled bamboo for at least an hour or overnight in cold water. In a mixing bowl, combine water and cake flour into a soft dough. Cover and set aside. Drain bamboo and squeeze dry. Cut pork belly into thick slices and cut the bamboo and long beans into 2–3 cm pieces. Chop ginger, garlic and spring onion finely.

Heat oil in a wok and fry ginger, garlic and spring onion, then add the pork and stir-fry for 2 minutes. Stir in bamboo and long beans. Add soy sauce and enough water to cover all the ingredients, and reduce heat to a simmer.

While the pork is simmering, divide the dough into two. Roll out each portion into a large thin disc, sprinkle oil and little salt over the whole surface, and roll the disc into a thick roll. Cut into 0.5 cm slices.

Arrange noodle slices to cover the pork mixture in the wok. Cover with a lid and simmer until noodles are cooked (about 10 minutes). Gently fold the noodles into the pork mixture and serve.

TIP

Pickled bamboo is salty so be restrained about adding salt to this dish.

TOFU 'SKIN' & LEEK SALAD

SERVINGS: 2–4 | PREP TIME: 10 MINS | COOK TIME: 10 MINS | SKILL LEVEL: 1 (EASY)

INGREDIENTS

4 sheets pressed tofu
1 leek
pinch of salt
25 ml oil
20 ml rice vinegar
10 ml soy sauce

METHOD

Boil or steam tofu sheets until cooked (about 5 minutes). Blanch in cold water and slice into 0.5 cm strips. Slice leek thinly. Put tofu 'skins' on a serving plate or bowl and sprinkle salt over. Stir-fry the leek slices in oil until lightly browned and add to the tofu. Add rice vinegar and soy sauce and mix well.

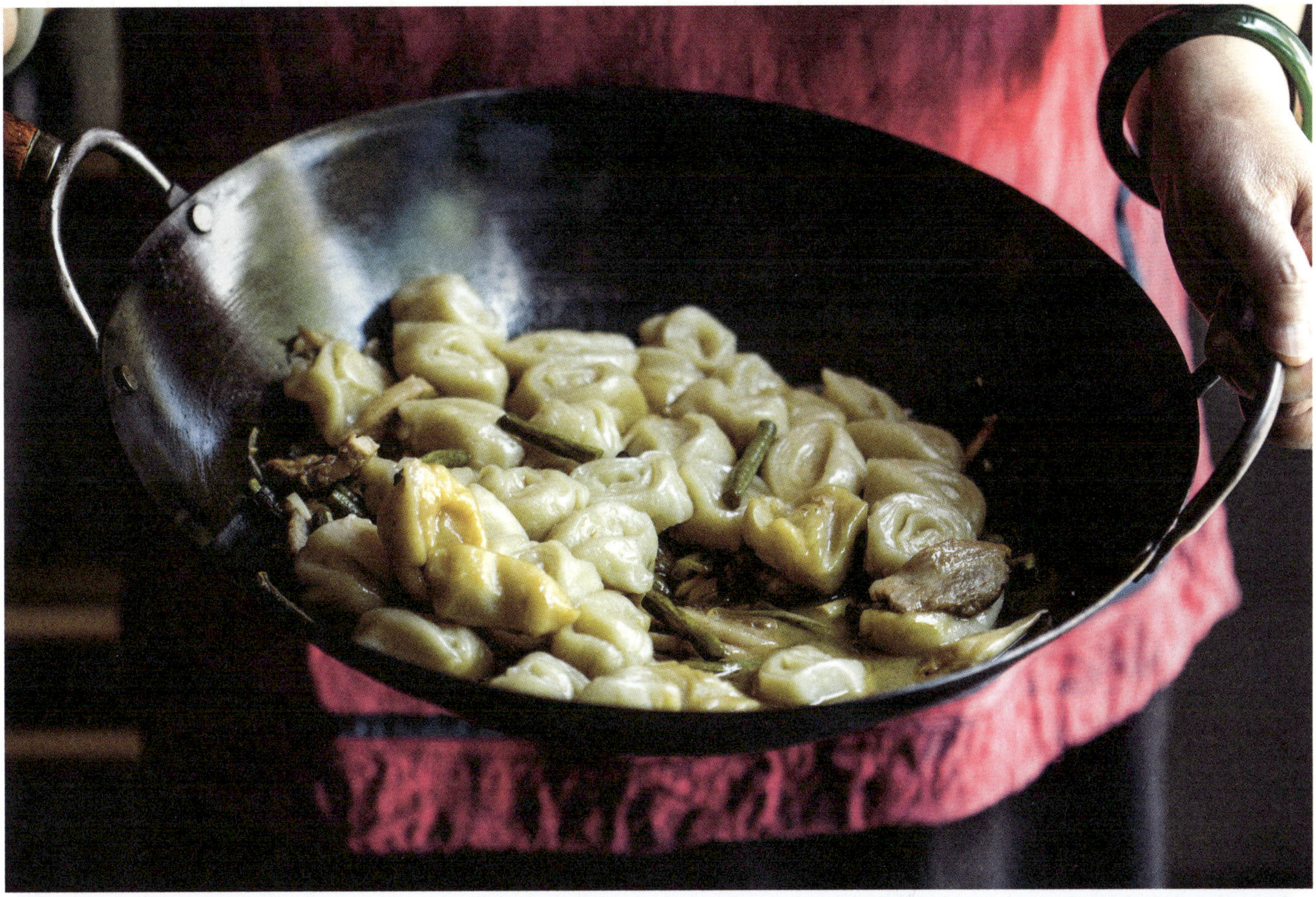

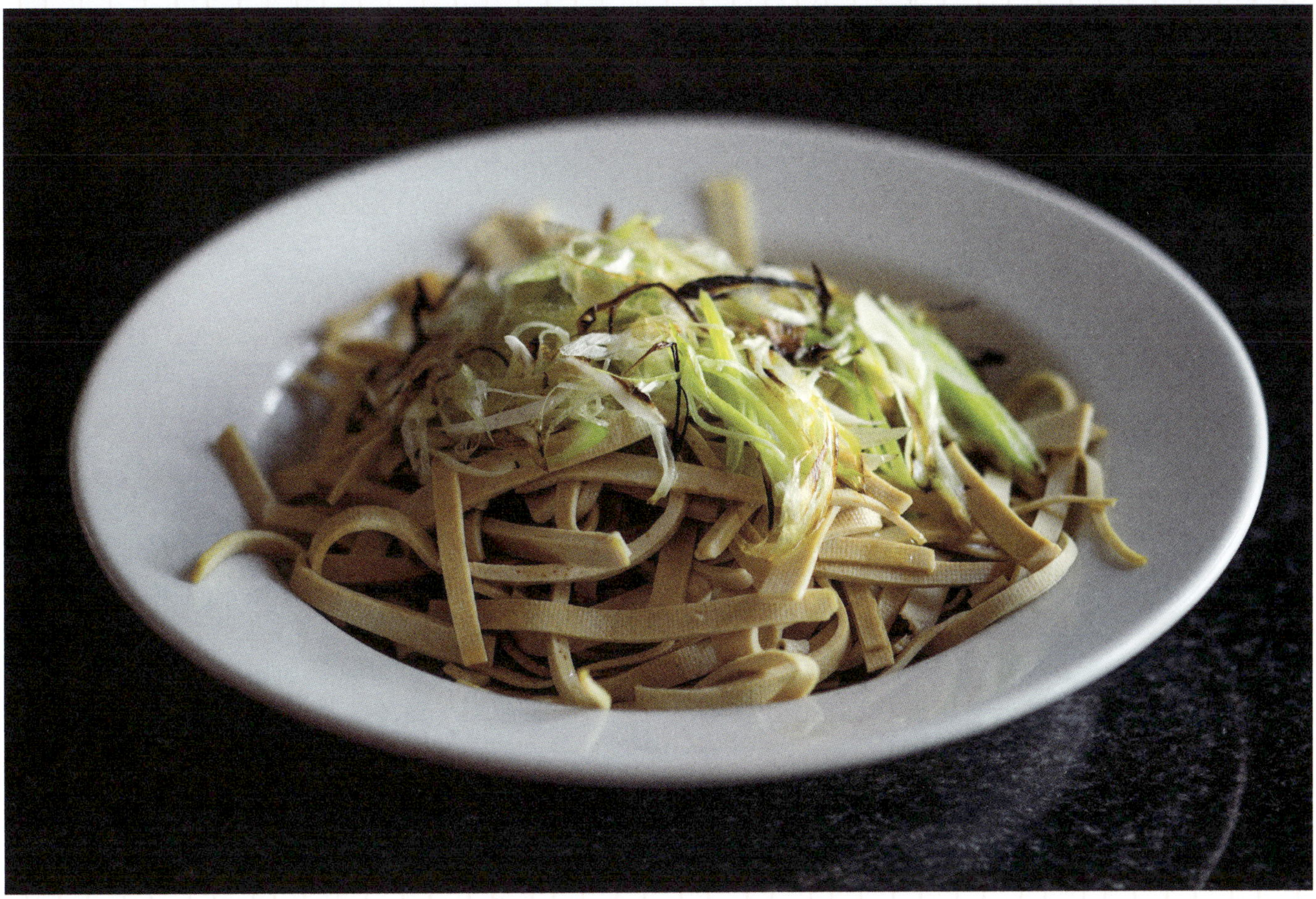

THE PATELS
WITH PATEL'S VEGETARIAN REFRESHMENT ROOM CUSTOMERS
PATEL'S VEGETARIAN REFRESHMENT ROOM

VEGETARIAN BUNNY CHOW

Patel's has been going for 100 years. The same shop, the same structures, the same bunnies – a tradition proudly continued by Manilall Patel. And these are the best bunny chows in Durban (if not the world!), hands down.

The Patels

Durban, KwaZulu-Natal

VEGETARIAN BUNNY CHOW

SERVINGS: 6 | PREP TIME: 15 MINS | COOK TIME: 45 MINS | SKILL LEVEL: 1 (EASY)

INGREDIENTS

2 onions, finely chopped

3 tbsp sunflower oil

2 cloves garlic, chopped

1 knob ginger, peeled and finely grated

2 dried chillies

2 tbsp cumin seeds

2 tbsp coriander seeds

1 tbsp mustard seeds

2 tbsp garam masala

1 tsp chilli powder

1 tsp turmeric

2 tomatoes, diced

2 cups brown lentils, washed

1½ litres water or vegetable stock

3 loaves 'government' bread

fresh coriander leaves, to garnish

red onion, sliced, to garnish (optional)

METHOD

Fry the onions in the oil until soft. Add the garlic and ginger, and cook for a minute. In a separate pan, fry the dried chillies, cumin seeds, coriander seeds and mustard seeds. When they start to pop and smell fragrant, remove from the heat and place in a pestle and mortar or blender. Grind to a fine powder, and then add the garam masala, chilli powder and turmeric. Add this spice mixture to the onion mixture and cook for a few minutes. Add the diced tomatoes and cook for a few more minutes. Stir in the lentils and water or stock. Cook until the lentils are soft (about 45 minutes).

To serve, cut each loaf of bread in half and scoop out the centres. Spoon in the lentils and garnish with coriander leaves and red onion, if using. Serve with sambals and raitas of your choice.

BUNNIES	
SMALL	R12
MEDIUM	R15
LARGE	R20
HALF-LOAF	R30

I made it from the streets of Joburg to being sous chef here at Londolozi, and I think that's very cool. Everyone knows me for my love of sauces – the peri-peri sauce is one of my particular favourites. Thoko, however, loves everything with chocolate, so we had to include her recipe for chocolate chip cookies.

Sipho + Thoko

Londolozi Game Reserve, Mpumalanga

SIPHO & THOKO KHOSA
WITH ANNA RIDGEWELL & SAMUEL
LONDOLOZI GAME RESERVE

BABY CHICKENS WITH PERI-PERI SAUCE
CHOCOLATE CHIP COOKIES

BABY CHICKENS WITH PERI-PERI SAUCE

SERVINGS: 6 | PREP TIME: 25 MINS PLUS MARINATING | COOK TIME: 45–50 MINS | SKILL LEVEL: 1 (EASY)

INGREDIENTS

3 whole baby chickens,
   cut in half

Marinade

1 bunch flat-leaf parsley

1 tbsp paprika

5 cloves garlic

½ hand-length piece fresh
   ginger

2 cups olive oil

Peri-peri sauce

olive oil

1 clove garlic

1 white onion, chopped

2 sweet red peppers,
   quartered and seeds
   removed

4 red chillies, seeds
   removed

125 ml white wine vinegar

2 tbsp white sugar

METHOD

Make the marinade by combining parsley, paprika, garlic, ginger and olive oil together in a blender. Cut the baby chickens in half and remove the backbones, then combine with the marinade in a large bowl or container. Cover and marinate for 30 minutes

To make the peri-peri sauce, heat some olive oil and sauté the garlic, onion and sweet red peppers until soft. Add the chillies, then the white wine vinegar and sugar. Stir to dissolve the sugar, then allow all the ingredients to simmer gently until they become soft. Remove from the heat and blend until smooth, then season to taste with salt and pepper.

To cook the chickens, prepare a braai fire or heat a griddle pan until smoking hot, then place the chickens on it, skin-sides down. Turn the baby chickens, basting them with the remaining marinade, for around 30–35 minutes.

When cooked, serve with the peri-peri sauce.

CHOCOLATE CHIP COOKIES

MAKES: 16-20 MEDIUM-SIZED COOKIES | PREP TIME: 15 MINS | COOK TIME: 10 MINS | SKILL LEVEL: 1 (EASY)

INGREDIENTS

1 cup butter
1 cup white sugar
1 cup brown sugar
2 eggs
1 tsp vanilla essence
2 cups flour
2½ cups oats
1 tsp baking powder
1 tsp bicarbonate of soda
pinch of salt
300 g dark chocolate
  chips
250 g dark chocolate,
  grated
½ cup macadamia nuts

METHOD

Pre-heat the oven to 200°C. Cream the butter and the sugars together. Add the eggs and vanilla essence and mix well. Add the flour, oats, baking powder, bicarbonate of soda and salt. Mix in the chocolate chips and the grated chocolate along with the macadamia nuts. Roll the mixture into balls and press out onto a baking sheet. Bake for about 10 minutes.

MIRA HARIE
WITH VINOD & CHANDRIKA
THE SPICE EMPORIUM

PUDLAS WITH RAITA
POTATO SAMOSAS
WITH GREEN CHUTNEY

Flavour is everything to us. Our food is simple, yet it's the fresh, high-quality spices that elevate it and make it special, an ethos we carry into our store. This is the food we love to cook at home – and share!

MIRA

Durban,
KwaZulu-Natal

PUDLAS WITH RAITA

SERVINGS: 6–10 | PREP TIME: 15 MINS PLUS RESTING | COOK TIME: 20 MINS | SKILL LEVEL: 1 (EASY)

INGREDIENTS

300 g wheat flour

50 g semolina

100 g chickpea flour

2 spring onions, finely chopped

1 tsp ground cumin

1 tsp ground coriander

½ bunch fresh coriander, finely
  chopped

½ tsp chilli powder

1 tsp green chilli, finely chopped

½ tsp fresh ginger, finely chopped

1 tsp salt

½ tsp black pepper

1 pinch ground asafoetida
  (available at The Spice
  Emporium or any Indian grocer)

2 tbsp plain yoghurt

500 ml water

oil for frying

Raita

1 cup plain yoghurt

2 tbsp finely chopped onion

1 tbsp finely chopped tomato

ground cumin, to garnish

chopped coriander leaves,
  to garnish

METHOD

To make the raita, mix together the yoghurt, onion and tomato. Garnish with cumin and coriander leaves.

To make the pudlas, mix together all the ingredients except the water and oil, and then add enough of the 500 ml water to make a batter. Leave to rest for an hour. Heat a flat griddle or non-stick frying pan and spread a little oil on it. Pour in a little of the pudla mix and spread it out with a wooden spatula so it thinly covers the pan. Cook for about a minute until browned, then turn over and repeat. Remove from heat and place on paper towel on a plate to absorb extra oil. Serve hot, dipped in raita and green chutney (see recipe following page).

Clockwise from top left:
pudlas, raita, potato samosas, green chutney
(see recipe following page)

POTATO SAMOSAS WITH GREEN CHUTNEY

MAKES: ABOUT 36 | PREP TIME: 15 MINS | COOK TIME: 2 HOURS 10 MINS | SKILL LEVEL: 1 (EASY)

INGREDIENTS

1 tsp chilli powder

½ tsp ground turmeric

½ tsp garam masala

oil for frying

500g potatoes, boiled and mashed

2 tbsp chopped fresh coriander (completely dry)

½ tsp salt

juice of ½ lemon

1 x 500 g pack pre-made frozen samosa pur (pre-cut pastry), defrosted overnight in the fridge (this is available at The Spice Emporium or any Indian grocer)

2 tbsp cake flour, mixed with water to make a thick paste for sealing

Green chutney

3 cups roughly chopped coriander

4 green chillies, roughly chopped

about 1½ tsp lemon juice

½ green pepper, chopped

salt, to taste

2 tbsp roasted peanuts, skin removed (optional)

METHOD

To make the green chutney, combine all ingredients in a blender and blend until smooth. Add a little water if the mixture is too thick. Keep refrigerated.

To make the potato filling for the samosas, heat a non-stick pan and fry the spices in 2 tsp oil on medium heat for 1 minute. Remove from the heat and mix thoroughly with the mashed potatoes, fresh coriander, salt and lemon juice. Allow to cool.

Remove pastry from the fridge. Place 1 strip of pastry on a flat, dry surface. Keep remaining pastry covered with a lightly dampened cloth to prevent it from drying out. Place 1–1½ teaspoons of potato filling on the bottom right-hand corner of the pastry strip and fold the tip over in a triangle shape to line up with left-hand side of the pastry. Fold the bottom left corner of the pastry over to line up with the left-hand side of the pastry. Again take the bottom left corner of the pastry and fold over and across to line up with the right-hand side of the pastry. Continue folding in triangular fashion, ensuring that corners, once folded, are tight. Tuck the final edge inside the samosa, trimming any excess, and seal with the flour-water paste.

Deep-fry the samosas, a few at a time, in medium-hot oil until golden brown. Remove from oil and place on paper towel on a plate. Dab with another paper towel to remove excess oil. Serve hot with tomato sauce and green chutney.

TIPS

The green chutney freezes well – simply defrost when needed. It is delicious with samosas, pudlas, toasted sandwiches and much more.

Freeze extra samosas in an airtight container. Lie the samosas flat and layer each row with greaseproof paper so they do not touch.

WATCH OUT
AVOID COW
Lick your lips for
LASSI
LET'S
CHAAT

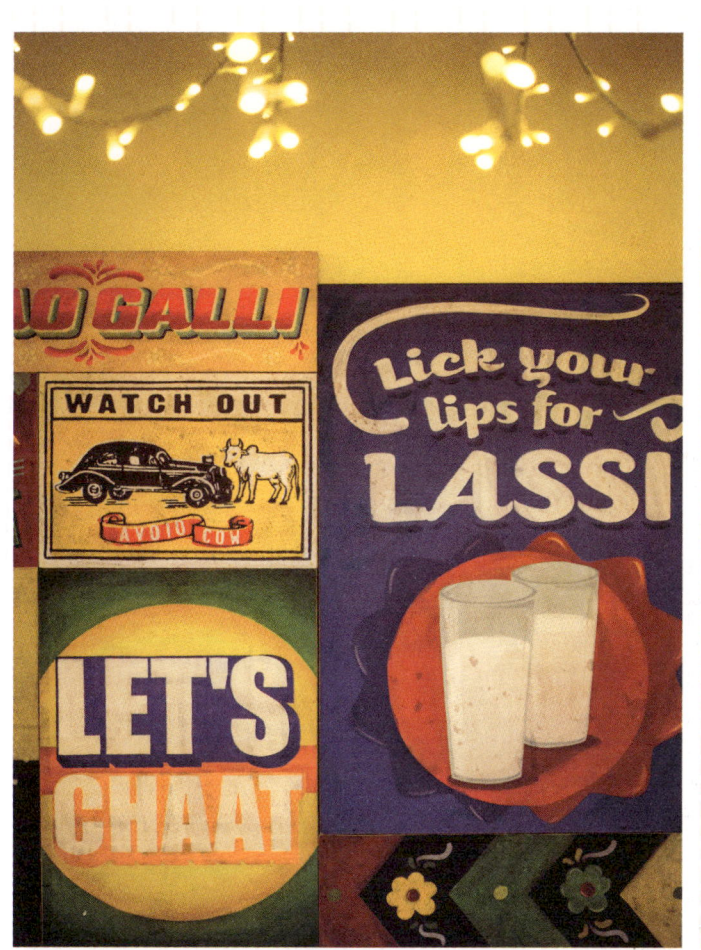

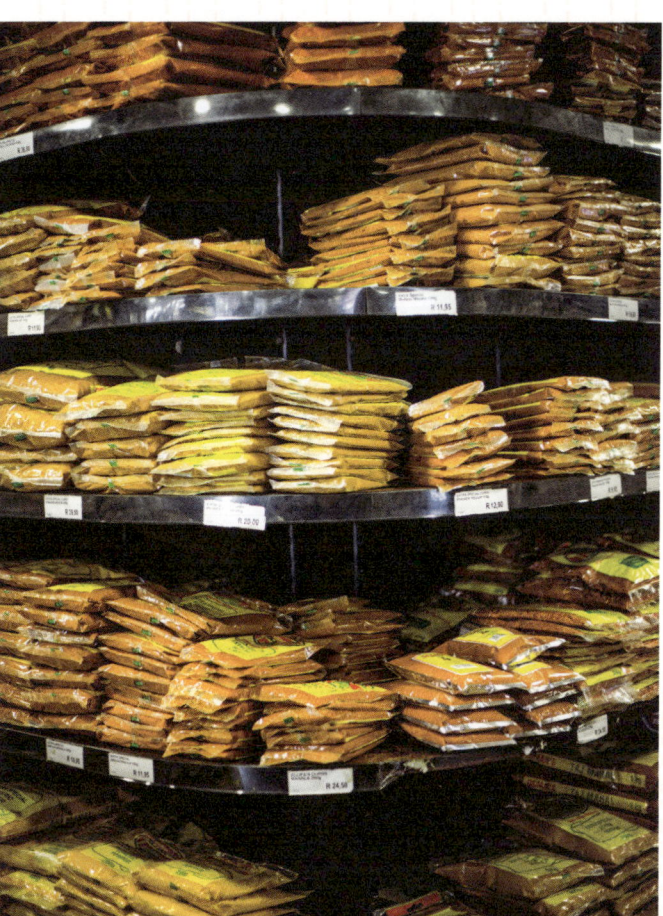

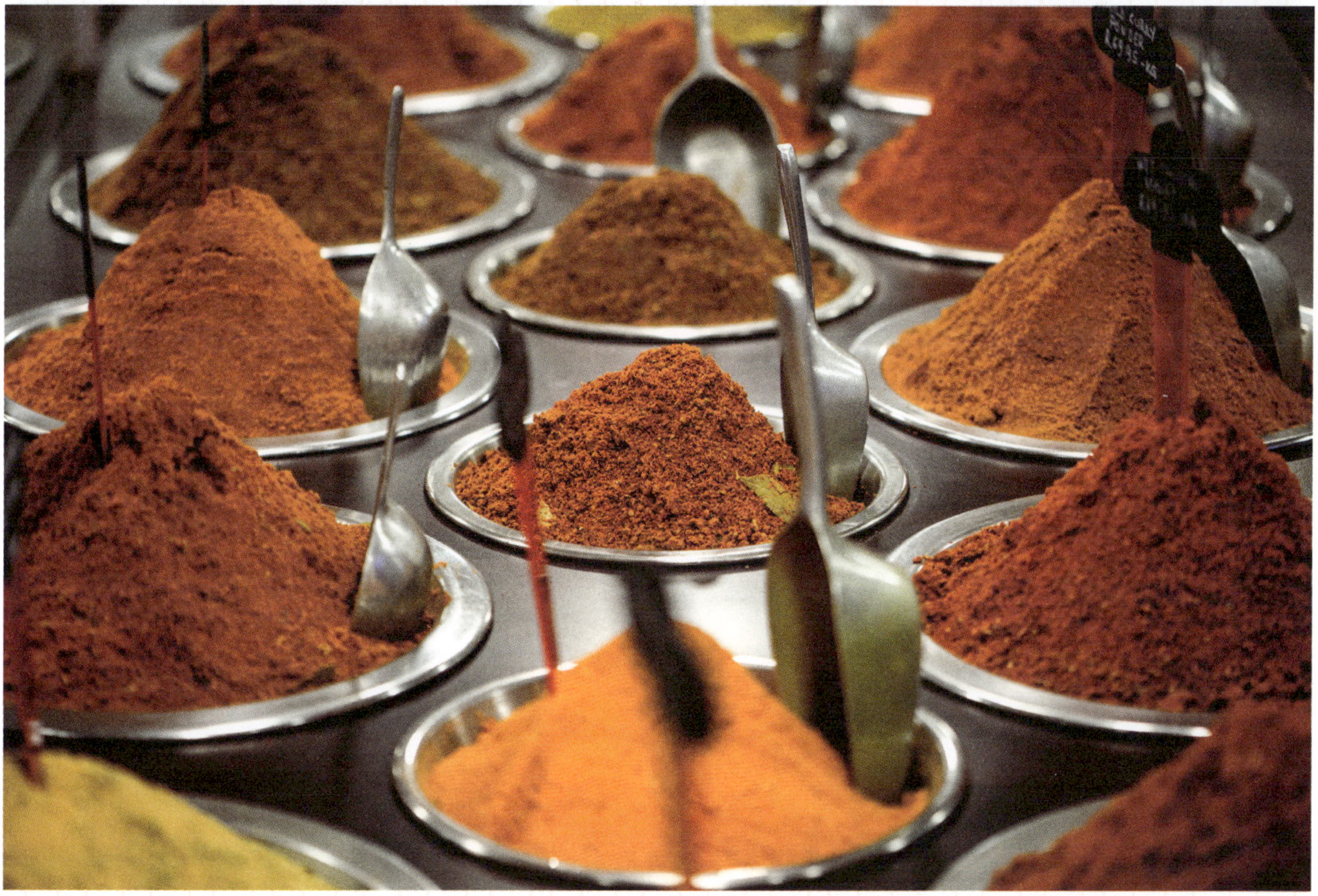

I try to instill a love of food in my family. I want my son to know how lekker a tomato off the vine is and how noisy peas are!

MARGOT

MARGOT JANSE

WITH DEAN JONES, GERALD VAN DER WALT & THE TASTING ROOM STAFF

THE TASTING ROOM

CRAYFISH & CAULIFLOWER

Franschhoek,
Western Cape

CRAYFISH & CAULIFLOWER

SERVINGS: 4 | PREP TIME: 55 MINS PLUS DRYING | COOK TIME: 45 MINS PLUS DRYING
SKILL LEVEL: 3 (CHALLENGING)

INGREDIENTS

Cauliflower & buttermilk purée
1 medium-sized onion, chopped
20 g butter
10 ml olive oil
½ cauliflower head, finely chopped
100 ml cream
50 ml buttermilk

Cauliflower crisps
½ cauliflower head
15 ml olive oil

Buchu crumb
10 g buchu powder
100 g breadcrumbs
30 g butter

Pickled bits
300 g tomatoes
10 g thyme
3 cloves garlic, sliced
20 g icing sugar
10 g coarse salt

15 g sugar
100 ml white wine vinegar
100 ml water
30 g cauliflower, very finely chopped
10 g chives, finely chopped
100 g hazelnuts, toasted and chopped

Crayfish
4 medium crayfish tails
butter
lemon juice

METHOD

Make the pickled bits the day before. Peel, de-seed and quarter the tomatoes. Place them on greaseproof paper and cover each piece with thyme and a slice of garlic. Dust a thin coating of icing sugar over them. Leave them to dry overnight in a warm spot. The next day, combine coarse salt and sugar with vinegar and water. Then, in a bowl, mix the small top florets of the finely chopped cauliflower with the pickling liquid.

Cook the onion for the purée in a heavy-based pot with the butter, olive oil and salt over a medium heat until the onion is soft. Add the chopped cauliflower and cook, covered, until the cauliflower is soft. Add the cream and reduce by a third. Once reduced, leave to cool and then blend with the buttermilk. Pass the purée through a fine sieve and store in an airtight container in the fridge until required.

To make the cauliflower crisps, thinly slice the cauliflower with a mandolin. Place slices on greaseproof paper, cover them with a little drizzle of olive oil and season with salt, making sure you cover the entire surface of the cauliflower. Vacuum-seal them on full, cook them sous-vide at 80°C for 10 minutes, then refresh them in an ice bath. Once cooled, lay the cauliflower out flat on greaseproof paper and leave to dry in a warm spot for a couple of hours, until crispy. Store in an airtight container until required.

To make the buchu crumb, blend the buchu, breadcrumbs and butter in a food processor until well mixed. Season to taste and store in an airtight container until required.

To serve, drain the pickled cauliflower and mix with the confit tomatoes, chives and hazelnuts. Poach the crayfish tails in butter in a heavy-based non-stick pan until they are slightly coloured. Once cooked through, squeeze over some lemon juice, remove from the pan and then slice each tail into four. Place a blob of purée on the plate, then place the sliced crayfish on top, then spoon a little bit of the buchu crumb on each of the crayfish pieces. Scatter the pickled bits over the top and finish with the cauliflower crisps.

JO BUITENDACH
PAST EXPERIENCES

EASY PEASY INJERA
KIK ALICHA
MISR WAT

Much of the food in Joburg's inner city has migrant influences, as it really is a city of migrants, where you can get great Ethiopian, Indian, Nigerian, Congolese and South African food. I always take clients to James XVI Ethiopian Café, not only for the incredible Ethiopian food, but also to see the smiling face of my friend James, the owner (see page 317).

Jo

Maboneng,
Gauteng

EASY PEASY INJERA
ETHIOPIAN SOURDOUGH FLATBREAD

MAKES: ABOUT 10 | PREP TIME: 5 MINS | COOK TIME: 10 MINS | SKILL LEVEL: 1 (EASY)

INGREDIENTS

2 cups teff flour (if you can't find
  teff flour, use all brown rice flour)
1 cup brown rice flour
2 tsp bicarbonate of soda
1 tsp salt
¼ cup yoghurt
2½ cups soda water
oil for frying

METHOD

Mix teff flour, rice flour, bicarbonate of soda and salt together in a bowl. In a separate bowl, mix the yoghurt and soda water together.

Mix dry and wet ingredients together. Heat up a frying pan to medium, pour in enough of the mixture to cover the bottom of the pan and cook for about 40 seconds. Cover and cook for another 20 seconds, then remove from the pan. Keep injera covered with a cloth as they come out of the pan so they don't dry out before serving. Serve with misr wat, kik alicha and other Ethiopian-style spiced dishes.

MISR WAT
RED LENTIL STEW

SERVINGS: 4 | PREP TIME: 10 MINS | COOK TIME: 1 HOUR | SKILL LEVEL: 1 (EASY)

INGREDIENTS

1½ cups red lentils, rinsed
water for boiling
5 tbsp olive oil
1 large red onion, chopped
5 cloves garlic, chopped
1½ tsp minced fresh ginger
2½ tsp berbere spice
  (see recipe)
1 tsp salt
1½ cups water

METHOD

Bring a pot of water to the boil, add lentils and cook for about 15 minutes. In a separate pot, heat the olive oil, add the onion and cook until soft. Add garlic and ginger, and stir in berbere spice (to make berbere spice, mix together 7 tsp chilli powder, 6 tsp paprika, ½ tsp salt, 1 tsp ground ginger, ½ tsp ground cardamom, ½ tsp ground nutmeg, ½ tsp garlic powder, ¼ tsp ground allspice, a dash of cloves and ½ tsp ground fenugreek) to form a paste. Add lentils, salt and 1½ cups water. Simmer for 15–20 minutes until most of the water has evaporated. Serve immediately with injera and kik alicha.

KIK ALICHA
YELLOW SPLIT PEA STEW

SERVINGS: 4 | PREP TIME: 10 MINS PLUS SOAKING | COOK TIME: 1 HOUR | SKILL LEVEL: 1 (EASY)

INGREDIENTS

1½ cups yellow split peas
vegetable oil
1 large red onion, chopped
7 cloves garlic, crushed
1½ tsp crushed ginger
2 cups water
1 tsp turmeric
1 tsp salt
1 chilli, de-seeded and chopped

METHOD

Start the day before by soaking the yellow split peas for 12 hours or overnight.

Rinse the soaked yellow peas. Heat oil in a pot and fry onion until soft. Add garlic and ginger, and fry for 1 minute. Add water, turmeric, salt and chilli, and bring to the boil. Add split peas, return to the boil, cover and simmer for about 50–60 minutes until soft. Serve with injera and misr wat.

SYLVIA DOROTHY WILLIAMS
WITH THE FISHERMEN OF KALK BAY
FISH SELLER

SOUTH AFRICAN SNOEK WITH APRICOT JAM & LEMON GARLIC GLAZE

I have a dream in my head, to one day live by the sea.
I'm not sure where – Simon's Town, Kalk Bay or Fish Hoek
– but to wake up every day with that glorious view, I can
remind myself that we live in the best place on Earth.
And I would eat fish every day. *SYLVIA*

*Kalk Bay,
Western Cape*

SOUTH AFRICAN SNOEK WITH APRICOT JAM & LEMON GARLIC GLAZE

SERVINGS: 6 | PREP TIME: 10 MINS PLUS FISHING | COOK TIME: 15–20 MINS | SKILL LEVEL: 1 (EASY)

INGREDIENTS

100 g butter
4 tbsp olive oil
2 cloves garlic, crushed
4 tbsp apricot jam
juice and zest of 1 lemon
1 kg fish of your choice
  (see Tip), filleted

METHOD

Pre-heat the oven to 180°C or light the braai and prepare medium-hot coals. In a saucepan, melt the butter, add the olive oil and garlic and cook for a minute. Stir in the apricot jam, lemon juice and lemon zest. Season the glaze to taste with salt and pepper. Spread half the glaze over the fish (flesh side up) and place in the oven or on the braai. Cook for 15–20 minutes: if using a braai, cook the fish either on a grid or a foil-lined grid, for about 15 minutes with the skin side towards the heat, and then flip to cook the flesh side for about 3-5 minutes. Remove the fish from the oven or the braai. Pour over the remaining glaze and serve immediately with lots of fresh bread and butter.

TIP

Traditionally we would braai snoek but our waters don't always offer us that, so sometimes we use Cape salmon or line-caught tuna.

LIESL BUSH
THE FARMERS DAUGHTER

ROAST LEG OF LAMB
PANCAKES
JAPIE'S PUDDING

*Upington,
Northern Cape*

My mom used to boil her leg of lamb on the gas stove first, because she was trying to save a bit on the gas for the oven! Then she would parboil the potatoes in the resulting meaty stock too – my dad liked the meat-flavoured potatoes, which were later roasted next to the leg in the pan.

Liesl

ROAST LEG OF LAMB

SERVINGS: 6 | PREP TIME: 15 MINS | COOK TIME: ABOUT 2 HOURS PLUS RESTING | SKILL LEVEL: 1 (EASY)

INGREDIENTS

2–2½ kg leg of
   Boesmanland lamb

3 onions

1 bulb garlic, cloves
   separated

glug of olive oil

3–4 stalks rosemary

1 tbsp coriander seeds,
   roughly ground in a
   pestle and mortar

METHOD

Take the leg of lamb out of the fridge about 1 hour before you cook it to bring it to room temperature. Pre-heat the oven to 220°C. Cut the onions into big chunks and place in the bottom of a roasting pan. Add the garlic to the onions – keep one or two cloves aside for rubbing onto the lamb. Rub lamb all over with olive oil, freshly ground salt and pepper, the reserved lightly crushed garlic cloves, chopped rosemary leaves and ground coriander. Place the lamb on top of the onions and garlic in the roasting pan. Cover tightly with foil. Place in the pre-heated oven and immediately turn the oven down to 170°C. Roast for 25–30 minutes per 500 g – so about 2 hours for a 2½ kg leg of lamb. Remove the foil for the last 45 minutes of the roasting time to brown the meat.

Rest for 10–15 minutes before serving with roasted vegetables including potatoes.

"We believe that our meat from the Boesmanland is even better than that from the Karoo, although both are called Karoo lamb. There is a saying that you just need salt and pepper for Boesmanland meat because the meat has enough flavour."

PANCAKES

MAKES: 14–16 | PREP TIME: 10 MINS PLUS STANDING | COOK TIME: 35 MINS | SKILL LEVEL: 1 (EASY)

INGREDIENTS

250 ml flour
5 ml baking powder
pinch of salt
2 free-range eggs
  (if possible, use plaas
  eiers – farm eggs)
200 ml milk
175 ml water
5 ml lemon juice
75 ml vegetable oil
vegetable oil for frying
mix of sugar and ground
  cinnamon, to serve

METHOD

Sift the flour, baking powder and salt together. Separate the eggs. Beat the egg whites until stiff and set aside. Beat the milk, water, lemon juice, 75 ml oil and egg yolks together. Add to the dry ingredients and mix. Gently fold in the egg whites. Set aside to stand for at least 30 minutes before cooking.

Heat a small frying pan over medium heat and add a drop of oil. Spoon in a little of the pancake batter and swirl the pan around so it covers the whole pan in a thin layer. Cook for a couple of minutes, flip over and cook the other side. Set aside to keep warm while cooking the rest of the pancakes or serve immediately, sprinkled with sugar and cinnamon.

TIP

The Boesmanland way to serve these pancakes is sprinkled generously with a mixture of sugar and ground cinnamon, but you can use them with savoury fillings too; golden syrup and cheese is also very good.

JAPIE'S PUDDING

SERVINGS: 14–16 | PREP TIME: 10 MINS PLUS STANDING | COOK TIME: 35 MINS | SKILL LEVEL: 1 (EASY)

INGREDIENTS

2 free-range eggs
  (if possible, use plaas
  eiers – farm eggs)
1 cup sugar
¼ cup flour
1 cup milk
3½ cups orange juice
1 tbsp lemon juice
zest of 1 orange
zest of 1 lemon
2 tbsp melted butter

METHOD

Pre-heat the oven to 180°C. Separate the eggs. Beat the egg yolks and add sugar slowly while continuing to beat. Add a little flour, then a little milk in turns, and mix well after each addition until both ingredients are incorporated into the mixture. Stir in the rest of the ingredients other than the egg whites.

Beat the egg whites until stiff and fold into the mixture. (This is a very wet mixture and I have doubted myself many a time – but each time it comes out perfect, so don't worry if it seems very wet.) Pour into a greased ovenproof dish and bake for 35–40 minutes or until nice and brown.

NWAMBENDHLA MHLONGO
WITH MARIA NWARELELA MKHARI & NWAMAGEZA HLUNGWANE
BALENI SACRED SALT

TIHOVE TINYAWA NA TIMANGA
MIROHO YA TIN'WHEMBE TIMANGA
MAJENJE
MATOMANI

I am 57 years old and I am still healthy and strong. I feel good being here and harvesting the salt. We want to teach the youth of the village these ancient traditions, because it will help them to have better lives.

Nwambendhla and the Baleni Salt Harvesters

Giyani, Limpopo

TIHOVE TINYAWA NA TIMANGA
SAMP & BEANS WITH NUTS

SERVINGS: 6 | PREP TIME: 10 MINS | COOK TIME: 2 HOURS | SKILL LEVEL: 1 (EASY)

INGREDIENTS

1 cup samp
1 cup dried beans, soaked overnight
2 tsp salt (we use Baleni Sacred Salt)
½ cup timanga (nut flour)

METHOD

Cook the samp and beans in a large pot of boiling water until cooked through, about 2 hours. Drain and return to a dry pan. Heat, adding a splash of water if the mixture starts to stick. Add the salt and stir in the timanga. Serve when the mixture has thickened slightly.

MIROHO YA TIN'WHEMBE TIMANGA
PUMPKIN LEAVES & FLOWERS WITH NUTS & TOMATOES

SERVINGS: 4 AS A SIDE DISH | PREP TIME: 10 MINS | COOK TIME: 20 MINS | SKILL LEVEL: 1 (EASY)

INGREDIENTS

2 handfuls pumpkin leaves and
  flowers
1 pinch bicarbonate of soda
1 cup water
2 tsp salt (we use Baleni Sacred Salt)
2 tomatoes, roughly chopped
½ cup timanga (nut flour)

METHOD

Cook the pumpkin leaves with the bicarbonate of soda in the water until soft, about 10–15 minutes. Add the salt, tomatoes and timanga. Stir and cook for another 5 minutes. Serve with pap.

Clockwise from top left:
Tihove tinyawa na timanga,
Matomani (see recipe following page),
Majenje (see recipe following page),
Miroho ya tin'whembe timanga

MAJENJE
ROASTED TERMITES

SERVINGS: 4 AS A SNACK | PREP TIME: 10 MINS | COOK TIME: 5 MINS | SKILL LEVEL: 1 (EASY)

INGREDIENTS

2 cups fresh termites
1 tbsp vegetable oil
1 tsp salt (we use Baleni Sacred Salt)

GF DF

METHOD

Place the termites in a saucepan and add the oil. Stir over a medium heat until they start to crisp up, about 5–10 minutes. Add the salt and stir for another few minutes to crisp. Serve warm as a snack.

MATOMANI
ROASTED MOPANE WORMS

SERVINGS: 4 AS A SNACK | PREP TIME: 10 MINS | COOK TIME: 10 MINS | SKILL LEVEL: 1 (EASY)

INGREDIENTS

20 sun-dried mopane worms
½ cup water
2 tsp salt (we use Baleni Sacred Salt)

GF DF

METHOD

Soak the dried mopane worms in a bowl of water for 1 hour. Remove, drain and place in a saucepan. Add ½ cup fresh water and salt to the pan and cook for 10 minutes. Serve warm as a snack.

SELLO HATANG
WITH THEMBI, TSHEGO & LETHABO
NELSON MANDELA FOUNDATION

SELLO'S BRAAIED LAMB CHOPS
THEMBI'S PEACH & CUSTARD TRIFLE

I am very excited to be part of *The Great South African Cookbook*. It's a showcase of what we have, rather than what we don't have, as a country. For both me and for the Nelson Mandela Foundation, it means we'll be able to touch and change lives with food; it's in everyone's hands to help make a difference.

Sello

*Johannesburg,
Gauteng*

SELLO'S BRAAIED LAMB CHOPS

SERVINGS: 6 | PREP TIME: 5 MINS PLUS MARINATING | COOK TIME: 6 MINS | SKILL LEVEL: 1 (EASY)

INGREDIENTS

4 tsp steak and chops
  spice
  (I use Robertsons)
½ tsp salt
80 ml olive oil
50 ml Worcestershire
  sauce
12 lamb chops

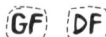

METHOD

The day before, mix steak and chops spice, salt, olive oil and Worcestershire sauce in a bowl to form a paste and coat the chops with the mixture. Cover and leave to marinate in the refrigerator overnight.

Braai chops for 3 minutes on each side or until done to your liking. Serve with your favourite braai side dishes.

THEMBI'S PEACH & CUSTARD TRIFLE

SERVINGS: 6 | PREP TIME: 15 MINS PLUS SETTING | SKILL LEVEL: 1 (EASY)

INGREDIENTS

1 x 200 g packet Tennis
  biscuits
1 litre fruit cocktail
  yoghurt
2 x 410 g cans peach
  slices (I use Koo)
1 litre vanilla custard
  (I use Ultra Mel)

METHOD

Place a single layer of Tennis biscuits in a large bowl and spread fruit cocktail yoghurt on top of the biscuits. Place a layer of peach slices over and top with custard. Repeat the layers, ending with a custard layer. Leave the trifle in the refrigerator for 6 hours or overnight to set before serving.

ENJOY
YUMMY
Enjoy Family Time.
Say Grace everytime
KISS THE COOK

CHEFS OF THE FUTURE

Tiger Brands, principal sponsor partner of *The Great South African Cookbook*, wanted to give South Africa's chefs of the future an opportunity to showcase their talent and love of food in this book. With the assistance of the Department of Higher Education and Training, it identified and approached culinary colleges in the heart of peri-urban communities in all nine provinces, and asked them to identify their most promising young trainee chefs. The students were invited to enter a competition in which they answered the same question as all the other contributors in this book: 'What do you cook for the people you love?' The 10 finalists' recipes, which appear on the following pages, are testament to the fact that the inspiration to cook always comes from the heart.

ISMAIL BEGGS
PORT ELIZABETH TVET COLLEGE, PORT ELIZABETH, EASTERN CAPE

It was my late great-uncle who got me into cooking. He showed me that food can be more than just nourishment; it's also an avenue for unleashing creativity. One of my regrets is that I never got to cook for him. I love to cook for my girlfriend. Her love of cheesecakes and chocolate brownies was the catalyst for my ballerina brownie cheesecake recipe.

BRONWYN CLOETE
WEST COAST COLLEGE, MALMESBURY, WESTERN CAPE

As a single mother, I decided that a future without education looked bleak, so I returned to the classroom. I began my cooking journey by selling rotis in college for extra income and I've now had the privilege of being nominated to prepare rotis for four hospitality lectures at a hotel college in France! I would love to have my own catering company one day.

KAMERON GANESAN
THEKWINI TVET COLLEGE, DURBAN, KWAZULU-NATAL

I am an experimental cook who is always on the lookout for new recipes. I love to create gastronomical masterpieces in my kitchen-cum-studio. My mother is definitely my biggest cheerleader and she always gets excited when I'm 'engineering' a new recipe. My dream is to work for one of the top hotel groups in the world, to travel and learn about different types of cuisine.

MAGDALENE JEANETTE GREEFF
NCR TVET COLLEGE, DE AAR, NORTHERN CAPE

As far back as I can remember, I wanted to be a chef. Cooking has always come naturally to me, so it wasn't a hard decision to choose a career in hospitality. I'm fully prepared to put in the long hours it takes to become a professional chef. I know that hard work and perseverance will bring me success in the long run.

PHUMZA HOLLAND
NCR TVET COLLEGE, DE AAR, NORTHERN CAPE

When I finish college I want to stay in De Aar and pursue my dream of one day opening a restaurant. My mother has given me so much support and encouragement and I've won three local cooking competitions. I regularly cook for my immediate family and I've also cooked for up to 50 extended family members. I feel like my cooking journey has only just begun.

OUMA MAFISHI
TSHWANE SOUTH TVET COLLEGE, CITY OF TSHWANE, GAUTENG

My passion for working with food motivated me to study hospitality at Tshwane South College. I now have a thriving small catering business, making traditional dishes for funerals and weddings. My greatest satisfaction comes from cooking for my husband and kids. They love feasting on my roast chicken and pap. I want to become one of South Africa's best chefs.

NOKUTHULA PORTIA MNGQOSINI
GERT SIBANDE TVET COLLEGE, STANDERTON, MPUMALANGA

I love being in the kitchen, cooking up a storm. My grandmother ran a bed and breakfast, so I was exposed to the hospitality industry from an early age. I used to help out with the housekeeping and cooking, and that is what inspired me to become a chef. I love cooking for my family. My cooking has led them to develop a palate for exotic dishes.

JOHN NKGWANG
ORBIT TVET MANKGWE, MANKWE, NORTH WEST

It was while I was volunteering at a local hotel that I developed my passion for cooking. I now work there as a part-time chef. My mum is definitely one of my biggest fans. Every Christmas my family asks me to make my coffee chocolate cake. There's something in it for just about everyone. It satisfies my father's love of coffee and my younger sisters' insatiable chocolate cravings.

SEBULA CHRISTOPH SEBUSI
CAPRICORN COLLEGE FOR TVET, POLOKWANE, LIMPOPO

I enjoy cooking for my mother and the people I love. While still studying hospitality at Capricorn College, I was selected to cook for the premier of Limpopo Province as part of a student showcase at a government function. The experience taught me that I can thrive under pressure. In a state of complete panic, I was able to create an inspired dish.

DIMAKATSO YOLANDA TAU
GOLDFIELDS TVET COLLEGE, WELKOM, FREE STATE

I come from a family with modest means. I relish the challenge of creating special dishes with limited ingredients because it forces me to think creatively. My 12-year-old brother is my designated 'masterchef' who reviews all my dishes and often gets to sample variations of my lamb shank recipes. His young age means he always gives me very honest feedback!

LASAGNE MEAT & SPINACH ROLL-UP

Recipe by **OUMA MAFISHI**, Tshwane South TVET College

SERVINGS: 4 | PREP TIME: 15 MINS | COOK TIME: 60 MINS | SKILL LEVEL: 2 (MODERATE)

INGREDIENTS

30 ml butter
1 small onion, chopped
2 ml garlic flakes
400 g beef mince
2 bay leaves
3 ml sweet basil
2 ml black pepper
60 ml beef stock
125 g spinach
1 x 250 g box Fatti's & Moni's lasagne sheets
30 ml margarine
30 ml Golden Cloud wheat flour
250 ml milk
60 ml grated Cheddar
2 medium-sized eggs
40 ml grated Parmesan
80 ml All Gold tomato sauce
40 ml grated mozzarella

METHOD

Pre-heat the oven to 175°C. Grease an oven dish.

Melt butter and lightly sauté onion and garlic flakes until soft. Add beef mince, bay leaves, sweet basil, black pepper and stock. Stir well and cook slowly until meat is just cooked, then season to taste with salt.

Submerge spinach in a pot of boiling water for 40 seconds, then drain and place in a bowlful of cold water, then drain again, squeezing any remaining water out. Boil the lasagne sheets in salted water until al dente and drain.

To make the cheese sauce, melt margarine in a saucepan over a low-to-medium heat, stir in wheat flour and mix until smooth. Gradually stir in the milk to form a smooth sauce and season to taste. Allow the sauce to simmer for 3 minutes, then remove from the heat and add grated Cheddar.

In a bowl combine meat mixture, drained spinach, eggs and half the Parmesan. Spread filling onto each piece of lasagna, roll up filled lasagne and place in greased oven dish. Pour cheese sauce and tomato sauce over top of lasagne sheets. Sprinkle with mozzarella and remaining Parmesan. Cover and bake for about 30–40 minutes until golden.

TIP

You can use chicken mince instead of beef mince if you prefer white meat.

CHICKEN CURRY WITH ROTI & A SALSA ON THE SIDE

recipe by **BRONWYN CLOETE**, West Coast College

SERVINGS: 8 | PREP TIME: 40 MINS PLUS RESTING | COOK TIME: 40 MINS | SKILL LEVEL: 2 (MODERATE)

INGREDIENTS

Chicken curry
30 ml oil
2 medium onions, chopped
5–6 cloves garlic, crushed
5 ml grated ginger
10 ml garam masala
10 ml 14-in-one curry masala
10 ml mild curry powder
10 ml all-in-one curry powder
10 ml bay leaves
10 ml curry leaves

8 chicken breast fillets, sliced into blocks
5 medium-sized potatoes, peeled, parboiled and sliced
1 x 410 g can All Gold chopped tomatoes
1 cup chicken stock
fresh coriander, plus extra to garnish

Roti
750 g Golden Cloud wheat flour
175 g butter or margarine, at room temperature

Salsa
1 red onion, diced
1 x 410 g can All Gold chopped tomatoes
½ green pepper, diced
1 chilli, chopped
⅓ cucumber, chopped
30 g coriander, chopped
125 ml vinegar
15 ml salt
15 ml sugar

METHOD

Heat the oil in a pot, add onions and sauté them until they turn golden brown. Add garlic and ginger and sauté for 2 minutes. Mix the garam masala, 14-in-one curry masala, mild curry powder, all-in-one curry powder, bay leaves and curry leaves together in a bowl and add 15 ml of this mixture to the pot on the stove with the sautéed onions, garlic and ginger. Leave to cook for 3 minutes. Add chicken breast fillet blocks to the pot and leave to cook until chicken turns white. Add sliced potato, chopped tomatoes and chicken stock and cook for 20 minutes. When potato is cooked, add remaining mixed spices and stir well. Spread coriander on top and simmer for 15 minutes, adding more liquid if necessary, to stop curry drying out.

To make roti, sift flour in a bowl, add a pinch of salt and mix the two together. Slowly add lukewarm water while mixing together with a wooden spoon until a dough starts to form. Once the dough starts to come together, use your hands to incorporate air into it, until the dough becomes firm. Rest dough in refrigerator for at least 20 minutes, then divide it into 100 g portions. Roll each portion out on a floured surface. Spread butter on the dough and roll the dough up. Then roll the dough in on one side and out on the other side. Place sides on top of each other to create layers and roll dough into balls again. Refrigerate dough for another 20 minutes. (This allows the butter to harden again and will make it easier to roll out the dough a second time.) Remove dough from fridge again and roll balls out into circles. Fry rotis in a pan, turning them over during cooking, until both sides are covered with golden brown speckles.

For the salsa, place diced onion, tomatoes, green pepper, chilli, cucumber and coriander in a bowl and mix together with vinegar, salt, sugar and black pepper to taste. Mix well.

To serve, place the rotis on a plate, top with some of the curry and a dollop of salsa. Garnish with fresh coriander.

TIP

Always make sure you use enough butter when making roti as this gives the roti its unique taste. Don't flour your surface too heavily when you roll out the dough as it can make the dough dry and minimise the buttery flavour.

CRUST ROAST CHICKEN FILLET WITH CHEESE & PAK CHOI

recipe by **SEBULA CHRISTOPH SEBUSI**, Capricorn College for TVET

SERVINGS: 4 | PREP TIME: 30 MINS | COOK TIME: 30 MINS | SKILL LEVEL: 2 (MODERATE)

INGREDIENTS

4 chicken breast fillets

1 egg, beaten

Crust coating

2 slices bread

30 g cornflakes

30 g Golden Cloud wheat cake flour

15 ml salt

15 ml pepper

Filling

125 g pak choi, blanched

30 g feta cheese, crumbled

20 ml Crosse & Blackwell mayonnaise

5 ml crushed garlic

15 ml dried mixed herbs

20 ml creamy Greek salad dressing

Sauce

30 ml olive oil

1 x 410 g tin All Gold chopped tomatoes

METHOD

Pre-heat the oven to 180°C.

Place bread, cornflakes, flour, salt and pepper in a food processor and pulse for 30 seconds or until a crumb consistency is reached. Place in a shallow bowl.

Place chicken breasts, one at a time, between 2 sheets of plastic film and using a rolling pin or meat mallet, gently pound until flattened and approximately 5 mm thick. Set aside.

Place beaten egg in a shallow dish. Chop the blanched pak choi and place in a bowl along with the feta, mayonnaise, garlic, herbs and dressing.

Lay the chicken breasts on a surface, divide filling mixture into four and place on top of each breast. Roll up each breast and secure with a toothpick. Dip each rolled chicken breast first in the beaten egg and then in the crumb mixture. Toss to coat evenly with crumbs.

Mix together olive oil and tomatoes, pour into the base of a shallow oven-proof dish and top with the crumbed chicken. Bake for 30 minutes, or until chicken is cooked through and crumbs are golden. To serve, halve the chicken breasts and serve hot.

TIP

For extra flavour, heat a drop of olive oil in a frypan and add 15 ml red wine with 2 tbsp All Gold mustard sauce. Allow to bubble for 2 minutes, then drizzle over the stuffed chicken fillet before serving.

Clockwise from top left:
Lasagne meat & spinach roll-up,
Chicken curry with roti & a salsa on the side,
Crust roast chicken fillet with cheese & pak choi

MINT & CORIANDER KEBABS WITH TOMATO CHUTNEY & ROTI

recipe by **KAMERON GANESAN**, Thekwini TVET College

SERVINGS: 4–6 | PREP TIME: 1 HOUR PLUS CHILLING | COOK TIME: 1½ HOURS | SKILL LEVEL: 2 (MODERATE)

INGREDIENTS

Kebabs
500 g mutton or lamb mince
5 ml garam masala
15 ml salt
5 ml turmeric powder
15 ml medium chilli powder
2 green chillies, chopped
1 onion, finely chopped
1 bunch coriander, finely chopped
10 ml crushed ginger
10 ml garlic paste
handful of mint, chopped

Tomato chutney
15 ml oil
2 onions, sliced
6 cloves garlic, crushed
2 green chillies, sliced lengthways
2 curry leaves
15 ml mixed masala curry powder, medium
5 ml turmeric powder
2 x 410 g cans All Gold chopped tomatoes
20 ml salt, to taste
20 ml All Gold tomato paste
5 ml sugar

Roti
500 ml water
5 ml salt
60 ml oil
500 ml Golden Cloud cake wheat flour
15 ml margarine or butter
250 ml Golden Cloud cake wheat flour, for kneading
melted butter (optional)

chopped coriander, mint and green chilli, to garnish

METHOD

To make the kebab mix, place mince in a bowl with garam masala, salt, turmeric powder, medium chilli powder, chillies, onion, coriander, ginger, garlic and mint. Wearing gloves, mix everything together with your hands until properly combined. With clean hands, break off little pieces of mixture of approximately 20–25 g and shape them into nice round balls. Chill in the fridge for 30 minutes. Pre-heat the oven of 180°C. Remove kebab balls from refrigerator and slide onto metal or presoaked wooden skewers. There should be 2–3 balls per skewer. Brush kebabs with oil and place on a baking tray and bake for 25–30 minutes. Remove from oven and set aside.

To make the tomato chutney, heat oil in a medium-sized pot and sauté onions until golden brown. Add crushed garlic, chillies and curry leaves and sauté for a minute before adding curry powder and turmeric. Sauté quickly, then add chopped tomatoes and salt. Leave partially covered, with the lid half on, to cook for 20–25 minutes, stirring occasionally. Stir in tomato paste and sugar and simmer for a few minutes. Add kebabs to chutney and gently stir so that each kebab is covered in chutney, being careful not to break them. Cover and simmer for 5–10 minutes.

To make roti, add water, salt and oil to a pot and bring to the boil. Remove from heat, add flour and stir. Return to the heat and add margarine or butter. Continue stirring until all ingredients come together. Remove from heat, cool dough, then knead it, adding the extra flour if too sticky. Form dough into balls approximately 50–60g in size and roll out into 20 cm circles approximately the size of a dinner plate. Fry roti one at a time in a hot frying pan (do not add oil or butter), turning each roti three to four times until golden brown spots appear. If you like, you can brush roti lightly with melted butter.

Garnish kebabs and chutney with chopped coriander, mint and green chilli, and serve with roti on the side.

WHOLE LAMB SHANKS WITH CREAMY SAMP

recipe by **DIMAKATSO YOLANDA TAU,** Goldfields TVET College

SERVINGS: 4 | PREP TIME: 1 HOUR | COOK TIME: 2 HOURS PLUS MARINATING
SKILL LEVEL: 2 (MODERATE)

INGREDIENTS

2 cups Ace samp, soaked for at least
  1 hour
750 ml water
30 ml olive oil
25 ml balsamic vinegar
4 sprigs fresh rosemary
10 cloves garlic, peeled
4 onions, peeled and cut into wedges

4 lamb shanks
1 x 410 g can All Gold whole
  peeled tomatoes
2 cups beef stock
250 g white button mushrooms
60 ml margarine
4 potatoes, peeled
375 ml low-fat milk

1 beef stock cube
1 sachet cream-of-chicken
  soup powder
sprigs of rosemary, to garnish

METHOD

Cook samp in 750 ml water over a medium-high temperature for 1½ hours, adding extra water if necessary.

While the samp is cooking, mix together 15 ml olive oil, all the balsamic vinegar, rosemary, garlic and onions in a small bowl. Pour over the lamb shanks. Cover and leave to marinate for at least 30 minutes. Then, place lamb shanks, marinade (including the garlic and onions) and remaining 15 ml olive oil in a casserole dish and brown the meat on a high heat. Add canned tomatoes and beef stock. Don't season yet. Cover the casserole dish with a lid and simmer the shanks over a medium heat. Baste them with the surrounding gravy at regular intervals, adding a little water if necessary. After 45 minutes, turn the shanks over and continue to cook for another 45 minutes, continuing to baste the shanks with gravy, until the meat is soft but still attached to the bone. Season to taste.

While the shanks are cooking, chop mushrooms, sauté them in 15 ml margarine until soft and set aside. Boil peeled potatoes in water until they are well cooked, then drain them and mash them roughly. In a bowl, mix low-fat milk, stock cube and soup powder to form a paste. Stir paste into mashed potatoes until well combined. Cover with a lid and set aside.

When samp is cooked, add the creamy mashed potatoes and stir until well combined, adding a little water if samp is too thick. Add mushrooms and stir a little. Season to taste.

To serve, dish samp into bowls and top with a lamb shank. Pour round gravy, onion and garlic. Garnish with sprigs of rosemary.

TROPICAL CHICKEN WITH SPICY RICE

recipe by **NOKUTHULA PORTIA MNGQOSINI**, Gert Sibande TVET College

SERVINGS: 2 | PREP TIME: 20 MINS | COOK TIME: 60 MINS | SKILL LEVEL: 1 (EASY)

INGREDIENTS

4 boneless, skinless
  chicken breasts
5 ml ground ginger
5 ml paprika
10 ml onion powder
2 cloves garlic, finely diced
2 tbsp olive oil
20 ml Holbrooks
  Worcestershire sauce

Sauce

125 ml All Gold tomato
  sauce
30 ml soy sauce
½ x 410 g can crushed
  pineapple in juice
30 g brown sugar

Stir-fry

30 ml olive oil
1 onion, chopped
2 cloves garlic, crushed
125 g frozen mixed
  vegetables, thawed
20 ml medium curry
  powder
250 ml Tastic parboiled
  rice
500 ml water
2½ ml salt

Garnish

1 spring onion, chopped

METHOD

Pre-heat the oven to 200°C. Spray a baking dish with cooking spray.

Cut each chicken breast into 3 or 4 pieces and arrange them on the bottom of the baking dish. In a small bowl, mix together the ginger, paprika, onion powder, garlic and olive oil, then add Worcestershire sauce and mix well. Set aside half the mixture and brush the rest of it over the chicken pieces. Bake for 10 minutes, then turn over the chicken pieces and baste with remaining sauce. Bake for another 10 minutes.

In a medium-sized bowl, combine tomato sauce, soy sauce, pineapple and brown sugar. Carefully spoon this mixture over the baked chicken, then return to the oven for an additional 30 minutes until caramelised and slightly charred.

While the chicken is cooking, heat olive oil in a heavy-bottomed saucepan and cook onion, garlic and vegetables over medium-low heat until softened. Set aside. In a separate pot, combine curry powder and rice. Add water and salt and bring to the boil, uncovered, without stirring. Reduce temperature to as low as possible, then cover saucepan with a tight-fitting lid. Cook for another 15 minutes. Stir in the cooked vegetables. Remove pan from heat and leave to stand for another 5 minutes before serving.

To serve, place chicken on top of rice and garnish with chopped spring onion.

Clockwise from top left:
Whole lamb shanks with creamy samp,
Tropical chicken with spicy rice,
Mint & coriander kebabs with tomato chutney & roti

BALLERINA BROWNIE CHEESECAKE

recipe by **ISMAIL BEGGS**, Port Elizabeth TVET College

SERVINGS: 8–12 | PREP TIME: 1 HOUR | COOK TIME: 1½ HOURS PLUS SETTING
SKILL LEVEL: 2 (MODERATE)

INGREDIENTS

Brownie base

115 g butter, coarsely chopped

100 g Beacon dark chocolate, chopped

4 eggs

225 g sugar

10 ml vanilla essence

100 g Golden Cloud cake wheat flour

2 ml salt

3 ml baking powder

Pavlova

2 egg whites

5 ml white vinegar

140 g caster sugar

5 ml vanilla essence

Filling

250 g smooth, plain cottage cheese, at room temperature

250 g cream cheese, at room temperature

250 ml cultured sour cream

5 ml vanilla essence

125 g caster sugar

30 ml gelatin powder

60 ml water

2 egg whites

METHOD

Pre-heat the oven to 180°C. Grease a springform pan.

To make the brownie base, melt butter and chocolate together in a heatproof bowl placed over a pot of boiling water. Beat eggs and sugar together until creamy. Add vanilla essence, then combine chocolate mixture with sugar/egg mixture. Beat well. Add flour, salt and baking powder. Pour the brownie batter into the greased springform pan and bake for 30 minutes or until a skewer comes out clean when inserted.

Reduce the oven temperature to 100°C. To make the pavlova, beat egg whites until foamy. Add vinegar and continue to beat until the mixture reaches the soft-peak stage. Add sugar, little by little, beating well after every addition. Do this until the mixture is glossy. Then whisk in vanilla essence. Line an oven tray with baking paper, then spoon the meringue onto it, forming a circle the same size as the springform pan the brownie base was baked in. Mould peaks and swirls into the meringue as required. Bake for 1 hour, then turn off the heat. Leave in the oven to cool.

To make the filling, place cottage cheese, cream cheese, sour cream, vanilla essence and half the caster sugar in a food processor fitted with a metal blade and mix until smooth. Tip this out into a bowl. Dissolve the gelatin in water over a low heat. Allow it to cool slightly, then slowly add the gelatin mixture to the cheese mixture, stirring vigorously, then finishing off with a quick whisk. Now, without wasting time, as the cheese mixture sets quickly, whisk egg whites until stiff in a separate bowl, then gradually whisk in the remaining caster sugar to make a meringue-like mixture. Fold into the cheese mixture, then pour onto the cooled brownie crust. The filling should be firm enough so that it sits on the brownie base and does not run down the sides. Refrigerate until firm.

When the pavlova has cooled, lay it on top of the cheesecake and decorate with fruit, nuts or chocolate as desired.

TIP

Do not let the cheesecake set completely before placing the pavlova top on it, but don't do it too early either or else it will absorb moisture from the cheesecake and go soggy. Timing is essential!

If you wish, garnish with chocolate, fruit or nuts.

HAZELNUT CAKE

recipe by **PHUMZA HOLLAND**, NCR TVET College

SERVINGS: 10 | PREP TIME: 60–80 MINS | COOK TIME: 30 MINS PLUS COOLING
SKILL LEVEL: 3 (CHALLENGING)

INGREDIENTS

100 g hazelnuts, toasted
and chopped

300 g light brown sugar

100 g unsalted butter

6 tbsp skim milk

1 tsp fine instant coffee
powder

6 large eggs, at room
temperature

2 tbsp cornflour

175 g Golden Cloud cake
flour

½ tsp salt

Coffee syrup

50 g light brown soft
sugar

4 tbsp water

1 tsp instant coffee
powder

1 tbsp Frangelico
(hazelnut) liqueur, or use
Kahlua or Tia Maria

Icing

400 g mascarpone

300 g Black Cat peanut
butter

1 tbsp fine instant coffee
powder

Decoration

100 g hazelnuts, toasted
and chopped, for the
side of the cake

METHOD

Pre-heat oven to 180°C. Generously butter two 20 cm sandwich tins (ideally about 4½ cm deep or deeper) and line the bases with baking paper.

Put hazelnuts into a food processor with 2 tablespoons brown sugar and pulse until finely chopped (don't expect them to be as fine as ground almonds and avoid over-processing, as this can make the nuts greasy).

Put the butter, milk and coffee powder into a small pan and heat gently until the butter has melted. Set aside.

To make the sponge, beat eggs and remaining brown sugar using an electric hand whisk or standalone mixer for 15 minutes until the mixture is thick and billowy and has almost doubled in size. It should leave a trail that holds for a couple of seconds. Mix cornflour, cake flour and salt together and sift onto the whisked mixture. Using a large metal spoon, fold flour mixture in carefully. Sprinkle in ground hazelnuts and fold in too. Pour warm milk mixture around the edge of the bowl. Fold in slowly, using a light lifting and cutting motion until ribbons of mixture stop appearing. Divide the batter between the tins and bake for 25 minutes until sponge has risen in the middle and is a burnished gold. Loosen the sides of the cakes with a palette knife and then cool inside their tins on a rack for 20 minutes (the cake will level off and possibly go a bit wrinkly, but that's normal). Then carefully remove from the tins and cool completely, paper-side down.

To make the coffee syrup, combine sugar and water in a small pan. Boil for 1 minute, then remove from the heat. Stir in coffee and liqueur.

For the icing, beat the mascarpone, peanut butter and coffee together with a wooden spoon until silky and even.

To assemble, cut the cold cakes horizontally across the middle using a long serrated knife. With a pastry brush, dampen the cut surfaces all over, using all of the coffee syrup. Put one cake layer onto a plate or cake stand, cut-side up. Spoon on 3 generous dollops of the icing and spread it to the edges with a palette knife. The icing should be about 5 mm deep. Repeat with the next two layers. When you come to the final layer, place it cut-side down, so that the top of the cake is smooth. Paddle the rest of the icing over the sides and top of the cake, creating a layer of icing on the top. Clean the knife, then use it to press a neat ring of nuts into the icing on the lower half of the side of the cake. Brush any excess nuts away.

The cake will keep for up to 2 days. Serve from the fridge or at cool room temperature.

NOUGAT CAKE

recipe by **MAGDALENE JEANETTE GREEFF**, NCR TVET College

SERVINGS: 10 | PREP TIME: 30 MINS PLUS SETTING | SKILL LEVEL: 1 (EASY)

INGREDIENTS

250 g butter

¼ cup caster sugar

1 x 385 g can condensed milk

1 tsp vanilla essence

1 tsp almond essence

1 tsp Tru-lem lemon juice

1 tsp cream of tartar

15 ml gelatin powder soaked in
  50 ml water

375 g combination of glacé
  cherries, glacé ginger and nuts

2 pre-baked sponge cakes, cut in
  half (or use 2 packets of Golden
  Cloud Vanilla Flavoured Cake
  Mix – bake 4 x 20 cm sponges
  and do not halve them, just
  trim the tops)

To finish
icing sugar for dusting

METHOD

Start the day before. Line a springform cake tin that is the same size as the sponge cakes with baking paper.

In a large bowl, cream butter and caster sugar together until fluffy. Add condensed milk, vanilla and almond essences, lemon juice and cream of tartar and blend again. Melt the gelatin and pour it into the filling mixture very slowly while still beating. Fold in the fruit and nut mixture.

Place a layer of sponge cake in the bottom of the cake tin and spread a layer of the filling over the cake. Add the next layer of cake and filling, repeating this process until all the filling is used up. Press the final layer of sponge cake firmly into the cake tin. De-mould the cake the next day and dust with icing sugar.

TIP

Remember to let the cake stand overnight in the refrigerator to enable it to set fully before you decorate it the next day.

Clockwise from top left:
Hazelnut cake,
Nougat cake,
Ballerina brownie cake

COFFEE CHOCOLATE CAKE

recipe by **JOHN NKGWANG**, Orbit TVET Mankgwe

SERVINGS: 16 | PREP TIME: 40 MINS | COOK TIME: 25–30 MINS | SKILL LEVEL: 2 (MODERATE)

INGREDIENTS

Cake

2 cups milk

1 cup butter, cubed

225 g Beacon 'Midnight Velvet' dark chocolate, chopped

3 eggs

2 tsp vanilla extract

1 tbsp instant coffee powder dissolved in a little warm water

3 cups Golden Flour wheat cake flour

2 cups sugar

1 tsp baking powder

½ tsp salt

Ganache

110 g dark chocolate (at least 70 per cent cocoa), chopped

280 g Beacon 'Midnight Velvet' dark chocolate, chopped

250 ml cream

3 tbsp soft butter, cubed

Filling variation

3 tbsp soft butter, cubed

115 g bittersweet chocolate, chopped

2½ cups icing sugar

250 ml cream

Garnish

cocoa powder, for dusting

fresh berries

METHOD

Pre-heat the oven to 170°C. Grease and flour three 20 cm round baking tins.

In a large saucepan over a low heat, combine milk, butter and 225 g dark chocolate until melted. Remove from heat and leave to stand for 10 minutes.

In a large bowl, beat eggs, vanilla extract and coffee mixture until fluffy, then stir in chocolate mixture until smooth. Combine flour, sugar, baking powder and salt in a separate bowl. Then gradually add flour mixture to chocolate mixture, mixing well. If the mixture is too thick, add more milk to achieve a runnier consistency.

Divide cake mixture evenly between three cake tins and bake for 25–30 minutes or until a skewer inserted in the centre of the cake comes out clean. Cool for 10 minutes before removing cakes from tins to wire racks to cool completely.

To make the ganache, place both types of chocolate in a small bowl. In a small saucepan bring cream just to the boil. Pour hot cream over chocolate and whisk until smooth, then stir in the butter. Continue to stir until ganache reaches a spreading consistency.

To assemble, place one cake on a serving plate, spread with half the ganache, then repeat process with the next layer. Top cake with remaining layer. Spread ganache over top and sides. Store in refrigerator. To serve, dust with cocoa powder and top with fresh berries.

Filling variation

In a small saucepan, melt butter and chocolate together, then stir in icing sugar and cream until smooth. Sandwich layers together with filling and spread ganache on top and sides of cake only.

GLOSSARY

amadumbe
Amadumbe (*Colocasia esculenta*) are starchy, quite mucilaginous root vegetables that form part of the traditional diet of KwaZulu-Natal.

amasi
Soured or fermented milk commonly used as a drink or accompaniment to uphuthu (crumbly pap). Also known as 'maas'.

askoek
Translates literally as 'ash cake': the 'askoek' is a traditional variety of bread roll cooked directly in the ashes of an open fire.

biltong
Marinated dried meat, usually seasoned with coriander. Widely consumed, usually as a snack.

biryani, also breyani and briyani
An aromatic spiced rice dish containing vegetables, lentils, meat or fish, which has its origins in the Indian subcontinent. Traditionally known as 'biryani', the name of the dish has various spellings, including 'breyani', which is commonly used in South Africa, and also 'briyani'

bobotie
A beef or lamb mince bake studded with dried fruit and topped with a savoury custard, distinguished from other minced or chopped meat dishes by the fact that is it is lightly spiced. The precise origins of bobotie are not known, but it is probably a fusion of Malay, Dutch and Middle Eastern culinary genres.

boeber
A thick, comforting, traditional Cape Malay milk drink or pudding that is made with vermicelli and/or sago and sugar, and flavoured with cardamom, cinnamon and rose-water.

boeremeisies
Boeremeisies are peaches or apricots preserved in brandy. Mampoer (see below) or witblits (see below) can also be used as preserving liquids. The Afrikaans word 'boeremeisies' literally translates as 'farm girls'; when grapes are preserved in this way, the result is called boerejongens (farm boys).

boerewors
Literally, 'farmer's sausage' in Afrikaans. Usually includes beef and coriander, but this wildly popular sausage comes in many forms. Annual competitions for the best boerewors recipe are held across the country and no butchery (or supermarket) would ever be without it.

bokkoms
Whole, salted and dried fish. This strong-tasting local speciality hails from the West Coast region of the country and is sometimes referred to as 'fish biltong'.

braai
South African term for barbecue. Literally, a fire allowed to die down to hot coals, over which meat and vegetables are cooked on a grid.

braaibroodjies
Toasted sandwiches made on a braai grid and cooked over open coals.

bredie
A slow-cooked, usually mutton-based stew seasoned with cinnamon, cardamom, ginger and cloves. See 'waterblommetjiebredie' below.

bunny chow
Street food developed by South Africans of Indian origin in which curry is placed inside a hollowed-out loaf of bread. There are no rabbits involved: the term 'bunny' is derived from the Gujurati word bhania, meaning 'trader class'.

chakalaka
A spicy township vegetable relish or salad that contains chillies (an essential ingredient) as well as onions, green peppers, carrots, beans and tomatoes. Traditionally served with braaied meat, bread, pap (see below), samp (see below), stews and curries.

gatsby
A street-food sandwich from Cape Town made from bisected, flattened, baguette-shaped bread stuffed with any combination of meat, melted cheese, fried eggs, chips and pickled chillies. The name is thought to refer to the flat cap worn by Robert Redford in the 1974 film of F Scott Fitzgerald's *The Great Gatsby* – the shape of the sandwich closely resembles that of the cap.

heerbone
A South African heritage bean variety, similar to lima beans or butter beans, that grows in the Sandveld on the West Coast.

inhloko
A slow-braised cow's head. Not to be confused with a smiley (see below).

koesisters, koeksisters
Koesisters are Cape Malay-style spiced, deep-fried, oval dough balls (rather like round doughnuts) dipped in a light syrup and sprinkled with desiccated coconut. The Afrikaner-style koeksister is made from twisted or plaited dough that is deep-fried and steeped in syrup.

kota
Township sandwich made from a hollowed-out quarter loaf, filled with a variety of meats, chips, cheeses and pickles. Also known as spathlo and skumbani.

maas
See amasi.

mala le mogudu
A traditional dish of stewed, uncleaned (meaning it has not been soaked or whitened) tripe, usually beef, served over pap (see below).

malva pudding
A syrup-drenched baked pudding containing apricot jam. There is much speculation – and mystery – surrounding the origins of the name of this dessert: some say that it is derived from the Afrikaans term malva lekker, meaning 'marshmallow' and referring to its light and springy texture, while others think it might also refer to a medieval fortified sweet wine, malvesy, or be derivative of the 'malva' plant, the rose pelargonium that was incorrectly named after the European mallow plant and used in the Cape as a flavourant in lieu of rose-water. What makes malva pudding different from the other brown baked puddings is that its creamy syrup topping (with some brandy or sweet wine added) is poured over it after it has been baked.

mampoer
Highly alcoholic 'moonshine' distilled liquor, generally homemade. Made from fruit including apricots, cherries, oranges, plums and pears.

melktert, also milk tart
An egg-custard tart topped with cinnamon and encased in puff pastry, the melktert is a South African teatime classic – so popular that there is now a National Milk Tart Day annually on 27 February.

mielie
Afrikaans word for a corn cob or maize plant.

mopane worms
A very nutritious and popular snack food in the northern part of the country. Sold fresh or dried – the dried variety is usually rehydrated in water before being cooked, but they are also eaten ground, as a kind of protein-rich seasoning. They aren't actually worms, but caterpillars of *Gonimbrasia belina* – the species that will become an emperor moth, if it doesn't get eaten first.

morogo
Sesotho term used to describe a variety of wild leafy vegetables including amaranth (*Amaranthus hybridus*) and blackjack (*Bidens pilosa*) leaves.

mosbolletjie
Made from lightly sweetened yeast dough flavoured with whole aniseed; the brioche-like dough is made into 'sausage' shapes and packed tightly into a loaf pan before baking. After being separated post-baking they are served fresh, or dried overnight and served with morning coffee. Traditionally seasonal and regional: the dough was originally made with grape must as a leavening agent, and mosbolletjies were thus a highlight of the grape harvest season in the Cape.

naartjie
An extremely popular, loose-skinned citrus fruit. In his book *Food Plants of the World* (Timber Press, 2005) South African Ben-Erik van Wyk describes a naartjie as a mandarin 'easily recognised by the loose segments and fruit wall that is easily peeled away by hand'.

padkos
Portable food packed for a road trip.

pap
Mielie-meal porridge cooked to a smooth and creamy consistency.

peri-peri, piri-piri
Piri-piri chillies, also known as African bird's eye chillies, are used to make peri-peri, a chilli sauce made from olive oil, garlic and chillies (other ingredients, such as herbs and citrus zest, may also be included). Peri-peri sauce is Portuguese in origin.

potbrood
Bread made in a pot, frequently on an open fire, but also in the oven. It might also contain beer as a leavening agent.

potjiekos
Stews made in a cast-iron, three-legged pot (known in Afrikaans as a 'potjie') over an open fire. The word translates literally as 'pot food'.

roosterkoek
Bread rolls cooked on a grid over a braai fire. A variation is stokbrood, (stick bread) when bread dough is wrapped around a stick and cooked over a fire.

roti
Flatbreads fried in butter, commonly eaten as part of the South African cuisines that derive from the Indian subcontinent and Indonesia.

rusk
A traditional biscuit-like snack. Frequently eaten dunked into hot coffee or tea.

samosa, also samoosa
A samosa is a triangle-shaped, deep-fried (or, sometimes, baked) pastry snack with a spiced savoury filling. The filling can be made of vegetables (such as potatoes, peas and onions), cheese or meat including minced lamb or beef, or shredded chicken. The word 'samosa' is often given the variant spelling 'samoosa' in South Africa.

samp
Dried, coarsely broken corn. Known in Afrikaans as stamp mielies, and frequently cooked in combination with beans, creating a popular staple dish that is known as umngqusho (see below) in isiXhosa.

shisa nyama
Township braai or steakhouse, often with an attached butchery. Customers choose their meat raw and it is cooked while they wait. Sometimes patrons cook for themselves.

slaphakskeentjies
A side dish or salad of baby onions pickled in a distinctively sweet-and-sour sauce. The word translates literally as 'little limp heels'.

slap tjips
Thick fried potato chips sold at takeaways wrapped in paper. Traditionally served with white spirit vinegar and lots of salt, but also popular with ketchup and other sauces. Frequently also served on a large white bread roll as a 'tjip roll'.

smiley
Roasted sheep's head. During roasting, the lips shrink and retract, exposing the animal's teeth and making it appear to smile.

snoek
Large, bony game fish with a silver body that is a relative of the barracuda. Common in Cape cuisine, it is often braaied with apricot-jam glaze, and frequently served with grape jam (korrelkonfyt) and sweet potato.

sosatie
The word 'sosatie' may have its origins in the Malay word sate, which means 'meat grilled on a skewer' or be an adaptation of the Indonesian term for minced meat, sasati. The meat, usually (but not exclusively) lamb, is marinated in a distinctive sweet-and-sour marinade and cubed before being threaded onto skewers, sometimes with the addition of vegetables and dried fruit pieces. Sosaties are usually cooked over coals on the braai (see above).

sousboontjies
Side dish of beans in a sweet-and-sour sauce, sometimes with a serious emphasis on the 'sweet'. Often referred to, and sold in supermarkets, as 'bean salad'.

tamatiesmoor, also smoor and tomato gravy
Afrikaans term for the tomato and onion gravy or sauce that is frequently served with braaied meat and pap (see above).

tameletjies
A traditional sweet in Cape Malay cuisine. Made from pine nuts added to caramelised sugar to form a nut brittle.

ting
Fermented sorghum porridge common in Basotho and Batswana cuisine.

ujeqe
A Zulu-style steamed bread; in the townships it's also called idombolo.

umleqwa
A township or farm chicken – a.k.a. a 'real' free-range chicken: umleqwa is an isiXhosa word meaning 'a chicken that you have to chase'.

umngqusho
This popular staple dish of samp (see above) and beans is often said to have been one of Nelson Mandela's favourites.

uphuthu
Mielie meal cooked to a crumbly – rather than smooth – consistency; frequently served with amasi (see above).

veldkos
Afrikaans term meaning 'field food' or 'bush food' and which implies foraged indigenous ingredients.

vetkoek
Fried dough balls similar in size and shape to a doughnut without a hole. Often sold by street hawkers and roadside vendors, and known as 'amagwinya' in the townships.

walkie talkies
Spiced, grilled chicken feet (and sometimes, but not always, heads too). Popular as a snack at soccer matches.

waterblommetjie bredie
A bredie (see above) featuring waterblommetjies, indigenous Cape water vegetables also known as Cape pondweed. Traditionally made with suurings (wild sorrel) added, which creates a distinctive sour note.

witblits
Another type of homemade liquor: colourless, made from distilled wine and thus similar to brandy. The Afrikaans word witblits means 'white lightning'.

INDEX

ACKNOWLEDGEMENTS

We are truly grateful to everyone who contributed to the making of *The Great South African Cookbook*. We would like to thank:
Najuwa Batiste, Shyama Batiste, Willie Botha, Marek Busfy, Troy Caltaux, Liam Cooper, Richard Davies, Richard Emmanuel, Zandra Emmanuel, Megan Goble, Amy-Jean Hahndiek, Lyn Jones, Cezanne Kouta, Nobuntu Lange, Stefanie Lim, Sheila McGillivray, Gerhard Pretorius, Kate Raven, Paul Sansom, Doug Young and Chris Wild.

A very special thank you to Sello Hatang and the team at the Nelson Mandela Foundation: Lee Davies, Yase Godlo, Verne Harris, Heather Henriques, Molly Loate, Nkateko Mabale, Reabetwe Makwela, Palesa Manare, Limpho Monyamane, Neeran Naidoo, Lunga Nene, Mongezi Njaju and Buyi Sishuba.
nelsonmandela.org

We especially wish to thank our principal sponsor, Tiger Brands, without whose support this book would not have been possible:
Bridgitte Backman, Nevashnee Naicker, Zandile Mlotshwa and Sithe Ngobese; and Moira Allison, Stella Fenster and the staff and students of the TVET colleges nationwide who found our 'chefs of the future'.
tigerbrands.com

Thank you also to the following organisations for their assistance in making *The Great South African Cookbook*:
Audi South Africa audi.co.za
ATC South Africa atcsouthafrica.co.za
JCDecaux jcdecaux.com

A very special thank you to the formidable steering committee – Cass, Hilary, Phillippa, David, Reuben, Dorah, Errieda, and Anna – for your never-ending enthusiasm and generosity of spirit in helping us find this rich and diverse collection of food heroes; and to artist Conrad, for going the extra mile and creating something beautiful, unique and proudly South African.

Thank you to Geoff Blackwell, Ruth Hobday, Helene Dehmer and the team at PQ Blackwell; and Libby Doyle, Craig Fraser, Ingeborg Pelser and everyone at Quivertree Publications.

And most importantly, to all the inspirational contributors who said 'yes' to being in this book and welcoming us into your homes, restaurant, boats and businesses, thank you. We couldn't have done it without you.

First published in South Africa by Quivertree Publications,
PO Box 51051, Waterfront 8002, Cape Town, South Africa
quivertreepublications.com, in association with PQ Blackwell,
PO Box 37692, Parnell, Auckland 1151, New Zealand
pqblackwell.com

EDITORIAL & PUBLISHING TEAM: Robyn Alexander,
Geoff Blackwell, Rachel Clare, Libby Doyle, Craig Fraser,
Ben Harris, Ruth Hobday, Jules Mercer, Diane Lowther
and Ingeborg Pelser
COVER ART: Conrad Botes
PHOTOGRAPHY: Toby Murphy
VIDEOGRAPHY: Brad Theron, Darren Ilett
FOOD STYLIST: Jules Mercer
ADDITIONAL FOOD STYLING: Justine Kiggen
DESIGN & LAYOUT: Helene Dehmer and Libby Doyle

Copyright © 2016 PQ Blackwell Limited/Quivertree Publications
Images copyright © 2016 Toby Murphy tobymurphy.com
Illustrations: front and back cover, pages 2, 6–7 and font
copyright © 2016 Conrad Botes conradbotes.com

Inspired by *The Great New Zealand Cookbook* created by
Thom Productions and PQ Blackwell.

The Nelson Mandela Foundation will receive all royalties from sales of *The Great South African Cookbook* to develop and support community food and agricultural projects to aid in the upliftment of the impoverished through food sustainability and empowerment.

Find us and follow us on:

thegreatsouthafricancookbook.co.za
ISBN: 978-1-928209-54-6
Printed in China by 1010 Printing Group Limited

10 9 8 7 6 5 4 3 2 1